Karmic Facts & Fallacies

Other Titles From New Falcon Publications

Cosmic Trigger: Final Secret of the Illuminati
Prometheus Rising
By Robert Anton Wilson
Undoing Yourself With Energized Meditation
By Christopher S. Hyatt, Ph.D.
Eight Lectures on Yoga
By Aleister Crowley
Info-Psychology
The Game of Life
By Timothy Leary, Ph.D.
Condensed Chaos: An Introduction to Chaos Magick
By Phil Hine
The Challenge of the New Millennium
By Jerral Hicks, Ed.D.
The Complete Golden Dawn System of Magic
By Israel Regardie
Buddhism and Jungian Psychology
By J. Marvin Spiegelman, Ph.D.
Astrology & Consciousness
By Rio Olesky
The Eyes of the Sun: Astrology in Light of Psychology
By Peter Malsin
Metaskills: The Spiritual Art of Therapy
By Amy Mindell, Ph.D.
Changing Ourselves, Changing the World
By Gary Reiss, LCSW
Soul Magic: Understanding Your Journey
By Katherine Torres, Ph.D.
A Mother Looks At the Gay Child
By Jesse Davis
Virus: The Alien Strain
By David Jay Brown
Phenomenal Women: That's US!
By Dr. Madeleine Singer

And to get your free catalog of *all* of our titles, write to:

New Falcon Publications (Catalog Dept.)
1739 East Broadway Road #1-277
Tempe, Arizona 85282 U.S.A
And visit our website at **http://www.newfalcon.com**

Karmic Facts & Fallacies

by

Ina Marx

New Falcon Publications
Tempe, Arizona, U.S.A.

International Standard Book Number: 1-56184-150-1
Library of Congress Catalog Card Number: 00-104174

First Edition 2000

Cover by Amanda Fisher

The paper used in this publication meets the minimum requirements of the American National Standard for Permanence of Paper for Printed Library Materials Z39.48-1984

Address all inquiries to:
New Falcon Publications
1739 East Broadway Road #1-277
Tempe, AZ 85282 U.S.A.
(or)
320 East Charleston Blvd. • #204-286
Las Vegas, NV 89104 U.S.A.

website: http://www.newfalcon.com
email: info@newfalcon.com

Attention

This life is a test.
It is only a test.
If it had been an actual life, you would have received
further instructions on what to do and where to go.

Table of Contents

Introduction 9

1. Yoga:
   A Rose Is a Rose and Yoga Is Yoga 19

2. Of Gurus and Cults:
   Don't Follow the Leader! 41

3. Religion and Dogmatism:
   Heavy Baggage 68

4. Meditation:
   My Mantra and Yours 94

5. About Health and Healing:
   Do I Have a Witch Doctor For You! 116

6. Psychic Phenomena:
   Shop Wisely 140

7. Mediumship and Channeling:
   I'm Four Thousand Years Old, But I Don't Look It 174

8. Death and Dying:
   "No Such Thing!" Shirley MacLaine Says 206

9. Karma and Reincarnation:
   Yes, Virginia, You *Do* Choose Your Parents 229

About the Author 252

INTRODUCTION

I trust that this book's message will provide inspiration and insight for the dedicated New Age seeker as well for the average person who may be bewildered by New Age lingo and puzzled by its ideas. While metaphysical practices and techniques are being accepted as part of everyday life by many, they are still being suppressed, ridiculed and misrepresented by the general media as esoteric flim-flam. But like it or not, as we enter the twenty-first century, we are engulfed in a wave of Eastern philosophy and mysticism. We have been besieged by such way-out (and to some, downright spooky-sounding) topics as celestial prophecies, near-death and after-death experiences, encounters with angels and extraterrestrials, UFO abductions and unexplainable crop circles. All these phenomena have been exploited in literature, TV, film and plays as well as sensationalized by the news media. The popularity of these subjects proves that both believers and disbelievers continue to be curious. And the eventual discovery of life on other planets is apt to shatter almost everyone's belief system.

At this historic juncture, all of us are confronted by the need to question our purpose on earth. It seems that most everyone is searching for a reason of our existence. While many still reject esoteric teachings, others accept and participate actively, and some are only vaguely aware of the subject or not at all interested. But the feeling that we need to change our consciousness is widespread.

I aim to de-mystify and clarify such topics as karma, reincarnation, faith-healing, Yoga, meditation, etc., and to motivate the seeker, the skeptic and the stoic to integrate them into their particular lifestyle.

This is hardly the first time that we've been confronted with esotericism and the occult. What we are experiencing is simply the latest revival of the persistent attempt to loosen our structured belief systems. The transcendental movement of the mid-nineteenth century also shook up our concepts of realism and logic. Transcendental philosophy regarded reality as fundamentally spiritual in nature, and claimed that knowledge is obtained through intuition and spiritual awakening. That movement was the forerunner to contemporary consciousness-raising, and stressed and encouraged the search for inner meaning and universalism. Many Americans were attracted to transcendentalism, and evidence of its impact can be found in the writings of Emerson, Thoreau, Whitman and others of that era.

At the end of the nineteenth century, spiritualism—not to be confused with spirituality—flourished and was perceived as a threat to orthodox Christianity. Communicating with departed spirits through seances became a favorite pastime in chic social circles. In the early part of the twentieth century, Swami Vivekananda brought his message from India to America. He lectured on Vedanta and the liberation of the soul, and attempted to unite Eastern and Western philosophies.

After World War I, most people who had been enchanted by spiritualism reverted to more mundane thinking, and the American dream of success through churchgoing and hard work became preeminent. We entered the age of technology, science, and reason, and witnessed the sanctification of the family, the president, and God. We weathered the Depression, prohibition, and gangsterism, and came out ready to fight another "just war," World War II. When the idealism dissipated, we allowed Senator Joe McCarthy and others to lead us back to the notion of supremacy and Americanism.

In the fifties, the United States became one of the most powerful nations and the savior of war-torn countries. The Vietnam War, however, drastically changed the comfortable complacency of the previous decade. American youth took a stand to protest the country's involvement in what they saw as senseless bloodshed. Rebelliously they embraced the age of psychedelics and found themselves steeped in a drug culture, where hippies and flower children threatened all that was holy to American society. Consciousness-raising became a new business enterprise, with groups like Scientology and the Unification Church of the Reverend Sun Myung Moon attempting to corporatize Eastern philosophy.

Famous show business personalities made pilgrimages to India, imported Yogis and Swamis, and guruism turned into a religion of the seventies. Meditation swept the country, and even straight folks became meditators, zealously guarding their mantras. Many experienced their highs through meditation; others were convinced that holy drugs like peyote and LSD would lead to even higher awareness. The literary works of the New Age and the Aquarian Age became bibles for a generation of seekers.

By the late seventies, the fun of deviating from the mainstream had mostly worn off. Some of our youth remained in Haight-Ashbury, but the majority entered the Yuppie generation of high finance, stock markets and computer-related enterprises, complete with sellouts and buyouts. Though mainstream thinking prevailed, and the drug scene had seemingly died down, the awakened continued in their pursuit of spiritual growth. We joined groups and organizations like Encounter and Synanon, est, Actualizations, and Arica, to name just a few of the mind-expanding techniques that swept the country in the sixties and seventies. We enrolled in T'ai Chi, Yoga, and Feldenkrais classes and availed ourselves of New Age healing methods, including chiropractic, acupuncture, Rolfing, color and flower and crystal healing. We felt well on the path to spiritual awakening, until Shirley MacLaine shook us up in the eighties with her book *Out On A Limb* with revelations about karma, reincarnation and the afterlife. Her book became a longtime bestseller, appealing to a non-New Age readership as well. Other prominent entertainers also came out of the closet to set the trend for spiritual search. The occult was In. Even Jane Fonda endorsed Yoga for physical fitness.

The spiritual seekers among us are perhaps more numerous now than at any time in history, and we are anxious to know what life is about and where it is leading. The majority of Americans are inclined to run with the crowd, and, just as hemlines and trouser cuffs go up and down and we switch from high- to low- to non-fat, we seem to get pulled into every New Age technique. Psychics, tarot and palm readers, astrologers and numerologists, seem to be flourishing in all major U.S. cities. Indian gurus are back in business and Zen Buddhist meditation centers are all the rage.

However, even our most sincere efforts to keep up with "the crowd" often lead to frustration, "Gee," you say, "I am really doing my best in this world. I'm earning my keep, voting at every election, and I'm drug free! What more do they want from me?" Or: "I'm eating wheat germ and sprouts, I consult psychics and astrologers, I exercise regularly, and I'm still not enlightened!"

Seekers tend to be more prevalent among the young, and Californians and New Yorkers seem to be more involved than perhaps those in the Midwest and Deep South. A large proportion of the American population steadfastly refuses to be taken in by all this "nonsense" and "ungodliness" and remains firmly entrenched in their familiar belief systems. And then there are the hard-core scientists who deny all that is not empirically verifiable.

There are also some very fortunate people among us who are so completely involved in absorbing, satisfying tasks that they are just too busy to explore the meaning of life and death. I am quite sure that Mother Teresa, occupied by caring for orphaned Indian children and the dying, found no time for philosophical debates about religion.

But for all of you who ponder the whys and wherefores of existence, I may have some answers.

I call myself a metaphysicist. I follow a philosophy removed from the norm. Webster's defines *metaphysics* as "a division of philosophy concerned with the fundamental nature of reality and being."

My New Age credentials include a career in Yoga, T'ai Chi, Sufi Dancing, shiatsu, and Judo. I've been Mensendiecked, Alexandered, Feldenkraised, and Rolfed. I have looked into Orgonomy, Bioenergetics, and Aryurveda. I covered the mind-expansion field with est, Transcendental Meditation, and possibly every technique that has ever been in vogue. I was psychoanalyzed, went through Primal Scream Therapy and took courses in astrology, aura reading and psychokinesis, crystal healing and various other New Age endeavors. I finally came to accept my ability to heal myself and others.

I experienced a near-death episode, an out-of-body trip, and past-life regressions. I have also become aware of the existence of the spirit world among us. I sense the spirits (also called guides or angels) that surround and watch over us and make us feel safe and protected. We can contact them when we need advice, and I can teach you how to do so. I have learned techniques to communicate with the departed, and it comforts me to know they are happy and there is no death.

"But what about life?" you ask. "What is that all about?" These are the facts ma'am. Life is definitely not just about being born, learning to walk and talk, going to school, finding a job, getting married and procreating. There is more to it than paying taxes and insurance premiums, voting for the right political candidate, and cheering for our favorite sports teams. We are not here on Earth because God split a rib, because we evolved from an amoeba, as result of a big-bang explosion or our parents were careless. A higher power *did* create us, but we were the co-creators, and we ourselves are responsible for the course of our lives.

"Does life have a purpose?" you may want to know. Yes, indeed. We entered this planet to strive, to grow, to progress, to achieve and to learn. We are here because we chose to correct errors and mistakes from previous lifetimes, heal past relationships, assist fellow men and women, and help create a better world. We also chose the body, the time and the circumstances best suited to our plan.

We open the way to enlightenment once we're able to rid ourselves of fear, anger, guilt, worry, and the concept of sin, as well as anxiety, envy and self-pity. When we have fulfilled the requirements and goals we set for ourselves, we are freely and wholeheartedly entitled to enjoy ourselves in the body.

This is the truth: *Earth is only a temporary residence and life is not real!* Hindus refer to it as *maya,* or illusion. Pedro Calderón de la Barca, a seventeenth-century poet, wrote, "Life is a dream, and dreams are dreams!" Or as Shakespeare put it, "All the world's a stage."

Life on this planet exists as a series of fleeting events and the length of a lifetime is but a sham. A lifetime on earth is most likely only a moment in eternity. As we came to realize through space travel, time does not exist except as a human concept. Time may seem expanded or endless when we are young, but runs rapidly away from us as we get older.

I personally go along with old Will's interpretation and believe that our lives are plays—both tragic and comic—or, more suited to this modern time, like movies or TV series. We ourselves write the script, we are the directors, and we are in charge of production. We assign the roles, and generally are the actors. Most of our time is spent on rehearsal to polish up the act and get it on the road. "Getting your act together" is a truly profound saying.

My own life definitely plays like an ongoing soap opera. I grew up in Germany during the Nazi regime, tyrannized by an abusive father and, as a Jew, by my peers. At age fourteen, I found myself alone in California, struggling to survive in a strange country. I nearly died in a fire, was forced to jump from the top floor of a burning building in order to escape, and was physically and psychologically disabled for many years afterward. I lost one daughter to a cult, another to mental illness, and my husband to drug addiction and eventually a plane crash. (Please don't be upset; I *did* manage to have some good times in between!)

For many years I suffered deeply and contemplated suicide. I literally beat my chest and cried to God, "Why me?" until the day came when I got sick and tired of being sick and tired and full of suffering, and I took a new approach. I decided to ask for help from a higher source. There was no crashing of cymbals but help came almost immediately, enabling me to switch my role from tragic heroine to successful character actress. In time, I came to believe that I had created all the events of my life to redeem myself for whatever negative acts I had committed in previous lifetimes. Undoubtedly, I must have been a hellion!

My own spiritual search began through Yoga, but yours can be initiated through any other venture. I've always been inquisitive and never wanted to miss anything, so I took the opportunity to experience each thing that I am sharing with you in this book. If you are just a spiritual thrill seeker, please proceed with caution; spirituality is a serious subject! But if you are truly curious, by all means explore and investigate every avenue open to you. It might be lovely to chant and meditate in the presence of an Indian guru, a Zen roshi, or a Sufi master, but I urge you: Don't get hung up on one guru, method, philosophy, or dogma. *Everyone and everything can assist you on your spiritual quest,* but no one person is omniscient and omnipotent, no system or philosophy presents the ultimate truth. All of them may fill a temporary need, but the answers to why you are on Earth can only be found within yourself.

To the skeptics among you, I say: It's okay to be skeptical; you don't need to swallow everything you hear and read. Every claim has a contradiction and the doubter's word is as valid as the believer's. For most of my life, I thought that the word *spirit* applied exclusively to alcohol. But I learned to keep an open mind to any evidence that could change my ideas about what is commonly accepted as fact.

To the scientist who is unwilling to consider that realities exist beyond the realm of the physical, I have nothing to say; I have learned to avoid such arguments. Nor do I attempt to convince the nonbeliever who denies that there is more to life than mere survival, and who shuts his door tightly to everything unfamiliar and threatening to his interpretation of normal existence. In my opinion, the rationalist who is intent on proving that concepts such as the afterlife are unrealistic and that life on Earth is all there is, accomplishes nothing more than the suppression of his innate spiritual nature.

I also don't have much to offer to those who are well advanced on the road to enlightenment without even knowing the meaning of the word or any of the language of spiritual phenomena. They may never have heard about karma or reincarnation, but live life in a way that naturally balances out their past actions. They may not sit on a mountain top and recite mantras or join a consciousness-raising group, but they remain centered and alert amidst all their activities. They most likely never need to see a psychiatrist or resort to Valium or Prozac. These are the childlike (though not by any means childish) among us who are not influenced by the presence of bad or evil. They may have encountered negative thought systems and teachings as they grew up, but they pay it no heed. They are too busy just having a good time, doing good deeds, and being creative. They refuse to knuckle under when they are hit with difficult circumstances, and are truly happy, finding life fulfilling and delightful. They are calm and peaceful within and without, and recognize humor in every phase of life, laughing frequently and wholeheartedly.

I very much believe that to laugh and play is part of our divinity and our mission on Earth. This is why I caution you that when we touch on supposedly serious subjects in this book, you need not take them all that seriously. Life itself is not that somber—we only make it so.

You need not be frustrated because you are not an ardent seeker or steeped in spiritual dogma. Being enlightened or spiritually conscious does not depend on knowing the lingo of holism or parapsychology. It is about being at peace with yourself, fulfilled in your strivings, and happy to be alive. It never depends on your material circumstances or relationships. Neither money, success, or another person can do it for you; all that is essential to your well-being and serenity has to come from within yourself. But if you choose to look into the reasons for your existence on Earth, I can help open some doors for you and guide you along the way. While you might not be able to cry out, "Look, Ma—I'm enlightened!" in this lifetime, I can guarantee you that you'll have fun exploring the possibilities. And most importantly, you'll develop the confidence to approach the unknown without fear.

Like my other books, this is a how-to book. I present you with some of the timely New Age and metaphysical topics I am familiar with and have participated in, or introduce you to qualified experts of my acquaintance for further elaboration. I share with you what I have learned on my personal journey, discussing the people, places, and situations that have added to or detracted from my own understanding and growth.

I may, at times, come across as judgmental, cynical, or harsh in my views and evaluations. This is because I feel that our current society and media often mislead, deceive, and confuse us about what is called the paranormal or supernatural. My intention is to demystify the esoteric or occult and present these phenomena in a more accurate light, as either a part of nature or as something that can be sensibly explained.

I seek to deflate groups and individuals who I feel are revered, exalted, and worshipped without cause, and often at much cost!

Some chapters offer information only, and others include practical methods to further your own exploration. I will teach you how to contact the spirit world, opening up new horizons of understanding. This can solve problems and create wholeness and peace of mind. I will offer you opportunities for expansion, while urging you to reject whatever does not seem right for you.

It is your choice: Do you want to jump in head first or do you need to proceed with caution? In either case, I urge you to apply common sense to everything new that is presented to you, both in this book, and in all the experiences that you will encounter. But while I respect your doubts about what I am about to present, I do appreciate your open mind.

I have written this book to motivate you to take charge of your life. I try to guide you to think independently without relying on self-appointed authorities or social dictates. I guarantee that a common-sense interpretation of sometimes unfathomable issues can lead each individual to freedom from guilt and fear, enjoyment of life on earth, mental and spiritual growth, and ultimately a better world. It is my sincerest hope that you will discover, as I have, that life makes sense and that existence is eternal.

Chapter One

Yoga: A Rose Is A Rose and Yoga Is Yoga

Yes, let's talk about Yoga! It's my favorite subject. Over the years, the topic has alternately enjoyed surges of popularity and faded into utter obscurity. It has invited ridicule as well as confusion and is still sometimes mixed up with Yogi Berra or yogurt.

The very name *Yoga* has been an obstacle to public acceptance. It connotes mysticism, the occult, and everything way, way out! It used to be associated with Indian fakirs lying on a bed of nails, charming snakes, or walking on burning coals. A few years ago, certain popular TV programs featured Indian Yogis performing incredible acts such as twisting themselves into pretzels and compacting their bodies into small crates. While their feats may have been admired, probably few, if any, viewers were inspired to attempt Yoga exercises. I have often thought to westernize the name *Yoga* to make it more palatable to the public, but decided that no substitute could suffice.

During the last thirty years, I have personally done my best to laud Yoga's virtues, trying to convince everyone I met that it is the most perfect exercise system in existence. As a Yoga teacher, I was fortunate to recruit a sizable number of students and converts who reaped benefits exceeding their wildest expectations. But it seemed that whenever I succeeded at putting Yoga on the map, one or another media personality, United States president, or medical authority would appoint a Jack LaLanne, Richard Simmons, Jim Fixx, or Arnold Schwarzenegger as the guru of physical fitness. Their particular method of staying in shape was heralded and promoted as the order of the day, and Yoga was relegated to the back seat, especially in my territory, New York. Yet Yoga never lost its popularity in Canada, Europe, Australia, and New Zealand, and it has continued to be popular in California.

Today I am no longer as involved in the Yoga scene as I was in the seventies and eighties, but I am happy to note that Yoga is making a comeback as part of increasing national concern about health and fitness. Jane Fonda, Raquel Welch, Ali MacGraw, and other personalities with great bodies have done their part, using tapes and books to restore the public perception of Yoga as a legitimate form of exercise. Madonna, at present, is gung-ho into Yoga, and so are many other entertainment personalities, greatly influencing the general public to join in the fun.

Also, while running, jogging, aerobics, and weightlifting are still in vogue, many medical experts, especially in the field of sports medicine, have cautioned us to proceed at a slower pace. They feel that the fitness mania contributed to too many injuries and are now advocating more sensible exercise.

My experience has demonstrated that Yoga is the most sensible and effective exercise system in existence and—contrary to certain medical opinions—foolproof to injury. Ironically, when Yoga was in its heyday about ten or fifteen years ago, quite a few physicians, especially orthopedists, advised their patients to try Yoga exercises. Serious athletes, incapacitated by sprains, pulls, or tendinitis, discovered that using Yoga as a warm-up system could help correct existing conditions and strengthen weakened muscles. Professional sports coaches recognized that Yoga stretches, relaxation, and breathing techniques could improve performance and prevent injuries if practiced prior to competition.

I sincerely hope that general public recognition and acceptance of Yoga as the perfect exercise will soon be forthcoming. It will enhance all aspects of the fitness movement and, most importantly, reduce the chances of injury.

* * *

At one time, Yoga was the last thing I would have considered. I believed it to be something strange and esoteric. I associated it with Indians sitting in a lotus posture and gazing at their navel. I was totally unaware that it could be practiced as a physical exercise. One day, I was sitting in the sauna of my health club, listening in on a conversation: "My brother had suffered from lower back problems all his life," said one naked lady to another. "He searched high and low for someone or something to help him, but nothing worked. Then someone steered him to Yoga. That was five years ago, and today he is free from pain."

I couldn't stop thinking about this comment. At that time, my own back pain was unbearable most of the time. Although eight years had passed since I injured my back when I had jumped from the burning building, I was still suffering. At first I had been put into a cast, then I graduated to a brace, and was eventually laced into a steel corset which I was instructed to wear for the rest of my life. "You will always have pain," said the medical doctor who supplied me with painkillers, uppers, downers, and barbiturates. "You must learn to live with your pain," said the psychiatrist as he used me as a guinea pig for literally every new tranquilizer on the market.

In addition to the medications, I drank numerous cups of coffee, gorged on junk food to compensate for my misery, and chain-smoked, as well. In short, I was a mess! I often felt like giving up and ending my life to escape from my unhappiness and pain, but innately I was a survivor, and my decision to fight was instinctual and strong.

My injuries eventually healed, but the pain persisted. I listened to and followed practically every piece of advice I received to reduce my pain. I tried heat treatments, massage, and traction, all to no avail. I finally let myself be persuaded to try exercise. I had never exercised or participated in sports, even as a youngster, mostly because I was fat, and ashamed to be seen in shorts or a swimsuit. I did lose some weight as a teenager, but had considered myself overweight throughout my adult years.

"I am sure exercise will help you," said one well-meaning therapist. "Your sluggish muscles need to be strengthened and restored." What he said did make sense; I made a heroic effort and joined a gym. Exercise had always meant calisthenics to me, so I sweated through the 1-2-3-4, up and down, left and right routines—and collapsed in more pain than before. I also made an attempt at machine exercises and isometrics, which didn't help at all. I finally gave up in disgust and retreated to the sauna. There, after overhearing that woman's comment about her brother, I asked myself, "Why not Yoga?" After all, I had tried everything else.

Although already popular on the West Coast in the early sixties, Yoga was still relatively unknown in New York. Looking under *Yoga* in the phone book, I found listings for a bookstore, a Yogi who turned out to be away in India, a disconnected number, and, finally, a male who answered the phone and said he was a teacher and available for private Yoga lessons. I made an appointment and decided to bring a friend along for protection because I vaguely associated Yoga with opium dens and white slavery.

Contrary to my expectations, we found a pleasant-looking Indian in Western dress. "I am Majumdar," he said with rolling *r*'s, introducing himself. Otherwise, his English was perfect. I estimated him to be in his forties, but he later revealed to me that he was in his late fifties. He was exceptionally well built, fit, and trim. He showed us his credentials: He had been a professor of Vedantic philosophy at the University of Bombay and had written a book on Yoga. My friend was duly impressed by his photos in unbelievable contortionist-like positions, but I was ready to run away and forget the whole thing. There was no way in the world that I could even attempt those exercises, as far as I was concerned.

Mr. Majumdar seemed doubtful as well, as he eyed my lumpy figure and most likely tried to estimate my age. I was forty years old, but I looked considerably older. However, he set out to convince me to give Yoga a try. 'He probably needs the money,' I thought, looking around at his modest living quarters, 'and anyway, this is my last resort!' I was positive that it wouldn't work, but I agreed to show up for weekly lessons anyway.

At first, my situation seemed as hopeless as teaching Yoga to an oak tree, and my stubborn muscles and unexercised anatomy resisted the demands made on them. But as the weeks went by, I loosened up more and more. After three months, I discarded the hated corset. From that day on, I never wore any kind of support, and my back grew stronger and stronger. Mr. Majumdar was a good teacher, though not an inspiring one. I had tried Yoga for the limited purpose of strengthening my back and easing my pain, and after accomplishing that within a year, I discontinued my lessons.

I did not backslide into my pre-Yoga days, however. I cherished my new limberness and my pain-free body, and I continued to practice more or less regularly. I was enormously proud of my headstand, which had taken me so long to accomplish. I cut down on coffee, reduced my intake of medications, and discarded other crutches. I still smoked heavily and I was still nervous, but my general health had improved considerably. My family, who had more or less suffered along with me, was happy with me, and I was happy with them.

I was convinced that Yoga was superior to all other kinds of exercise, but I was completely ignorant of its full spiritual and philosophical meaning. I don't remember whether my teacher ever alluded to any other aspects of Yoga besides the physical, or whether I just wasn't interested. Yoga, I believed, had had all the impact on my life that it was ever going to. But it turned out that I was mistaken.

I began religiously following a daily yoga TV program broadcast from California, featuring Richard Hittleman and his beautiful wife, Diane. One day, after watching the program, I heard about a mother-daughter yoga class being offered in Manhattan. Enthusiastically, I enrolled myself and my younger daughter. At eight, she was as roly-poly as I had been as a child, and I was always on the lookout for physical activities for her. I chauffeured her to dancing, acrobatics, ice skating, and tennis lessons. She became extremely agile, in spite of her weight, but she thoroughly resented my interference.

I almost dragged her to the Yoga class, and she rebelled from the very beginning. "Yoga is stupid, and besides, it's embarrassing to be taking classes with your own mother," she would whine and gripe. After three lessons I could stand it no longer and let her drop out, but I completed the course because I had paid for it in advance. I discovered that practicing with a group was fun, and I caught a glimpse of a more hopeful future.

When I first started the lessons, I felt terribly out of place. Everyone, including my child, was more graceful and flexible than I. I was utterly awed by the gorgeous, pencil-slim instructor who taught the course and by her flawless demonstration of the Yoga positions. 'I would give anything to look like her,' I thought with envy, 'but I can't imagine how it could be possible.' Yet, after completing the course, I re-enrolled and progressed to an intermediate, and eventually, an advanced level.

The impossible happened! My body turned incredibly limber, even though I possessed no inherent flexibility. My muscles and tendons became elastic and strong. The exercises were now rewarding and fun to do. When a teacher-training course was announced, I found the nerve to sign up for it, although the idea that I could teach Yoga was incomprehensible to me.

Mr. Hittleman himself flew in from California to teach the course, and my first class with him was a humiliating experience. I noticed him looking at me disapprovingly as if to ask, "Who in hell signed her up?" I saw the other students as uniformly slim, trim—and young! I stuck out like a sore thumb, overweight and over-aged. I expected to be ousted from the course, but Mr. Hittleman either took pity on me or decided that my tuition—a rather handsome sum—justified my presence. It was up to me to make the choice to quit the class or lose weight. With grim determination, I opted for the latter. From day one, I strictly adhered to my self-imposed regimen of a Spartan diet and two hours of Yoga practice per day. My family and friends knew I meant business, so they refrained from teasing and tempting me; in fact they supported me.

Sheer mechanical practice, combined with good eating habits, started producing results. The pounds rolled off and stayed off. My fellow students applauded me, and the once-supercilious teacher noticed the change and invited me to demonstrate positions in front of the class. As my figure became more shapely and my Yoga poses more polished, my confidence grew. I saw that Yoga was something I could do well. I realized with sudden certainty that I was meant to be a teacher and help others. And I, who had never directed my energies toward a goal, suddenly knew how to achieve this new dream—by applying myself with discipline and hard work. In the past, I had always worked belligerently, but now I set about it with a slow, steady deliberation born of a true sense of purpose. Once I realized the direction I had to take, I stopped being frantic; I slowed down to an hour of practice daily and spent more time with my family.

Everything seemed to fall into place. Not only had I lost weight, I had lost inches—in all the right places. Jubilantly, I noticed that my hips and thighs had slimmed down considerably. I had been a size fourteen top and size sixteen bottom, and now, with my weight evenly distributed, I was able to fit into a perfect size eight. I was healthier and more energetic. For the first time in years, I fell asleep easily. I gradually eliminated all tranquilizers and barbiturates, and one day, naturally and painlessly, I gave up smoking forever.

As my body changed, so did my mind. My entire mental outlook and attitude became different. I developed more patience, understanding, tolerance, and compassion.

At the same time, I was better able to stand up to those who tried to browbeat me and impose their values on me. I also experienced a surge of hunger for knowledge of all kinds, and I felt a whole world of learning opening up for me. I stopped blaming people and circumstances for my failure to have a college education and for the fact that I had never had a satisfying career. I had always dreamed about being a teacher of some kind because I felt that I had something to offer to this world. Now I knew that I was meant to teach Yoga, to pass on to as many people as possible the benefits I had received.

When my training program ended, I sought out other Yoga teachers to learn about all aspects of Yoga. I read all the books in print on the subject. I immersed myself totally, enjoyed myself totally. By this time, Yoga had infiltrated New York, and teachers were widely available. Most of them were associated with the Sivananda, Integral Yoga, and Yogi Gupta schools, each teaching their specific method and adhering strictly to their particular guru. Their centers resembled Indian shrines, pungent with incense and decorated with Indian artifacts, numerous portraits of the guru, and pictures and paintings of Hindu gods and goddesses—variously multi-armed, flute-playing, and elephant-headed. The classes were generally taught by the disciples, young men with shaved heads and pious demeanor, wearing saffron robes or dhotis.

Yet, they taught me to perform such intricate *asanas* (Yoga poses) as sitting in the full lotus seat, standing on my forearms or hands, or wrapping both feet around my neck. The thought often came to me: 'If only all the doctors who predicted that I would end up in a wheelchair could see me now!' I learned to meditate, chant in Sanskrit, reverberate to the sound of OM, recite mantras while fingering *mala* beads (similar to rosaries), gaze at mandalas (holy symbols), and indulge in other rituals.

Anxious to experience even more intricate practices, I sought out private teachers and discovered that Yogi Vithaldis was the man for me. He knew everything that I ever needed to know and then some. He taught me *vastra dhauti* and *sutra neti*—two of the most disgusting Yogic rituals ever devised. He insisted that I needed to cleanse my intestines and sinuses to purify my system to attain higher physical and mental powers. *Dhauti* involved learning to swallow yards and yards of gauze and regurgitating it. *Neti* required running heavily waxed, stiff strings through my nostrils and into the back of my throat and then out the mouth (my throat was sore for months).

Yogi Vithaldis was an acclaimed gourmet who had published cookbooks on Indian vegetarian cuisine. He taught me how to prepare curry and dal, bake Indian bread, and eat daintily with my fingers. He chose to ignore that whenever he forced me to sample his concoctions, my eyes would tear and my tongue would catch fire from the fierce Indian spices. He was also an expert on impotence and would regale me with anecdotes of his male clientele. He claimed that he could draw milk through a straw into his penis, but I declined his offer to demonstrate this feat.

Thankfully, I learned many extremely useful practices from him. He taught me a back somersault and promised that if I did this every day of my life, I would never get old (I have never skipped this practice). When I felt sufficiently versed in all aspects of Yoga, I felt qualified to attempt teaching it. I decided, however, that my Yoga would be a westernized version, devoid of dogma and ritual, similar to the teachings of Richard Hittleman.

I drummed up six more-or-less skeptical neighbors and friends and got them to come to the basement of my house for weekly Yoga lessons. This experience gave me the courage to apply and teach at various Y's, community centers, and adult education programs on Long Island. Within a short time, I rented my own little studio, graduated to a bigger one, and arrived at the position of owner/director of probably the largest Yoga exercise center of its kind in the United States.

By then, Yoga was reaching the heights of its popularity on the East Coast, along with other New Age innovations. I had to employ four instructors to teach the three hundred fifty beginner and intermediate students who took classes each week, and we had a long waiting list. I taught all the advanced classes myself and offered free meditation instruction for anyone who wished to explore the non-physical practices of Yoga. In addition to running the school, I instituted a volunteer program for teaching Yoga in schools and colleges, and in drug and alcohol rehabilitation centers, as well as to the physically and mentally disabled.

In the early seventies, I became an acclaimed Yoga authority, especially after the success of my first book. I received invitations from all over the country to lecture or conduct workshops, was frequently interviewed as a guest on TV shows, and conducted a weekly radio program. I was proud of myself for the part I played in the progress of almost all my students. The thought that I was able to enrich other people's lives and give new hope to many was deeply satisfying for me.

While I basked in the admiration of my students, I was sad that my family didn't share my enthusiasm. It hadn't been easy for me to adjust my home life to cope with the demands of my teaching schedule, but I honestly felt that I had done the best I could not to neglect my family. When my children were small, I had sincerely tried to be there for them at all times and support them emotionally, and also to fulfill my social obligations to my husband. I did my best to interest him and my daughters in my work, without much success. My husband came to one class and declared, "This is not for me!"

My older daughter reluctantly attended a few classes but accused me of pushing her into it. I managed to motivate the younger one by promising her that she could pose for pictures in my next book if she thinned down and practiced. She was willing to oblige and was delighted to show off, but she also made it clear that she was not happy with my time-consuming involvement in Yoga. As far as I know, no one in my family, except my mother, ever read either of my books. The girls *did* make an effort to tolerate my new career and modest fame, but did not rejoice with me now that I looked svelte and ten years younger. I sensed that they had preferred me as an old-fashioned mom. While my husband supported me in my business affairs, praised me to others, and accepted their praise of me, I knew that he resented my success. "It all started with that damn Yoga!" he was heard to exclaim in later years when we became bitter enemies.

When my family eventually fell apart, I was able to use the inner strength and confidence I had gained from Yoga to absolve myself from blame and guilt. I shudder to think what my life would have been like without Yoga, especially as more and more tragedies and heartbreak descended upon me. It saved me from another breakdown and gave me the courage to face up to life. And, *serene in the knowledge that I can always help myself and others, I am equipped to keep meeting all life's challenges.*

* * *

Before I tell you how Yoga can save *your* life as well, let me acquaint you with some of its history and tradition. Yoga originated in India possibly between three and five thousand years ago, when a great civilization flourished, offering an impressive example of culture and education for the rest of the world. Its beginnings have been traced back to the Upanishads and the *Bhagavad Gita,* part of the ancient Sanskrit epic of Hindu philosophy called the Vedas. Yoga and its philosophy are intertwined in Hinduism and its offshoot, Buddhism, two of the major religions of the East. However, being a Yogi requires no affiliation to a religion, nor does adherence to religion make you a Yogi. The *Bhagavad Gita,* perhaps the most quoted work of all Eastern literature, can be considered the original Bible, encompassing all moral concepts. It is a seminal guide to ethical behavior and action, teaching that the better individuals we are, the more we can benefit our fellow men and women, and the world in general.

Around the second century B.C., the basic principles and practices of Yoga were set down in the *Yoga Sutras* by Patanjali, sometimes called the father of Yoga. All these works were written in the ancient language of Sanskrit, which is extremely difficult to translate and therefore open to a broad range of interpretation. Consequently, a multitude of Yoga societies and schools of thought have arisen, each with its own particular advocates, each claiming to represent *the* true Yoga. I sincerely believe that the Yoga I teach, based on common sense, is true Yoga. It follows the classic rules of an ancient wisdom, philosophy, and science, but custom-tailors them for practical application to life in our present civilization. Most importantly, Yoga has worked and continues to work effectively for me and for my students.

The word *Yoga,* most simply interpreted, means "union"—the union of body, mind, and spirit. There are many forms and schools of Yoga: Hatha, Raja, Bhakti, Kundalini, and Tantra, to name a few. The ultimate goal of all Yogas is the same—the supreme realization of the self. To acquaint you with the Yogas I have mentioned, I offer below a brief sketch of each.

Hatha Yoga

This is the Yoga of physical culture, combining body-stretching postures and regulated breathing, designed to produce the utmost flexibility, health, and vitality. The word *hatha* comes from the Sanskrit word *ha,* meaning "sun," and *tha,* meaning "moon." It refers to the balance of these two forces, corresponding to the positive and negative polarities of the body.

The classic postures, called *asanas,* are patterned after the natural movements of animals and augmented by other exercises developed by various Yoga teachers. Any movement held static for a period of time with proper breath control, can become a Yoga position. By remaining motionless, we allow the body to stretch naturally to its own limits. We maintain the posture without forcing, and then let the body itself do the work of elasticizing unused muscles, ligaments, and tendons. Just by stretching and holding, we firm our muscles, increase our flexibility, and build up physical endurance.

The other vital aspect of Hatha Yoga is regulated breathing. Although the need to breathe properly in conjunction with exercise is stressed in popular fitness methods, the kind of breathing usually taught is shallow, utilizing only partial lung capacity. In Yoga, the breath is drawn in from the area of the diaphragm, utilizing the entire lung capacity by inhaling slowly and deeply through the nose only, which filters and purifies the breath. Obviously, the deeper we breathe, the more air we inhale, and the more oxygen our body receives. Increased oxygen intake means a healthier and more efficient heart and cardiovascular system. It also decreases tension and directs more oxygen to the brain. This results in greater mental alertness, clarity of thought, and increased serenity.

Marvelous as the results of Hatha Yoga are, most Eastern teachings relegate the practice of *asanas* to the bottom rung of the Yogic ladder. They concede that the body should be in perfect shape, but only as a step toward perfecting the spiritual state. Traditional Hindus, including many sects of Yogis, are only indirectly concerned with the body. They consider it just a temporary abode for the spirit, which for them is the one reality. They regard the soul, or self, as a complete entity and believe that the more the soul can separate itself from the body, the greater the experience of bliss will be. The ascetic strives to liberate the soul from the body and reunite it with the universal soul. Freed from its bondage to the physical world, it joins with the Divine, home at last.

Bhakti Yoga

This is the Yoga of love and devotion. To be a Bhakti Yogi means to surrender one's self completely to God. It is the Yoga of the Hindu masses, the most widely practiced form in India. It is also called the Yoga of the simple man because it is free from all dogma, and in its simplicity appeals to those who are highly religious and yet untutored. All other Yogas require a degree of learning and are not suitable for the majority of Indians, who can't even read. In contrast, Bhakti Yoga is a path of the heart, not the intellect.

With its major focus on love, adoration, and service, Bhakti Yoga is practiced through constant chanting of devotional Sanskrit hymns, prayers, and poems often accompanied by cymbals, tambourines, other instruments, and the clapping of hands. Its gatherings are uninhibitedly exuberant and emotional and generally evolve into spontaneous dancing and twirling. Bhakti also encourages self-sacrifice and acts of devotion and humility. Tending the sick, visiting the lonely and aged, and helping other people carry their burden are part of this religious practice.

Bhakti Yoga is probably the oldest form of Yoga, dating back to the pre-Aryan civilization. While it is devoted to the worship of Vishnu and Krishna, these two are not considered to be deities, but rather representatives of the one Supreme God. The Bhakta is not concerned with the abstractions of Brahma, the Atman, or the Absolute as are other Yogis. Like the Christian, he worships a single God who is seen as pure and divine love. Bhakti is similar in other ways to the Christian religion. Just as the Virgin Mary is venerated as the Mother of God, the Goddess Kali is revered as the Mother-Goddess of the Universe. Prayer and meditation are part of daily ritual, and chanting with prayer beads, or *malas,* is akin to saying the rosary. The names of ceremonies may differ, but many of the basic beliefs and acts of adoration are similar.

Karma Yoga

This is the Yoga of action and is sometimes recommended for Western students whose lives are deeply involved in action. It teaches that human beings are responsible for their actions, and that these actions shape both present and future destiny.

The ideal of the Karma Yogi is work for work's sake, not for the fruit of the work. The true Yogi does not regard his daily duties as labor or toil but as an act of love and worship for the Divine. Freed from desire and attachment to worldly things, he finds spiritual liberation in pure action.

Work, therefore, represents joy, happiness, and love. While this may be a beautiful ideal, it is unfortunately often misused by employers in India who exploit the poor and ignorant, and by gurus who take advantage of their disciples for their own gain.

While the emphasis on Karma Yoga is self-realization through action, the word *karma* describes the relationship of cause and effect. It can be interpreted as action and reaction, or, as Jesus said, "As ye sow, so shall ye reap!" It is the doctrine of responsibility for all of one's acts in all incarnations and the justification for good or bad fortune during one's lifetime.

During each lifetime on Earth, individuals have the chance to work out their karma and encounter the consequences of their past life and amend them, either through atonement or by progressing to a greater level of understanding and responsible action. Generally speaking, this involves two steps forward and one step back because there is always old karma to be worked out and new karma to be taken on. The doctrine of karma teaches us that nothing happens by accident; everything that occurs—be it momentous or insignificant—is both the action of a previous cause and the cause of a later effect. Nothing happens in isolation; everything is ultimately related. Unfortunately, in some teachings, this principle has become distorted and karma is misunderstood as fatalism. Believing that they have "bad karma," some people accept that they have no control over their life circumstances and no ability to alter them.

Yoga teaches us that we are here on Earth to gain experiences not possible otherwise, and that life is a series of lessons designed for our spiritual development. The principle of karma reminds us that each of us has a set of lessons to learn that are specific to our particular path of development. It is these experiences or lessons that lay the foundation for the quality of our present existence.

Raja Yoga

This form of Yoga is generally accepted as the King of Yogas, or the Royal Yoga. Its adherents believe it is the ultimate Yoga that will lead us to the highest level of being, called *samadhi, nirvana,* or enlightenment, in which one experiences permanent conscious union with the Absolute. An accomplished Raja Yogi has conquered his body and mind, his sense and passions, to merge with the Universal Self.

The higher meditative states achieved in Raja Yoga are most easily attained via the practice of Hatha Yoga. The *asanas* are designed to strengthen the Yogi's body to enable him to sit unmoving in the lotus seat for hours at a time. The breathing rituals purify his respiratory system and induce stillness of mind, and the cleansing techniques energize and purge his entire organism. The next preparatory step is concentration, learning to focus the mind on a single object or sound. This is the discipline required for meditation to be successful, for developing the ability to abandon the ordinary mind or the intangible part of it, the ego. Such concentrated focus enables one to turn deep within one's self, beyond the realm of thought and emotion. Once the body is sufficiently controlled, one can attempt to enter into a state transcendent of mind through timeless, undisturbed meditation. That is the essence of Raja Yoga.

Some Yogis say that by controlling our internal nature we control everything; others say that by controlling our external nature we control everything. Because in nature the internal and external merge into one, both statements are true.

The aim of life on Earth is to develop our Real Self to manifest the spirit within us. Like Karma Yoga, Raja Yoga claims that each of us holds our destiny in our own hands. One of the most important lessons we have to learn is that spiritual progress and development come from within. Human beings possess a consciousness of self not found in other forms of life. We have the awareness of ourselves as an "I," as a unique being, able to think and define ourselves and reach the highest manifestation of creation. We have the ability to evolve to higher levels of being while we are on Earth, leading us to greater spiritual heights when we depart.

Kundalini Yoga

Basic to every type of Yoga is the concept of *prana,* the life force. Essential to all life, it is found in every living thing, from the most elementary plant life to the most complex animal forms to huge celestial bodies. It is *in* matter, but it is not matter itself. It is *in* the air, but it is not air. Too subtle to be observed, *prana* exists as surely as does electricity and cosmic rays.

The Yogi believes that pranic energy is preserved throughout the body in six storage centers called *chakras*—literally translated, "circles" or "wheels." These subtle centers of consciousness are located along the spine and the head. The first is located at the base of the spine, the second at the genitals, the third near the navel, the fourth in the area of the heart, the fifth at the throat, and the sixth between the eyebrows. In a category by itself is the *chakra* at the top of the brain, containing what is referred to as the thousand-petaled lotus flower. This ancient scheme of *chakras* was, no doubt, the counterpart of what we call the autonomic nervous system, the regulator of involuntary anatomical functions. *Chakras* are plexes, and the third *chakra,* the solar plexus, is referred to as the abdominal brain by both the Yogi and the modern scientist.

Kundalini can be translated as spiritual energy or basic power. According to Yoga legend, intensive concentration on the *chakras* awakens Kundalini, the "coiled serpent" sleeping at the base of the spine. Meditation on the six basic *chakras* forces the energy depicted as the female Kundalini to move upward through a channel along the spinal cord, penetrating and awakening each *chakra* along the way. When she pierces the *chakra* at the top of the brain, its lotus petals open and the journey of the Kundalini is complete. She is symbolically united with her spouse, the male deity Shiva. Sexually, this process is comparable to the release of the libido (Freud's term for the sex urge, the psychic energy or force motivating human action), which thereby reveals itself as the source of man's creative, emotional, and spiritual drives. When the Kundalini bursts through the final *chakra, samadhi,* also called *nirvana* or *satori,* is achieved. Hindu teachings say that *samadhi* can be experienced many times, ultimately resulting in complete enlightenment. Then Shiva and Shakti (the personification of the divine feminine) are united forever in a permanent state of blissful oneness.

Tantric Yoga

In Tantric Yoga, the conscious direction of sexual energy resulting in divine union is synonymous with spiritual awakening. Tantra is a cult of ecstasy, a personal religion based on the mystical experience of joy rather than established dogma. It is the worship of sex as energizing, lifegiving, and sacred. The Tantrika believes that conscious sexual union most closely approximates the bliss of union with the Divine. Tantric practices include meditation, breathing techniques, and rituals, involving all the senses in a deeply respectful cooperation with mind and spirit in order to reach mystical peaks. They are usually performed with partners of the opposite sex.

Tantra recognizes the benefits of Yoga exercises in sexually stimulating and energizing all the organs, intensifying their function. The emphasis is on stimulation rather than ejaculation and reproduction. Tantra places high value on moment-to-moment awareness and a deep experience of relatedness with your partner, rather than goal-oriented sexual performance. However, any form of sexual expression can be Tantric if approached with the attitude that all is divine. And, ultimately, the energy made available through Tantric practice is for regeneration of vital energies, resulting in the expansion of consciousness.

(Tantric yoga, along with Kabbalah, an ancient teaching of Jewish mysticism, has evolved in to a New Age undertaking of special appeal to those in the entertainment field.

Both practices engage in similar rituals, and share the conviction that the semen needs to be preserved.)

* * *

Though the paths of Bhakti, Karma, Raja, Kundalini, and Tantra Yoga can all be tread on the road to enlightenment, consider this before you jump into them just yet. Although some traditionalists may say that Hatha Yoga is not the way to spiritual purification, I believe that it is as profound as any other Yoga. Is it not said that the body is the temple of the spirit? Isn't it respectful to this temple to keep it in as perfect a condition as possible? So, I will make my case and entice you to look into Hatha Yoga as something that can be of great value to you, and that, in addition, can be easily incorporated into your daily lifestyle.

Yoga is the science of life and the art of living. It is the common sense path to overall physical and mental fitness. For me, there exists no other exercise system that reaches every part of the musculoskeletal system, and no other method that exercises the inner organism as well as the outer body.

For the body to be in perfect condition, every single part must be involved. Today, the greatest emphasis in the fitness movement is on cardiovascular performance. However, the heart is just one of six hundred thirty-six muscles in the body. In Yoga you will find all the physical movements you need for superb overall physical health. It also offers a multitude of relaxation and meditation techniques to achieve mental fitness, calm, and vitality.

To practice Yoga, you don't have to join a gym or a health club. No gadgets or special equipment are required. You don't need a personal trainer at your side every day. All you need is a towel, a little space, and some preliminary instruction, through attending a Yoga course or following a book or a video.

When pushed against the wall, most people who shun exercise have the ready excuse: "But I don't have time!" Can't get away with that one! Regardless of how busy we are, everyone can spend ten to fifteen minutes a day on exercise, five minutes on breathing practice, and fifteen minutes on meditation. Consistently practiced, these three aspects of Yoga can make the difference between feeling "blah" or feeling great every day of your life.

Other popular excuses I won't accept are the complaints: "I'm too overweight... too out of shape... too weak... too out of breath... and definitely too old! And I'll never be able to stand on my head!" "Nonsense!" I answer. "Yoga can benefit everyone from eight to eighty!"

My experience is that virtually everyone, regardless of age and physical condition—even those afflicted with health problems—can be helped. I have worked with people suffering from such chronic degenerative diseases as arthritis, rheumatism, asthma, and hypertension who have improved their conditions. Others have experienced relief from tendinitis, bursitis, respiratory afflictions, allergies, obesity, digestive disorders, and a slew of gynecological problems. I know many people who, through practicing Yoga, have been successful in relieving, alleviating, and curing every kind of back problem, often eliminating the need for surgery.

Yoga can be started in kindergarten and practiced by someone of seventy, or even eighty. It's not uncommon for older practitioners to display more physical vigor than someone half their age. And they don't have to stand on their head or sit in the lotus seat unless they opt to do so. There exist a multitude of nonstrenuous, yet challenging, yoga poses and stretches suited to every kind of body, all of which increase vitality, restore flexibility, control weight, and firm up muscles.

When it comes to the aging process, Yoga cannot stop the clock, but it can slow it down. I offer myself as a fitting example. I am seventy-five years old and in extremely good shape. I am healthier, more energetic and vital than I was in my twenties. I feel great all the time and am rarely sick. And yes, I am still a size eight! Although my back injuries have healed, with age I have developed severe disc deterioration and spinal curvature. Those who have viewed my X-rays couldn't believe that I am even able to walk. Yet my back is incredibly strong, supple, and pain free.

Which brings me to the subject of flexibility, which I feel has been sadly neglected by both advocates and adherents in the fitness world. We are led to believe that we are in top physical shape if we participate in marathons and triathlons, rock climbing, weight lifting, and step aerobics, etc. Yes, we may be strong, muscular, and trim, but unless we balance these activities with proper stretchings, we forego true flexibility. The stretches currently practiced in most sports and fitness programs do not fill the bill as far as I am concerned.

We used to be able to touch our toes; now the average person can hardly touch his knees! The Yogi believes that the spine is our lifeline, and that a flexible spine and good posture are insurance for healthy, pain-free old age. Fortunately, the spine is constructed to gain and regain flexibility, regardless of whether we've exercised it or allowed it to deteriorate, and all Yoga exercises are geared to promote elasticity.

The increase of flexibility and agility is only one of the numerous benefits that will become evident in a relatively short time of Yoga practice. You will sleep better, feel better, look better, and your energy and endurance level will increase considerably. You'll notice that you are able to more easily release tension and relax. Soon you will develop good balance and coordination and your posture will improve. In time you can normalize your weight and firm sagging muscles. Flab, sags, bulges, and wrinkles can be prevented or reduced. Yoga restores and maintains youthfulness and, as a bonus, has been known to rejuvenate sexual performance and counteract impotence!

In Yoga, a most important factor in restoring and maintaining good health is proper breathing. The scientifically based method of Yogic breathing that I described earlier relieves and combats all respiratory diseases, sinusitis, and nasal blockages, and can prevent and cure colds. It also helps relieve pulmonary diseases such as asthma and emphysema. And, Yoga can most certainly help you to stop smoking—I can personally vouch for it!

I realize, of course, that I can't convince everyone to jump on the Yoga wagon, especially the young and competitive among us who may deem Yoga to be too slow, too rigid, and too disciplined to fit their lifestyle. And, it may be possible that for some people Yoga might not be exactly the right thing—though I rarely met anyone who felt that way once they tried it! But if you are devoted to your particular exercise system and are receiving benefit from it, continue by all means. Just be aware that all exercise methods work only if you apply them consistently. To achieve significant, lasting results that will enhance your life and health, further your growth, and promote self-satisfaction, daily practice is the answer. It is the key to success in every endeavor.

Traveling a spiritual path does not require that you sit on a mountain top and chant OM all day long, sit in a lotus position, or emulate saints. You just need to devote a short period of your day to exercise, breath control, and meditation.

As we stretch and hold the poses and breathe deeply and regularly, we become aware of our body, its functions and its ingenuity, and experience its deep connectedness with our mind. As we effortlessly include meditation into our practice, we find a sense of oneness with ourselves and the universe.

Through a more fit body and a finer mind, we learn to assume responsibility for ourselves, which can positively influence world thinking and help bring about world peace. As we realize our power to change our bodies, our health, our thought system, and therefore our life, we can effect change in others as well. We realize that though we did not intentionally create the disease, poverty, starvation, and wars in our midst, we are not just innocent bystanders. We allowed it to happen. But now we know that with our newfound strength and our capacity for transformation, we can make a dent in the task of creating a better world.

CHAPTER TWO

OF GURUS AND CULTS: DON'T FOLLOW THE LEADER!

The guru crusade of the sixties was one of the offshoots of the youth rebellion against society, materialism, and governmental and parentally imposed structures. The disillusioned generation discovered their spiritual path in Eastern religions; of these, Hinduism, Buddhism, and Zen attracted the lion's share of followers.

The guru (from *gu*—"darkness" and *ru*—"light") was acclaimed as the spiritual teacher who leads the student from darkness to light, and, it is said, from the unreal to the real and from death to immortality. Only *he* is qualified to guide you toward the achievement of *samadhi,* or enlightenment. Today the term *guru* has become part of our vocabulary, referring to a charismatic leader in any field of enterprise.

Herman Hesse's book *Siddhartha,* the story of the Buddha, became the "in" book on campus, and American youth longed to go to the sacred river to free their souls from bondage. They believed that they could only find peace and spiritual enlightenment by journeying to India and placing themselves under the guidance of a spiritual teacher—the guru. Many young Americans dressed themselves as Sikhs, in white robes and turbans; as Yogis, in saffron-colored garb; or as sannyasins, in shades of red and orange. They wore prayer beads or a *mala* with a picture of their guru around their neck. The men let their hair grow or shaved it off completely. Children born John, Mary, Bob, or Nancy were renamed Gopala, Devi, Krishna, or

Satya after a legendary Hindu god. They proclaimed their love for the Indian teacher and his God, or for the teacher as a god himself.

Many made pilgrimages to India to seek a guru, a procedure initiated by the Beatles and other pop figures who sponsored the guru immigration to this country. A fair number of these gurus happily traveled to the States, anxious to address and serve the eager multitudes. I met some of these newcomers, who arrived with only the clothes on their backs, when they came as guests of various established *ashrams* (Sanskrit for spiritual communes). They appeared to be humble, grateful to be in our country, and eager to please. But thanks to the generosity of enthusiastic, spiritually starved, and wealthy patrons and seekers, it took no time at all to set them up in their own *ashrams* and launch the promotion of lucrative enterprises.

Everyone is probably familiar with the Maharishi Mahesh Yogi, also called the giggling guru and sometimes falsely credited with inventing meditation. Transcendental Meditation, or TM, became a howling success and served as one of the finest examples of good PR. TM was copyrighted, widely advertised, cleverly packaged, and sold as the panacea for all our ailments and an instant source of peace and enlightenment. The little guru emerged both as a genius and as a multimillionare. He lost some of his credibility when it was discovered that his supposedly "secret" mantras were shared by thousands of people, and when his teachings of levitation were denounced as bogus (the practice was then renamed Yogic hopping). I have, however, been informed that he personally is a humble soul, uninfluenced by fame and riches.

Another guru who hit the headlines in the eighties, Bhagwan Shree Rajneesh, was perhaps best known for supposedly owning ninety-three Rolls Royces. It is said that he had already accumulated tremendous wealth in India, but this apparently multiplied when he came to Oregon, where thousands of his followers lived on a sixty-four-thousand-acre ranch. His original *ashram* in Poona, India, was renowned for therapies that included group sex. (I once witnessed a movie segment of the goings on in the *Ashram* and it was heavy porno indeed!) Many young people, mostly Europeans, flocked to his commune to share his philosophy that sex is natural and divine. Rajneesh's emphasis on sex as a door to enlightenment apparently simmered down in the Oregon city that was named after him, Rajneeshpuram, and issues surrounding the abuse of power moved into the limelight. The nearby township of Antelope voluntarily disincorporated as a way to escape the influence of the Rajneeshees, and people in the surrounding area became extremely nervous that the powerful group would expand and eventually take over their towns as well. As he preached his message of world peace attainable through nonattachment to materialism, he and a number of his disciples set out to accumulate their riches through various profitable enterprises, such as drug trafficking, prostitution, abuse of charitable funds, and exploitation of his free labor force.

Rajneesh, a former philosophy professor, was considered to be the most intellectual and profound guru of them all, and he was definitely the most mesmerizing. When he spoke in his beautiful, velvety voice on his vision of the New Man, he dispensed energy that could produce a hypnotic trance, and followers were apt to confuse this with authentic meditative states. He also recommended the daily practice of Dynamic Meditation, a process that included a catharsis that left the meditators high and enraptured after a period of releasing pent-up emotions by screaming, shaking, and crying.

Eventually, corruption, dissension, and internal political conflict caused the Oregon commune to collapse. Rajneesh was indicted for immigration fraud by the United States government and expelled from the States. He did, however, have a sizable sum left when he went back to India, where he returned to the site of the original *ashram* in Poona. He died there in 1990, insisting that the United States government had poisoned him while he was briefly jailed before being deported.

* * *

When my children left home and I knew my husband to be wrapped up in his own affairs, I became a full-time Yoga junkie. Other than my involvement in my school, public appearances, and lectures, I spent my weekends and free time attending Yoga seminars or visiting Yoga *ashrams.* They had sprung up *en masse,* almost overnight, in New York and surrounding states. For a week each summer, I visited the Sivananda Ashram in Val Morin, Canada, in the Laurentian Mountains. The *ashram,* plus a Sivananda Yoga Camp in the Bahamas and several smaller retreat centers throughout the country, were all established by Swami Vishnudevananda, generally addressed as Swami Vishnu or Swamiji. (*Ananda* means "bliss" in Sanskrit and is appended to the name of most Swamis; *ji* is a term of affection.) He was the first Swami I had ever encountered. He was clad in a saffron-colored wrap-around that consisted of yards of material that clung to his body and which, amazingly, never slipped—not even when he performed a handstand. It looked like a sari, and it exposed his arms and one shoulder in winter as well as in summer. I never saw him wear shoes. Swami Vishnu did not at all fit my image of a holy man; he looked too sexy and vital.

He must have been in his late forties when I first met him, and I thought him to be quite attractive. Although short and stocky, he was well built and muscular, with gray wavy hair, dark velvety skin, and a beautiful smile—when he chose to display it. He had immigrated to Canada many years previously, and his was the first established Hatha Yoga *ashram* in the Western hemisphere. I had been truly impressed when I first came across the book he had written as a young man about Yoga exercises. But when I witnessed his demonstrations of the most intricate poses in obvious middle age, I was filled with awe.

Swami Vishnu was of modest background and had trained in Yoga as a youngster. He had spent a few years in the Indian army where, apparently, his training inspired him to run his *ashram* like an army boot camp. He taught most of the classes, and when he didn't teach personally, was always around to supervise, criticize, and often terrorize. The exercises were hard work, performed on wooden platforms for two hours twice each day. I worked like crazy to compete with everyone younger than I. But I loved the challenge and the way my body responded to the almost acrobatic gyrations that were expected from us, and I was thrilled that I could keep up.

I waited and hoped and prayed (as did everyone else) for a compliment or even a nod of recognition from the great guru, but none was ever forthcoming. When we passed each other, he acknowledged my silent *namasté* (a respectful greeting honoring the divine nature in all of us, conveyed by pressing palms together under the chin), but in all the years that I came to the Canadian *ashram,* he never learned my name. He ignored me as he did all his paying guests, leaving all their needs to be handled by his disciples, who emulated and adored him. The disciples treated us efficiently but impersonally, and their attitude toward us implied that they, who served the master directly, were "the chosen ones." They taught us to be disciplined, uncomplaining, and unquestioning.

The camp was situated on acres and acres of beautiful countryside high in the mountains and was equipped for at least three hundred guests. Visitors flocked there from everywhere in the world, but most came from the States. We had to rise at five a.m. to be in the meditation hall promptly at five-thirty. Mornings in the Laurentians were bitterly cold and generally rainy, summer and winter. We sat on the hardwood floor, barefoot and preferably in the lotus seat, wrapped in the scratchy, wet, smelly blankets from our beds. For one hour we chanted, then sat for another hour in silent meditation. The same ritual took place every evening after dinner. Nonattendance was inexcusable and resulted in immediate expulsion. In between, we attended compulsory Hatha Yoga breathing sessions and Sanskrit classes, as well as instruction in various

Hindu rituals. Periods of organized hiking and walking were combined with the practice of silence.

Free time was sparsely and reluctantly doled out. At night, we had to attend lectures by visiting swamis or other dignitaries from India, who all spoke a heavily accented English that was impossible to understand. On other nights, Swamiji would lecture, and his English was not much better. His favorite topic was the evils of meat-eating, and his talk was usually accompanied by gruesome slides of animals in agony as they were being led to the slaughterhouse. He could rant for hours about the carnivorous inhumanity of American cuisine and loved to warn us of the diseases in store for us if we were to thus indulge. He, himself, was a dedicated junk eater. He seemed to live on pizza, ice cream, and chocolate, and each year when I returned I noticed he had gained more weight, until finally he could no longer exercise. He had no use for clothes, wearing his *schmatte* for every occasion, yet he was a hedonist, indulging himself to the *n*th degree. He was not into luxury cars or motorcycles, as were some other gurus, but he owned a valuable art gallery and a series of small planes that he flew himself. He appointed himself an ambassador of world peace and would periodically fly to one or another war- or strife-torn country and distribute peace flyers. His ego was boundless, and to his disciples he was God.

Most of them he turned into swamis, demanding that they be celibate. He also bestowed the honor of swamihood to the middle-aged ladies who left their families—and left their worldly possessions to him. He shipped them off (on a one-way ticket) to remote places throughout the world to open and run Sivananda Ashrams. He preached that swamihood—a pure life unbesmirched by carnal desires—is next to godliness, but did not practice what he preached. Although the secret was kept for many years, it was eventually discovered that the good Swami fooled around. This resulted in a public scandal, which soon died down and was considered just a temporary blemish on his image.

You may wish to know, "Why did you keep going back to Val Morin if you were so critical?" and you have a point. It is true that I was offended by the guru reverence and adulation that I had always resented and spoken against. (At times, my own students indicated that they wished me to be their guru and addressed me as such. I always firmly refused their request.) I most certainly detested the rigid and ritualistic practices I allowed myself to be forced into and I objected to Vishnu's antics. I did, however, respect his expertise as a practitioner and teacher of Hatha Yoga and I learned much from him that I was able to share with my students.

I perfected my breathing techniques while I was there and I learn to meditate. In the beginning, during meditation periods I sat in the dark, dank hall, shivering in my disgusting blanket and wished I were anywhere else. I tried to keep myself from drifting off to sleep by picturing all the good food I would eat once I got back to civilization. But gradually I learned to concentrate—the first step in meditation—usually on somebody's snoring. I learned to harness my mind and then let it dissolve into nothingness. I eventually came to experience meditation as a beautiful and meaningful discipline.

I also learned to fast, and once I got over the initial discomfort of hunger pains, it was a wonderful experience. I was able to be without food for as long as six days, feeling light, refreshed, and rejuvenated in body and mind. The breathing and *asana* practices became joyful experiences, and afterward I felt stronger and healthier than ever. The beauty of nature, clarity of the air, and purity of the water were all conducive to fasting, but what made it so easy was the vileness of the food at the camp. I didn't object that it was vegetarian, but I abhorred the unloving, tasteless, and often unsanitary way it was prepared and served.

Despite Vishnu's obnoxiousness, I admit that I admired his chutzpah, and I did have a certain fondness for him, perhaps because he gave me my first mantra. It took me a long time to receive it because everyone else seemed to be standing in line for it (I suspect that he gave the same mantra to one and all). But I use it to this day, and his face still appears before me during meditation.

The last time I saw Vishnu, he was in his late sixties but looked as old as Methuselah. He was so fat that he could hardly walk, and he had become senile. I could not help feeling sad. Somehow he got back to India and died shortly after.

Another well-known guru I sometimes visited was Swami Satchidananda, who resided in an *ashram* in New York State. He founded Integral Yoga Societies in every major city of the United States and in almost every other country and continent. He had been one of the sponsored ones from India and came to the States in 1966, leaving his wife and children behind. In no time at all, he amassed a sizable force of benefactors and disciples and was well on his way to spreading his particular message and gospel around the world. Like Vishnu, he was an adept Hatha Yogi and had published a book that pictured him in intricate poses. He did not teach the exercises himself, but he had no problem accumulating a huge teaching staff who taught under his supervision. I wasn't crazy about the classes I took there; too much emphasis was given to spiritual rituals and not enough to *asanas,* as far as I was concerned.

When I first visited the *ashram,* I was amazed and repelled by the goings-on. All the guru-disciple formalities described in ancient Sanskrit writings were carried out here. The acolytes walked ten feet behind their master, with their palms touching in *namasté* and head bowed toward the ground. They ate the leftovers from the Swami's dish after each meal and constantly fanned him to protect his skin from the sun. I witnessed at least ten disciples attending to him simultaneously as he reclined in his chair. They were massaging his back, manicuring his nails, washing and anointing his feet, and combing his hair and beard. The Swami was very tall and well built, but I always thought that his beautiful white beard was the only impressive thing about him. Judging from his lectures, he was neither mesmerizing nor intellectual, and I thought to myself, 'Take away his beard and what do you have?'

Swami Satchidananda liked fast cars, motorcycles, and Rolex watches, in addition to collecting property. I am sure the he is still one of the richest yogis alive. He was also exposed for breaking his chastity vows, having demanded sexual favors from young girls. For a while, this made headlines around the Yoga circuit, but the scandal subsided within a short time.

Swami Muktananda was undoubtedly the most eminent of all the gurus. He had well-established *ashrams* in India even before he came to the States. Each weekend, hundreds of devotees made the pilgrimage to his retreat in the Catskill Mountains to receive *shaktipat*, or Kundalini awakening, via a touch on the head with his famed peacock feather. Out of sheer curiosity, I went to see him one Sunday and had to stand in line for hours in the broiling summer sun until it was my time to be "hit." I didn't experience anything in particular, but around me everyone who had been "graced" by the feather seemed to be in ecstasy. They were screaming, weeping, moaning, tearing off their clothes and, I could swear, having orgasms. I decided that they were all unhinged and that I was the only person there in my right mind.

Although he was acclaimed as a genius, to me Muktananda was a ridiculous, funny-looking little bearded man in a woolen stocking cap, whacking away with his peacock feather. He never learned to speak English, yet he accumulated a worldwide following and became increasingly famous, successful, and wealthy over the years. He died a few years ago, and when the rumors of *his* sexual exploits reached his people, many were disenchanted. His teachings had emphasized sexual abstinence as the key to spiritual growth.

Every guru I have ever heard speak has delivered the same message: God is within you, and you are God. You are divine. Be your own teacher, your own savior, your own master, your own God. And, with the exception of Rajneesh's sannyasins, disciples are taught to regard sex and possessions as obstacles to their spiritual growth. Yet, each of the westernized gurus I have met set himself up as God. He claimed to possess all the answers to the puzzle of human existence and to be the only one who can lead you to truth.

The guru maintains that he has something that you cannot know through ordinary channels and offers you access to hidden realities—as long as you bow to his authority, hand your life over to him, and submit to him unquestioningly. He promises you *samadhi, nirvana,* enlightenment, but in return demands absolute discipline, obedience, and unconditional service. You must accept whatever the guru preaches, and every doubt is proof of your unworthiness. You are led to believe that the more bizarre his actions are, the more likely he is to be right. To the guru, the disciple is a nonentity. He who claims to be enlightened should demonstrate not only great wisdom, but compassion as well. Yet, I have never met a guru who paid heed to his disciples' personal needs or who showed the slightest interest in his students as individuals. The guru is supposed to be loving, but instead demonstrates self-love and self-importance.

"Are there any true gurus?" you may want to know. "Do they exist?" Yes, they do exist, but most of us never get to hear about them. True spiritual gurus who believe and live by all the precepts of Yoga—cleanliness, austerity, nonviolence, harmlessness, truthfulness, spirituality, and self-knowledge—can be found. However, they mostly dwell in isolated regions, living ascetic lives in the Himalayas. They descend into the world only on rare occasions, when they feel that they have an important message to deliver. Then they come forth without fanfare. Otherwise, those sincerely in search of peace and fulfillment must seek them out in their isolated retreats.

To strive toward enlightenment under the guidance of these teachers, one must adhere to rigid rules and disciplines for months or even years. One has to withstand great hardship and self-denial that only very few can endure. True gurus possess the knowledge, the expertise, and the power to raise the Kundalini of those they deem worthy and ready to progress. The ritual involves careful and loving guidance on the part of the guru and requires disregard of time by the disciple.

"But don't we need a guru to lead us on a spiritual path?" you ask. It is through this very perception—which is evidence of our dependence on someone else for our growth—that *we* have created gurus in our midst. We cannot fault them. They did not deliberately intend to defraud, mislead, or enslave us, becoming the symbol of intimidation and arrogance. And I am certain that they did not expect such fame, power, and riches to come their way. Many originally came to our country with sincere desire to inculcate us with Hindu concepts and values, purportedly for our own good. People from the East and the Middle East generally believe that we in the West are devoid of spirituality, and that North Americans especially are steeped in worthless religions, materialism, depravity, and lawlessness. While he proselytizes Yoga, the guru in fact involves his disciples in the principles and precepts of his religion, which are by no means one and the same. The principles form a philosophy and the precepts make up a religion—in the case of Hinduism, possibly the most dogmatic of them all. As dedicated followers of the guru, we allow ourselves to become enmeshed in a foreign culture, absorbing its symbolism, practicing its rituals, and worshipping its Gods. In this sense, guruism is just another religious cult, on a par with the Hare Krishnas and other similar movements.

As a devout religionist, the guru is only fulfilling his spiritual obligations, so we cannot blame him for deceiving us. It is *we* who empower him to take advantage of our gullibility, and we are the ones who permit him to treat us as immature dependents. *We* listen, enraptured, as he speaks to us in metaphors, parables, and riddles that only a few can comprehend, yet all pretend to grasp. While he keeps us guessing, *we* insist that he is profound. In our immaturity, *we* need to believe that the guru is omniscient and omnipotent, that he is perfect and wise and we are not. Our willingness to identify with his Eastern religion and its belief in karma, reincarnation, and striving toward *nirvana* may be motivated by true spiritual yearnings, but our discrimination is often faulty in the face of that desire.

If we think that the guru has misrepresented himself, exploited us, or betrayed us, we must be aware that we gave him license to do so. We chose to idolize him and put him on a pedestal. Taking responsibility for this is the first step for disentangling oneself.

I have often attended lectures by J. Krishnamurti, an Indian educator and philosopher who died in the eighties. He spoke about relying on one's intuition and railed against guruism and guru worship. He begged his audiences, "Don't think of me as your guru! There is only one guru and he is within you!" Invariably, after his lectures people would huddle together outside to discuss forming Krishnamurti gatherings or study groups.

No, we do not need a guru. We should never depend on one person as our guide; if we do we won't progress and reach new plateaus of consciousness. What we require are teachers for inspiration and guidance to help lead us to our inner teacher. In reality, everyone can be a teacher and we can learn from all.

How can you tell who is a good teacher? A good teacher never intimidates. He is humble, honest, and patient, and encourages the student to search for the answers himself before resorting to books or other outside sources for ready solutions. He allows the student to make his own decisions and teaches him to trust their validity. The objective of a true spiritual teacher is to help the student understand that all his suffering and self-doubt are of his own making. He may act as a travel guide, but he lets the student journey on his own; he supports each student along his own unique path of initiation, without imposing his personal will or selfish demands.

I hear your concern: "Can't you say anything good about the guru?" Of course I can. Many people have sought spiritual refuge and have found it in the seclusion of an *ashram*. Many who have been overcome by sorrow and tragedy and overwhelmed by life have come to peace through participating in seminars and retreats led by gurus. Practicing Yoga, meditation, chanting, and inwardness has changed their lives. Many people who have lost hope and trust have found the courage to go on through the guidance of a spiritual leader.

Despite the dangers and drawbacks, I believe that of the large number of people who joined *ashrams* in the sixties and seventies, adolescents benefited the most. Many had run away from home, had been ousted from society for their behavior, or were addicted to drugs and alcohol. The *ashram* offered them shelter and protection and taught discipline and clean living. I must say, in all honesty, that these groups may have saved many lives in this way. Yogi Bhajan, a well-known, wealthy Sikh guru, established drug rehabilitation centers where Sikh religious practices, healthy food, Yogic breathing, and meditation were successful in counteracting the effects of the drugs.

The son of good friends of mine, hopelessly addicted for many years, was cured after staying in Yogi Bhajan's Arizona center for one year. He is fine and functional today. He did, however, have the good sense and courage to leave the *ashram* once he knew that he was cured. It was not easy because he was enticed and besieged with pleas to stay on and was warned of the consequences that would befall him if he didn't.

That is the crux of the guru strategy, as I see it. Learning and serving under the guru is *never* accepted as a temporary arrangement; it is considered a commitment for life. Gurus say that discipleship is forever, so those who break away are regarded as traitors. The disciple is made to feel that the *ashram* is his true home, the guru is his protecting parent, and that he cannot face the outside world by himself.

From all of this, you might think that disciples are an unhappy lot, but I would say that the exact opposite is the case. Most *ashram* residents consider themselves fortunate that they do not have to face the uncertainties of the job market and compete in the business world. They are grateful that all their needs are taken care of and that all decisions are made for them. They have surrendered their individuality, but are loathe to leave the safety of their cocoon to regain it.

The guru mania has subsided somewhat; there is no influx from India at present, and some of the better-known gurus have passed on to the next world. But the guru business is still very much alive and prospering. Established *ashrams* and Yoga societies bearing a guru's name are in existence all over the world, and all are doing well. Quite a few disciples of Vishnudevananda, Muktananda, and Rajneesh still serve their masters, propagating their practices of Hatha Yoga, *satsang* (celebrating in the presence of the guru), silent sitting, or Dynamic Meditation. Muktananda's chosen successor, Gurumayi, has amassed a group of her own disciples and travels all over the world to uphold her guru's teachings. Rajneesh's sannyasins still meet in groups, and though they no longer wear red, they still practice Dynamic Meditation and are devoted to each other and the vision of their master.

"Is there a difference between guruism and cultism?" you may ask. Yes, there is. And differences also exist among the gurus and cult leaders themselves. While Rajneesh's empire embodied corruption and violence, Satchidananda, for instance, may have been arrogant but was otherwise harmless. Some cults are law-abiding and others are radical and dangerous.

A cult is generally the projection of one person's psyche and philosophy, whereas guruism adheres to an established religious dogma. In guruism, it may seem that you are offering devotion to just one person, but you are actually aligning yourself to the beliefs and doctrines of the guru's entire lineage. So, while a cult extols a particular individual, guruism promotes an ideology that has developed over time through many individuals.

In both cases, the followers make the leader of central importance—whether he is a swami, lama, or roshi; an evangelist, scientist, psychotherapist, or politician; or a pied piper. The cult leader or guru almost always possesses charismatic, mesmeric, or magnetic powers, or at least believes he does. If not, he deliberately develops them. All leaders of this type boast of their supremacy and expect their doctrines to be accepted as absolute truths. Each one professes to have a unique message that benefits humankind and to possess *the* solution for a better world.

Some cult organizations and guru-oriented communities allow contact with the outside and with family; others create a group autonomy and isolate themselves from the rest of the world. Members of some of these groups are coerced to forsake former lives, friends, and family, and are persuaded that a better life can be achieved only within the confines of the *ashram* or cult. Initiates are expected to surrender their identities and ego and give up or share their possessions with their new family. Some groups demand all your worldly goods; others expect you to contribute all or part of your salary to the divine cause.

Exploitation of the devotee—be it financial, physical, emotional, or sexual—is the common denominator in all constrictive structures. Cults may employ brainwashing techniques, sleep deprivation, scare tactics, or disciplinary measures to subdue their flocks. In *ashrams,* compulsory, almost incessant incantation of mantras, prayers, and chants produces the same effects.

Who worship those who keep them enslaved and are therefore typified as freaks, fools, or weak-minded by "normal" members of society? Generally speaking, they are young and restless, purposeless, lonely, insecure, afraid to make decisions for themselves, and scared to face the world. Regardless of age, they are almost always immature. Some are disenchanted with family, friends, lovers, and societal structure. Many think themselves different from anyone else, or feel they don't belong—they aren't one of the crowd. Others believe themselves to be nonconformists, idealists, or potential saviors of humanity.

Regardless of public image, I believe that everyone who has joined such a group did so willingly or allowed themselves to be converted. Cults, especially, employ high-powered recruiting techniques. Many ex-members and so-called cult-snatchers insist that innocent victims have been duped, betrayed, lied to, coerced, or abducted, but I doubt this is true. In my view, no one can be talked into something that is repugnant to his nature. Most everyone who joined found their niche of gratification, especially at the beginning. The leader was the a substitute for a father or mother figure and the group represented the rest of the family.

Those who became involved experienced friendship, affection, a sense of belonging, and often, sexual satisfaction. They were fawned upon, flattered, and praised for their courage in abandoning the outside world of cruelty, corruption, and evil. This was especially true in the beginning of their affiliation. They were made to believe that they were the chosen ones, the elite—more knowledgeable, idealistic, and powerful than those on the "outside." They felt privileged to lead a meaningful life on the path to spiritual fulfillment.

Many remained because they felt that they had no life outside the group and that they were lucky to be included. Others didn't know if this was really the case but let themselves be convinced of it. However, they all were aware that they had committed themselves to the leader and were expected to serve him or his ideas for the rest of their lives. In groups like these, there is *never* a legitimate reason for leaving, and everyone is indoctrinated with the belief that terrible consequences will befall them if they do. Many eventually become disenchanted and, fortunately, find the courage to break away, returning to society to carve out a new life or continue where they left off. Others choose to resign themselves to remaining, afraid to face the world and its responsibilities. Or, having abandoned their outside relationships, they feel that they have no one else to turn to.

It is interesting to note that everyone who belongs to or has been part of a leader-controlled group rejects the word *cult*; none of them will admit that theirs is or was a cult. And, in all likelihood, nobody ever said, "Let's make a cult!" I assume that all cult leaders started out with the sincere belief that they had the solution that would end all human suffering and keep the world from falling apart. (It is quite possible that Hitler, in his demented state of mind, sincerely believed that he was saving Germany by exterminating the Jews.)

Of the various cults with which we are familiar, most are religious cults. We find new-age religions and old-age revivals, worshipping God, Jesus, Jehovah, Eastern deities, Satan, and the almighty dollar.

One of the first cultists to turn away from traditional religion and turn out the profits was Father Divine, a black man who came to fame in Harlem during the Depression years. He believed that he had been chosen to lead the poor and the oppressed, principally those of his own race, to dignity and prosperity. He established communes to house and feed his fast-expanding flock, whom he called his children. In return, he demanded that they unconditionally surrender their earnings from outside jobs, abstain from sex, and have no relationships with outsiders. Individual thought was totally suppressed. In time, his messianic fervor developed into business acumen, and his kingdom became one of lucrative enterprises and accumulation of valuable property.

The most extreme examples of religious cultism were, of course, the Hare Krishnas and the Moonies, primarily because of their public solicitation schemes. The Hare Krishnas were certainly the most colorful on the cult scene, in their orange robes and shaved heads, beating drums, shaking tambourines, and playing finger cymbals. An Indian businessman named A.C. Bhaktivedanta Prabhupad, who was committed to integrating Hindu religious tradition into American culture, brought the movement to the United States. He died in the seventies, and to the best of my knowledge, appointed no successor, though the movement still continues without a central figure. It is still widespread, especially in Europe, renamed as Iscon, or the International Society of Krishna Consciousness.

Hare Krishnas deem themselves to be the exclusive disciples of Lord Krishna, whom they exalt as the highest manifestation of the Godhead, and all worship and ritual is dedicated to his image. The practice of Bhakti Yoga, including dancing and endless, monotonous chanting of "Hare Krishna" seems to be the devotees' sole purpose in life.

* * *

The Unification Church, whose members are known as the Moonies, is the brainchild of Sun Myung Moon, or Reverend Moon, a self-ordained, charismatic preacher (like Muktananda, unable to speak English). He claimed that he received direct orders from God and Jesus to save the world. In reality, his religion represents a mishmash of East Asian folk religion and fundamentalist religion.

His movement began in South Korea, but it rapidly spread throughout the United States, Europe, and other countries. Like other self-styled messiahs, he predicted that the end of the world was imminent, but retracted his prophecies each time this failed to happen. He attracted his followers through highly organized and well-financed recruiting and publicity schemes. Beneath his facade of religious fervor, he was a shrewd businessman with political ambitions. His intention was to control corporations and political organizations, and he very nearly succeeded. He amassed millions of dollars and probably close to a million followers.

* * *

The Children of God, though not as flamboyant as the Moonies and Hare Krishnas, received their share of attention as a religious cult. They were part of the Jesus crusade of the sixties and seventies. Their leader, David Berg (Moses), a second-generation evangelist, appealed to hippies who had become disillusioned and burned out with the drug scene and were seeking new, meaningful directions. The cult started out as a fundamentalist Christian movement, attracting its followers from college campuses, communes, and the streets of Haight-Ashbury. His group also solicited donations on a large scale from the society it condemned as corrupt, and prospered sufficiently to establish COG societies, communes, and colonies in practically every continent.

When Berg's predictions—various catastrophes he foresaw based on a combination of Bible prophecies and his own imagination—did not materialize, he fell into disfavor, especially in the United States. He retreated to foreign shores to live in seclusion, but his movement is still very much alive. Although the cult aroused a furor during its heyday, and many members were undoubtedly psychically scarred and maimed, no one was reported to have been killed.

* * *

The horrors of Jonestown and Waco, however, created an unparalleled nightmare when mass murder/suicide was committed, in one case via cyanide-laced Kool-Aid, and in the latter, through immolation. (It can be assumed that the cult members themselves were unaware of their destiny.) The leaders of established religions held up The People's Temple of Jim Jones and the Branch Davidians organized by David Koresh as the epitome of the evils evoked by New Age religions.

It seems that both men started out as traditional religionists committed to teaching the scriptures of the Old and New Testaments, with no intention to create a holocaust. Jones began as a typical Midwestern evangelist and was later ordained as a minister. His original Christian Assembly of God was regarded as a legitimate church, and he was highly esteemed for his charitable projects. His congregation created soup kitchens for the poor, day-care facilities, and drug-counseling programs. He stressed racial equality and preached against discrimination of any kind.

But, when his following increased rapidly and began adoring him as their idol—female members practically begged for his sexual favors—and he amassed fame, power, and wealth, all this apparently overwhelmed him. Already emotionally unbalanced, he eventually became paranoid. He spoke of visions of nuclear holocaust, claimed that he could resurrect the dead, and stated that he was the reincarnation of Jesus, Buddha, and Karl Marx.

Certain that he was being persecuted in the United States, Jones moved most of his congregation to Guyana, where he reigned as spiritual leader, political enforcer, and, eventually, assassin. His cult was atypical of those of the seventies, which largely recruited white, middle-class, young adults. Most of his followers were older people and children, and the majority were black and poor. More than nine hundred of them died.

David Koresh also started out as an evangelist, coming from a family of evangelists who followed the teachings of the Seventh-Day Adventist Church. At the beginning of his career, he strictly adhered to their distinctive brand of Bible prophecy. While Jim Jones seemed to lose his cool over the years, I have read that David Koresh was eccentric even as a child. He did have a remarkable memory and memorized all the scriptures of the Bible, though he was otherwise a poor student. He evidently possessed charismatic powers and a talent for leadership and membership recruiting, because his followers came in droves when he proclaimed Branch Davidianism as the only true religion.

David Koresh was a doomsday prophet on an apocalyptic mission who created the Armageddon that he had predicted. It was perhaps not as extensive as he had hoped—only about eighty people were killed—but he made enough ruckus to shake up the whole country. He stirred up the Texas police, the FBI, and even the President, and provided a field day for the media, who reported on the negotiations between the Branch Davidians and government authorities on a twenty-four-hour basis.

It is still unclear what he intended to accomplish, but I imagine he believed that he was going down in glory. Doomsday prophets have always existed in religious history, but seem to be most evident in our dawning Aquarian Age. With the approaching end of the millennium, we became inundated with fanatics and cultists representing all types: almost all sects and denominations in Christianity, Jewish fanatics, and Muslim, Tibetan, Chinese, Japanese and various other zealots. Each group proclaims that theirs is the one true belief, their God or symbol of worship the only authentic one.

Any principle or ideology can be made into a cult. Besides religious and mind-expanding cults, there are political cults, mystical cults, sacred cults, sexual cults, satanic cults, old-age and New Age cults, psychic awareness cults, pro- and anti-cults of every variety and description. As the major Eastern religion, Hinduism is the most fanatically interpreted and proselytized religion, and the most widely represented by the Indian guru outside his country.

Why are religious cults, sects, and strange, foreign religions so widespread, especially in the United States? Is it because people are so starved for religion, or could it be that all religions and organizations that incorporate church, God, or Jesus in their name are tax exempt? This is how the Church of Scientology came about: One day, L. Ron Hubbard, a science fiction writer and the author of *Dianetics*—an innocuous, common sense method of self-improvement—said (as told to me by his former secretary), "Let's invent a religion. It's tax free and there's a lot of money in religions."

Based on *Dianetics*, he created Scientology, a lopsided therapy system that incorporates notions of reincarnation, extraterrestrial life, and the spiritual dimension. Hubbard had the money to get Scientology off the ground, and successfully advertised and presented it to a sophisticated and well-heeled audience as an exclusive mind-healing system. His prediction came true—he did make a fortune. He is no longer with us, but Scientology is still going strong, expanding in power and property and, apparently, still tax exempt.

Scientology is definitely not a religious cult, and neither was est. What they have in common is that both were conceived as get-rich-quick schemes. They were part of the self-help supermarket that flourished in the seventies. I don't think that either Ron Hubbard or Werner Erhard, est's founder, intended to become gurus and lead a cult; all they wanted was to make some easy money. Both, however, were overcome by their unexpected success and got drunk on their power.

* * *

Est, loosely based on Buddhist philosophy, was packaged as a sixty-hour course to imbue participants with assertiveness and self-assurance, and to convince them that selfishness is our birthright and therefore divine! While many of its principles were sound, it snowballed into a cult when the movement was deluged with members and their fees; Erhard and his associates realized that people could be milked for life if they could be enticed into one workshop after another. (It's trade-name dissolved several years ago when Werner Erhard's personal life was exposed as a series of sexual scandals and financial illegalities. Est, however, was renamed The Forum and today boasts of a large membership, paying large fees for learning "The Truth.")

Consciousness-raising groups like est, too numerous to mention, continue to exist because there is still a fortune to be made in the self-improvement field. Their lingo may differ, but they all claim that they have the answer to the mystery of life. Their methods and contrivances are generally a conglomeration of religion, self-help methodology, and Freud.

While their basic philosophies may be based on logic and common sense, they most often employ disciplinary measures, fear tactics, threats, and violence. In the public mind, militant groups and cults seem to be synonymous with brutality, weaponry, mass suicide, murder, and psychotic leadership. They may manipulate their members through brainwashing, hypnotism, sleep deprivation, and other mind-altering techniques, yet they are rarely associated with therapeutic practices. However, those operating under the guise of psychotherapy are the most dangerous of all group structures, because they insidiously destroy the mind and the soul, all the while pretending to be sophisticated and scientific. Their members appear to be ordinary, sober citizens, mostly white, well-mannered, and unobtrusive; they don't cause riots, wear robes and turbans, or chant. The majority are highly educated and degreed. Many psychiatric cult members are professionals—teachers, lawyers, physicians, and even psychiatrists. Most often, no one on the outside is aware that the cult even exists—especially not the grief-stricken families who have, uncomprehendingly, lost a loved one to it.

I have had first-hand experience with one of these cults. I lost my beautiful, loving, brilliant daughter to one of them for almost twenty years, and as a result my family was destroyed. She was a member of a group who called themselves the Sullivanians, after Harry Stack Sullivan, an eminent psychiatrist who died in 1949. Sullivan's therapeutic ideas, which emphasized the influence of parents on human personality development, became perverted by the Sullivanians to suit their personal agenda of ultimate control. Members became convinced through almost daily radical therapy sessions that the nuclear family stifles individual growth and creativity. Sullivanian dogma dictated that all mothers are monsters who deprive children of their natural instincts, and that they are the cause of all childhood and adolescent trauma. Members were brainwashed to hate their parents until they couldn't remember one decent or loving thing about them. They were ordered to break all contacts with the outside, and told that only within the protective confines of the group—their new, supportive, healthy family—could they be freed from the evils of their former family and friends, and the rest of the corrupt and dangerous world.

My daughter, a child of the sixties, who was involved in the college rebellions and idealism of the era, was recruited by the cult at a time when she was searching for direction and meaning in her life. Although highly educated and sufficiently degreed, she was indecisive about her future. In need of structure and purposeful existence, like many young people of that era, she responded to a messianic, charismatic leader, authoritative guidance, and a regimented atmosphere. In the group she found her home (in a commune apartment on Manhattan's Upper West Side), friendship, sympathy, and freedom from decision making. The cult took charge of her lifestyle, career, sex life, and sleeping habits, determined how much money she was to contribute, and involved her in deceptive fund raising. She, like everyone else in the group, was turned into an automaton, deprived of individual action or thought.

The cult leader, Saul Newton, a lay analyst who fancied himself on the same level as Freud and Jung, ruled with an iron hand, along with his appointed hierarchy. From an eccentric he turned into a lunatic, so paranoid and controlling that he forced the group to live in virtual isolation except during working hours. He and his immediate family amassed real estate worth at least twelve million dollars, mostly from funds extracted from his members.

The group dissolved upon Newton's death, and eventually my daughter found her way back into society. Like all the members of her cult, she had been discouraged to marry and procreate. When she left, she did both, and made me a grandmother.

You may be horrified by my story and, if you are a parent, might insist, "This could never happen to my child! I am too good a parent!" I am certain, however, that it can happen to anyone. There are no guarantees. You may delude yourself into believing that cults have dwindled, just because you haven't recently been approached by a Hare Krishna at the airport or a Moonie selling peanut brittle or flowers. Soliciting of this type may have stopped, but don't kid yourself! Statistics on the number of cults, sects, and secret organizations, and those involved in them, show just the opposite. Those in search of ultimate commitment are every bit as likely to find their way into a cult today as they were ten years ago. As of 1999, there are at least five thousand such groups in the United States, ranging from very large to very small. The Cult Awareness Network reports that it receives around eighteen thousand inquiries a year. Former members of cults (including the Sullivanians) which are officially dissolved, still function underground in splinter groups.

As we reached the new millennium, apocalyptic cults increased. They range in membership from a dozen to thousands. They reside in private homes, in apartment houses, in mountain caves, or in desert hide-outs. Doomsday cults prepare for Armageddon in special training camps, stock-piling food and weapons. The Church Universal and Triumphant is preparing for the apocalypse in a magnificent 12,000 acre ranch equipped with underground bunkers. Public awareness, if any, is geared to be tolerant of religious and cultist fanatics, unless they step out of line. We are generally incensed and shocked only when confronted and aroused by the media with facts of the meticulously planned and executed UFO journey of the Heaven's Gate members, mass suicide in Switzerland, and the killing of innocent passengers in Japanese subways. The increase of cults in Asia, especially China, presents a tremendous threat to the government. Cults exist, generally underground, in the Near- and Mid-East, Australia, South America, Europe—in almost every civilized and quasi-civilized society of the world. Recently, the originators of a cult in Uganda immolated and buried thousands of its members and disappeared from the face of the earth.

The way of life in the United States is geared toward manipulation, and cults are an integral part of our present society. They exist only because we put them in existence, because we need someone or something to admire, emulate, and put on a pedestal. We may ridicule guru worship, but see it as normal to idolize rock groups, movie stars, and pop culture heroes. We may shun cult leaders, but make sports figures into heroes and immortalize dead luminaries such as Elvis and Marilyn through devotional rituals and shrines.

Being impressionable is not an exclusive characteristic of the young; gullibility transcends all considerations of age. Though we live in countries which nurture individualists, we have allowed ourselves to follow the dictates of the media and are receptive to the continuous brainwashing of salespeople, hucksters, profiteers and politicians. We are told how to live, how to dress, what to eat, how to vote, and what brand of toothpaste to use. Every person who appears to be more knowledgeable than we are is able to convince us that we are babes in the woods, and, feeling devalued, we are cowed into obeying a set of rules imposed by others. We are terrified to think for ourselves and risk trusting our instincts, because doing so may bring negative consequences. We are afraid to make our own decisions because they may prove to be wrong. It is so much easier to make someone else responsible for our actions and for the direction of our life, so we shift the blame for our failures to our parents, teachers, government, the medical profession—or God.

Spiritual evolution does not mean that you need to disobey authority or refuse advice from those more qualified and experienced. By all means, take courses and attend workshops and seminars on subjects that attract you. You might even reside in an *ashram* or Zen monastery for a while if you are curious about their ways. Each person and group has something to teach you, and it is sensible to suspend doubt, disbelief, and criticism and listen with an open mind. Just don't trust anyone who demands your unconditional devotion and/or your life's savings; and please run like a rabbit from whoever says: "I have the answer to everything!" "Mine is the only truth!" or "Only I can lead you to salvation!"

Learning to follow your own instincts, plus astute observation and reasoning about what you experience externally and internally, will lead you safely to the path of enlightenment. If you trust your own faculties, you will know what is right for you and what is not. You will be able to rely on your own judgment rather than waiting for the "go ahead" signal from some outside authority.

You have the right to use your own mind and change it at any time and in every situation, regardless of the opinions and actions of others. Never allow the desire for approval to keep you from following your truth. It can be confusing to sort out all the complexities and uncertainties along the way, but always remember that you are entitled to make mistakes and to correct them.

To be spiritual means to acknowledge the power of your thoughts and to learn to channel them in the right directions. It is the awareness that positive, purposeful and loving thoughts for yourself and all mankind can prevent disasters, wars and diseases; eliminate hate and negativity; and help create a better universe.

It may not be easy for you to trust your intuition and rely on your decisions; you may have to work at it. But you will find tools and practice routines in this book to lead you on the way, and I assure you that it feels great to become the master of your mind.

When you accept the truth proclaimed by all religions—"Thou art That," "God helps those who help themselves," or "The guru is within you," you are well ahead on the path home to your true self.

Chapter Three

Religion and Dogmatism: Heavy Baggage

From the beginning of existence, humankind has searched for the answers to the conundrums of life and death and has explored the realms of the unknown by creating religious rites, idols, and objects of worship. Primitive people—who lived in hostile and unpredictable environments—constantly struggled against dangers and disasters and believed themselves to be controlled by either benevolent or evil spirits, which they tried to appease or ward off. Throughout the ages, symbols and objects of either adoration or adversity appeared in various forms, and superstitions and myths have flourished throughout history. Religions arose out of humanity's need to seek assurance that life has a purpose and that death is not the end.

Ancient tribes worshipped animals, trees, the sun, the moon, stars, rivers, mountains, and stones. Later civilizations prayed to deities in human or animal likenesses, demigods, nature and fertility gods and goddesses, and revered their gods in man-made statues and sculptures. Mysterious and legendary religions prevailed during the earliest centuries recorded in history. Zeus was the supreme ruler in Greek mythology, and Wotan reigned as the chief honcho in German mythology. The Romans had their own gods to whom they paid homage, and the rest of the civilized and uncivilized world found their explanation for existence and survival in a variety of schemata.

Those who adhere to the Old Testament or New Testament trace back to Abraham the shift from paganism and polytheism to monotheism—the worship of no god to many gods to one God. The Hebrews had idolized the image of various gods in statues constructed of fine metals, among them the golden calf. One day, either Abraham or his father, Tenach, supposedly cried out: "Destroy your idols—there is only one God!" However, the Hebrews strayed again in years to come, worshipping Yahweh as God along with his subgods and goddesses, represented by Baal and Astarte.

Around two centuries after Abraham, it is said that Moses heard the voice from the burning bush proclaim: "I am the God of thy father, the God of Abraham, Isaac, and Jacob, the only true God to follow!" Yet, it was not until Moses had confronted God on Mount Sinai and presumably received the stone tablets bearing the Ten Commandments that the concept of one God was firmly established. It has led to battles, bloodshed, persecution, and discrimination throughout the ages, but it has survived to this day. Jews have never swerved from their allegiance to the "Only One." Most Christians have accepted Jesus Christ as God's son, others consider Jesus as God himself—but the image of God as the father figure, the protector of mankind, and the all-powerful one is still intact. Feminists prefer God to be in female form.

This God or Goddess is holy and sacred, loving and just, and yet at the same time, forbidding and stern. He or she is prayed to and cherished, revered, worshipped, and died for—but is always remote and unattainable. In Judaism, his name may not be uttered; when written, it is abbreviated to *G-d*. God is generally pictured as an old man with a long beard who is sitting on a throne in heaven, looking down at us all. He apparently keeps ledgers about all the people in the world. If Johnny has lied to his mother, that is a minus; if he helped an old lady to cross the street, that is a plus. In Christianity, all the pluses and minuses are evaluated and computed at the Pearly Gate when you die, and St. Peter and his helpers determine whether you enter heaven or go to hell. In heaven you rest on a cloud and play the harp, and in hell you roast.

I am exaggerating, of course, but many rational grown-ups *do* believe that there is a God who keeps tabs on all the people on our planet. I wonder if they ever reason that this Earth is just one minuscule planet with one puny sun, and that our solar system is part of a vast number of other suns in the galaxy called the Milky Way. Billions and billions of other solar systems exist, and no one knows where the universe begins and ends. For an adult to believe that there is one personlike entity in charge of us all seems pretty farfetched to me—to put it mildly. It is as ludicrous as someone past age ten believing in Santa Claus or the Easter Bunny.

As a child, I had been indoctrinated with the idea of one God in heaven; I believed it because I was told it was so, and I was not allowed to question. In Judaism there is no hell, but we incite the wrath of God if we are bad. Since I was more bad than good, I was sure that one day he would catch up with me and that I was destined to doom.

I became an atheist as I grew older. I was still terribly afraid of death, but I never confronted my fear. And I refused to believe in a white Jewish man somewhere in heaven who was in charge of birth and death. If he did exist, I wanted nothing to do with him! He was partial and unfair, allowing people to suffer poverty in the midst of plenty. How could he be good if he allowed Hitler and the holocaust to happen?

I had no use for religion of any kind. In my childhood, I'd learned about Jesus and the Blessed Virgin when my governess sneaked me into Mass on Sunday mornings when we were supposed to be at the park. I loved the ornateness of the church: its smell of incense and all the rituals involved. But when my parents found out about it the governess was fired, and I was punished and lectured to about the evils of Catholicism and told that Jesus, most likely, was an anti-Semite.

I also enjoyed going to my mother's parents' house in the country for the High Holy Days, where I greatly relished my grandmother's delicious kosher food and attended synagogue with my grandparents. The men were downstairs, chanting and praying, and the women sat in the balcony listening to them. I thought the services were sacred and holy, and I felt like a good person just for being there. But once I got home, my father took me aside and warned me that my grandparents were obsessed with religion and were fanatic about their eating habits, and that I must not be influenced. In Berlin we belonged to a Reform Temple where everyone sat together and the men wore neither skullcaps nor prayer shawls. I surmised that the women were there mostly to show off their clothes and to gossip. I went because I was forced to go although I thought that it was all very senseless. I kept it to myself, however.

When Hitler came to power we no longer went to synagogue, and I became ashamed of being Jewish. I was told by my gentile classmates that the Jews were evil because they had killed Jesus Christ. I never felt at ease at the mention of Jesus, even in later years, and I experienced distaste in viewing depictions of his crucifixion in all the churches and cathedrals I visited when I traveled. I especially condemned the Catholic Church when I went to South America and other Latin countries where the rich were very rich and the poor very poor. I felt that the people were deliberately kept ignorant and were taught to dedicate their lives and belongings to the Church—the wealthiest group of all.

I was equally upset when I lived in Israel after the 1948 war. Living conditions were at their lowest level, but our lives were dictated by the Orthodox. We were not allowed to travel on the Sabbath, which was the only nonwork day of the week. Some who disobeyed had their tires slashed and were beaten and even killed by fanatic members of ultra-Orthodox sects. We were forced to adhere to the antiquated laws of the Talmud, and although food was minimal, we had to eat kosher food only.

I always thoroughly detested Christmas when my children were small and we lived in the suburbs. I experienced the alienation between Christians and Jews when each house identified itself by either a Christmas tree or a menorah. Each Christmas my children howled, "Why do we have to be Jewish? Why can't we have a tree?!" I was overruled by my husband when I wanted to comply; I truly sympathized with the girls because a tree was much more colorful and fun than a mere candle holder.

I've always felt queasy about the way religion became an issue in schools and institutions. In the past, children in grade school were routinely questioned by the teacher in front of the whole class, "What is your religion?" The children were never sure that theirs fit into the correct category. Students were also apprehensive when asked to fill in their religious affiliation on a college application.

I continue to feel that the very word "religion" still stands for identification, differentiation, and isolation, and I further believe that it is used incorrectly. While we think of religion as faith or denomination, or we link it to a particular house of worship, it applies to God-consciousness only. What we refer to as *religion* is, in fact, *organized religion, religiosity,* or *religionism*—all three contributing to the separation of humankind.

The majority of world religions can be traced back to one specific person, generally an actual historic figure: Judaism to Moses, Christianity to Jesus, Zoroastrianism to Zoroaster, Taoism to Lao Tzu, Buddhism to Buddha, and Confucianism to Confucius. The founders of religionisms were either learned and wise or powerful and purposeful. Each possessed dynamic, mesmeric, or charismatic characteristics. Many religions arose because someone proclaimed that they had heard a voice or had a vision or an otherwise spiritual experience: Moses heard the voice of God, Paul the voice of Jesus, Mohammed the voice of the Archangel Gabriel. All three were told to spread their particular message. The Mormon faith evolved when Joseph Smith encountered two luminous apparitions that guided him to the golden plates inscribed with the laws of Mormonism. Others claimed to have experienced psychic or mystical prophecies and dreams that compelled them to lead their people to the truth.

Religionisms are perpetuated through history, heritage, family values, and hearsay. They are upheld and adhered to for protection, to meet human dependency needs, and are considered necessary for our existence. In ancient times, religionisms *did* fulfill these needs. They helped to allay fears of mysterious and uncontrollable forces, and they prevented people from destroying and consuming each other. They subdued and prevented lawlessness, and in the Judeo-Christian tradition the Ten Commandments became the guide for moral conduct. In Judaism, the Talmud embodied the laws of justice, government, and social behavior, as well as providing nutritional and other practical guidelines. Eventually, however—as people became separated and disunited by geography, language, culture, and race—ideologies multiplied and led to dissent, hate, and wars.

Throughout history, numerous wars have been fought in the name of religion, dividing the world into battle zones. Religious wars, strife, and persecutions still rage all over the globe. Catholics clash with Protestants in Ireland, Muslims with Christians in Bosnia, and Jews with Muslims in the Middle East. Shiite and Sunni Muslims fight each other constantly and Buddhists and Hindus are involved in never-ending conflicts. Religious fanatics try to eliminate everyone who disagrees with their views, and at present few countries exist that don't fear attacks from zealous terrorists.

Modern ideologies, perhaps more than ever before, keep people apart and fragmented—largely due to the plurality of religious beliefs. At least seven hundred organized religions exist on our planet, nearly one hundred seventy in Japan alone. Each religion, sect, faith, order, or denomination professes to be the true one that holds the answers to the mysteries of life and death.

Each religionism is caught up in rituals, rules, and regulations that it glorifies as more profound than all others. Each one insists, "*My* truth is the only one and yours is not truth! My religion is exclusive. If you believe as I do, you are special. If not, you are inferior to me!" Individual religions offer salvation for their members only: everyone else is doomed. (There are a few honorable exceptions, such as Quakerism and Ba'hai.)

What are the reasons for the survival and conservation of the multitude of outdated, obsolete, and generally senseless ideologies and superstitions and their dogmas and rituals? Why are they not buried along with the mythologies of the past? Why do they continue to exist in our supposedly rational, progressive, and scientifically oriented society?

One reason may be that organized religions are often promoted by governments for political reasons and sometimes for tyrannical motives. Fanatic religionists can become troubleshooters in arenas of conflict, as is happening in the Middle East. Some dedicated followers of Islam intend to wipe out Israel as the Zionist threat to their lives, while Arab monarchs assume their roles of innocent bystanders. The same situation has occurred in Europe, India and other Asian nations throughout the centuries. At times dictators demote religion to suit their political pursuits; this happened in Russia and China not long ago.

Governments endorse religionisms because they provide structure and encourage morality, lawfulness, and compliance to rules and regulations. In many countries of the world, people are deliberately kept ignorant and uneducated so they will share their earnings with the religious and political hierarchy. Anti-feminism, as well, has been an important issue in religious and political oppression. This was most prominently demonstrated in Iran under the rule of the Ayatollah Khomeini. The majority of the male Islamic population had been offended by the Shah's liberation of womanhood. The Ayatollah, however, won their approval when he ordered the female back into her veils. Female equality has been disdained by other religionisms as well—especially Hinduism, where the role of the woman is restricted to serving her husband and bearing his children. In Catholicism, only men can become priests or officers of the church, and there is a passage in the Talmud that refers to a woman as "A Thing with a Hole"! Extreme ultra-Orthodox Judaism considers females to be mere vehicles for reproduction.

The holds of organized religions over the individual person are many—fear being the most common denominator. People remain intimidated by the threats of religion such as the Christian concepts of the devil, hell, purgatory and damnation. Fear of dying is interwoven with guilt of living, and everyone is looking for a way to come to terms with death—free of pain and blame. Religions have existed, and continue to exist, to ease fear of the unknown and to serve as a security blanket for all who cannot face death and oblivion. People cling to their religionism and Gospels, their religious leaders and houses of worship, for safety and protection from outside evils. The exclusivity of their inner circle is their shield against threats from the rest of the world. Many are loath to let go of their childhood traditions and fables; they are unhappy when their cherished beliefs no longer hold true and they realize that they may have to revise their thinking. To relinquish concepts is like losing one's identity or experiencing anomie. It creates doubt and leaves a void. Thus, they tenaciously hold on to their religious dogmas—no matter how outmoded they may be—because there is safety in familiarity. They find comfort and explanation for their otherwise meaningless and often miserable lives only in religious doctrines; it is their sole way to cope with their existence.

Along with newspapers, TV, and political monopolies, organized religion is designed for the masses—and the masses, according to Thoreau, "lead lives of quiet desperation." Speaking of the masses, Karl Marx said, "Religion is the opiate of the masses." (However, his substitution of Communism didn't work too well either!)

Those in the United States are among the most active churchgoing and synagogue-attending people of all, and take great pride in their religious freedom. Being liberal and tolerant, they welcome Eastern religions and sects into their midst and respect their temples, mosques, shrines, and ways of worship; yet they emphasize that they are, first and foremost, a Judeo-Christian culture of Protestants, Catholics, and Jews. The belief systems of the Protestant faith comprise the majority: Episcopalians, Presbyterians, Lutherans, Baptists, and Quakers are among the most respected Protestant denominations. Christian Science, the Seventh Day Adventist Church, Mormonism (Church of Jesus Christ of Latter-Day Saints), and Jehovah's Witnesses—to name only a few—are tolerated as established religions. Born-again Christians, Satanists, and witchcraft practitioners are considered to be low on the totem pole by mainstream Christianity, but nevertheless are recognized as bona fide religions by the U.S. government and are therefore tax-exempt. Billy Graham, the friend of presidents, is without a blemish, but even tarnished evangelists who have openly defrauded and deceived the public—such as Jim Bakker, Jimmy Swaggart, Oral Roberts, and others—still have their share of faithful followers.

In the Catholic religion, Roman, Greek Orthodox, and Russian Orthodox are the dominant persuasions. Roman Catholicism, which adheres to either Anglican or Old Catholic principles, is subdivided into various lay categories and Franciscan, Jesuit, Dominican, and other monastic orders. Greek and Russian Orthodox and other Eastern Churches embrace vastly different dogmas, rituals, and beliefs in their worship and do not recognize the Pope as the head of the Church.

Contemporary Judaic practices include Reform, Reconstructionist and Conservative factions as well as various degrees of orthodox sects—such as Sabbatists, Satmars, and Chassidim. In Israel, members of the ultra-Orthodox Shas, Chabad and Haredi movements are the most fanatic followers of their faith. Judaism is also divided into Ashkenazic and Sephardic sects, which follow different laws, holidays, rites, languages, and houses of worship. Ashkenazim are those of Western heritage and Sephardim are of Spanish, Portuguese or Mid-Eastern descent.

All three major Western religions are divided within themselves, and every splinter group, denomination, sect, or belief system claims superiority over the next one. Each one feels that they are special and unique and that only their members have a handle on the truth. It seems to be impossible to merely call yourself a Christian or a Jew without being questioned as to what kind you are. To an ultra-Orthodox Jew, for instance, someone belonging to a Reform or Reconstructionist congregation is considered to be a "goy," or non-Jew.

Christians and Jews share many beliefs. Along with Islam (which proclaims Allah as the only God), these are the only monotheistic religionisms. Their common God seems to demand unceasing homage and assurance of his greatness through prayer (five times per day for Muslims), chanting, affirmations, and rituals. He inspires fear because man is born sinful (both Christians and Jews trace their beginnings back to the Garden of Eden). Catholics reveal their sins in confession and atone through penance prescribed by the priest. Protestants make sacrifices during Lent, and Jews fast all day on Yom Kippur. All are but temporary absolutions; it taken for granted that one will probably sin again.

Many Christians and Jews regard their priests, ministers, and rabbis as direct representatives of God and therefore consider them to be authorities not only on religion but on virtually every subject—be it social, political, or humanistic. Most people have either little or inaccurate information about the origins of their faith; they blindly trust that the knowledge their clergymen imparts to them is authentic. Devout congregants will unhesitatingly seek and accept counsel and guidance for their personal life from the head of their church or synagogue. Both Christians and Jews are apt to staunchly support their leaders and their religious institution—morally, civilly, and financially. Another common bond is the disregard of Judeo-Christians for all other religions of the world. Generally, they either deny the validity of Buddhism, Hinduism, and other Eastern religions or else regard them as weird or unholy. Many members of various Christian and Judaic sects actually profess unawareness of the very existence of other religions.

The irrevocable rift, however, between Christians and Jews is the conviction that Jesus is the only begotten Son of the Lord and therefore is the Messiah who will save the whole world in his Second Coming. Jews have never swayed from their denial of the prophetic Jesus. They are awaiting their own Messiah, and they neither recognize Jesus as the son of God nor view the New Testament as relating to Judaism. The Christian interpretation of the New Testament and the rejection by the Jews of its authenticity have resulted in two thousand years of anti-Semitism. Jewish persecution was rampant in Byzantine, Hellenic, Egyptian, and Roman times, but it did not reach its peak until Catholicism pronounced that the Jews were responsible for killing the Christ. This very concept—promulgated throughout the centuries—was as absurd and illogical as all religious claims.

The Crucifixion itself is subject to various interpretations and questioned by many. While Judaism concedes that Jesus, or Yeshua (in Hebrew), did indeed exist, numerous historians and statistical researchers of that era voice their doubts. Some claim that if he *did* live, he was not famed in his lifetime. Historic evidence attests to the lives of persons mentioned in the Old Testament, also authenticated by the discovery of the Dead Sea Scrolls. History books provide approximate dates pertaining to the existence of Emperor Tiberius, Herod, Pontius Pilate, Nicodemus, John of Arimathea, and others supposedly associated with Jesus, but he himself is not recorded in history. Those who unquestioningly accept the writings of the New Testament as containing direct quotes from Jesus must also believe that the Apostles followed him around with steno books or portable computers to record his words verbatim. It has been asserted that it was at least forty years after Jesus's death that Paul (Saul in Hebrew) related the story of the Nazarene whom he had heard about but had never met. Historical experts have also ascertained that no written word about Jesus appeared until at least two hundred years after his demise.

Most biblical researchers maintain that each evangelist wrote a different version of the events at a different time, using different languages—either Aramaic, Latin, or Greek. Each Gospel was translated, retranslated, and rewritten numerous times to suit the specifications of its sponsors. Common sense dictates that neither Mark, Matthew, Luke, nor John undertook the tedious task of creating a New Testament of their own volition. We can more reasonably assume that all four authors were commissioned by the ruling political or church powers. I believe that Matthew's version of the testament is the one particularly geared to incite anti-Semitism; most likely it was written that way to please the ruler of that period. The teachings of the Bible were definitely written by flesh-and-blood men—wise men for sure, but professional scribes without a doubt.

It is also a fact that the concept of "Maryology," which upholds the Immaculate Conception and the myths surrounding Jesus's birth, was first conceived during the reign of Emperor Constantine in the first century A.D. The doctrine of the Trinity, as well, was not formed until the second century, under the leadership of the Catholic Church.

Christendom in general seems to ignore the opinions of anybody who questions the validity of "Jesusism." Even those who are intellectually aware of the discrepancies surrounding the Jesus figure are apt to argue: "What difference does it make whether the Bible was authored by God or not? It tells the truth about the fate of mankind, it inspires people to lead a moral life and love each other, and its writings are profound and beautiful!" This, of course, cannot be denied—but is it reasonable to believe that the teachings of the Bible provide *all* the answers for our existence? To my thinking, all religionisms are illogical, and I cannot comprehend that devout Christians insist that the whole world believe in Jesus Christ as the savior of mankind and trust in his Second Coming. Christ, as applied to his name—many actually think of it as his surname—also makes no sense. Christ comes from *Christos* in Greek and is translated as "the anointed one."

Numerous Christian sects, including the fanatic Fundamentalists, maintain that those who don't accept Jesus as the Messiah stand no chance to get into heaven. This explains why they believe that Judaism is doomed: The Jews knew of Jesus and admitted that he was one of them, yet they refused to idolize him. But what about the aborigine of North Borneo—is he guilty as well? And what happens to all others who inhabit this planet, the two-thirds of the population who practice their own religionism? Most are unaware of his name, just as many people in this country have never even heard of Mohammed, Buddha, Lao Tzu, Confucius, or Zoroaster. What happened to the trillions and zillions of people who inhabited Earth prior to the birth of Jesus? Are all their souls burning in hell? I have not been able to receive a logical or nonevasive answer whenever I have raised this question.

* * *

I came across the Course in Miracles in 1979. My husband had died a year earlier, and I found myself entangled in legal, financial, and personal problems that seemed insurmountable. A friend suggested that I look into the Course. "It may help you to see your way clear, and I know that you like to investigate all that is new," she said. The Course was composed of three leather-bound volumes: Text, Workbook for Students, and Manual for Teachers. It was for sale at $22.95, a steep sum at that time, and it was as heavy as lead to tote around. It read like an outdated theological scripture and made no sense whatsoever to me. I was convinced that I had, once again, wasted good money on New Age paraphernalia, and I relegated the books to the rest of my vast collection. By coincidence (I know today that no such thing exists), I heard via the holistic "hotline" about a study group that had formed in my neighborhood. It met once a week to interpret the

Course with the help of a moderator. When I went to investigate, I met kindred souls who were as puzzled as I was. The meetings were held at night at someone's home (free of charge)—and they ended with coffee and cake, as well as hugs and kisses that often turned into lasting friendships.

We first learned how the Course had come about: Two clinical psychologists, Dr. Bill Thetford and Dr. Helen Schucman, had been engaged in psychological research at Columbia University for almost ten years. Their experiments were tedious and exhausting, and they worked long hours side by side in cramped quarters. Bill was in his forties and had been raised as a Christian Scientist. Helen, fourteen years his senior, was born a Jew; at one time, she had converted to Catholicism, and later she became an atheist. Their personalities clashed: Bill was an optimist, a basically "up" person, and Helen was insecure and pessimistic about practically everything. Although they respected each other and became close in many ways, they got on each other's nerves and bickered constantly. The tension had built up to the extent that somebody or something had to change. One day one of them said to the other, "There must be a better way!"

Shortly after that, Helen heard an inner voice that said: "This is a Course in Miracles. Please take dictation!" She tried to ignore the voice, but it persisted, and she feared that she was going insane. Her husband didn't know how to advise her, and she finally confided in Bill that she was panicky because the voice didn't stop. He advised her to calm down and listen, and because she was fluent in shorthand, he suggested that she take down what the voice had to say. Eventually Helen allowed herself to respond to the inner voice, which could be shut off and resumed at will. It never interfered with her daily tasks. Its first words were: "Nothing real can be threatened and nothing unreal exists. Herein lies the peace of God!" It continued with a personal message: "There is an urgency that calls you. Do not delay. In a little while you will understand. You have been given charge to one way to God. It is direct and sure and there is a need for it."

Helen was hesitant to continue with the writing, mainly because it was religious in concept and foreign to her nature. She did, however, admit that it had provided the answer to their request, "There must be a better way." Always reluctant and constantly encouraged by Bill, she took down verbatim all that was being dictated, and Bill typed it up. It took seven years to compile the manuscript; by that time both Helen and Bill agreed that the principles of the Course differed from all the teachings of their scientific, worldly, and religious backgrounds. They decided to simply lock up the manuscript and forget about it.

A while later, Judy Skutch, a well-known and successful parapsychologist, was at a point where she felt restless and unfulfilled and was searching for greater meaning to her life. She was introduced to Helen and Bill at a luncheon at the university and immediately sensed that it was a fateful encounter. She sat next to Helen at the table, and during dessert she mustered up her courage to say, "I know that you have something for me." She watched Helen blanch and tremble, but there was no reply. Afterward, Helen conferred with Bill; at first they argued, but then they invited Judy to come to their office. As Bill unlocked his filing cabinet and handed her the manuscript of about fifteen hundred pages, he said, "It is yours to do with as you wish." Judy knew that she had found her purpose in life. With the help of her husband, and the expert practical and financial support from friends, relatives, and strangers, she managed to convert the manuscript into print.

As a group, we plodded through the Text and Manual for Teachers; the Workbook, which consisted of three hundred sixty-five lessons, provided our homework assignments. Some of the headings read: "I am one of the monitors of God." "I will not value what is valueless." "Forgiveness is the key to happiness." I practiced each lesson as a meditation and never missed a day. The exercises helped me to deal with my daily complications; they gave me the courage to go on and the assurance that I was not alone.

The Course material was never easy; often it was discouraging. When we learned that it was Jesus who was said to have authored the Course, I, like most of my fellow students, were ready to quit. Paul, our moderator, did his best to calm us down. He told us that he, being Jewish, had been greatly upset at first and that Judy Skutch, as well, had found it difficult to accept that the voice came from Jesus. He said that Helen, in fact, had tried to deny his identity but could not ignore his message to her: "The name Jesus Christ as such is but a symbol. It stands for a love that is not of this world. The symbol is safely used as a replacement for the many names of the God to whom you pray. This Course has come from Him because He wishes to reach you in a language you can love and understand."

Paul continued: "I was able to reconcile myself to the evidence that the Jesus of the Course does not directly relate to the Christian concept of the Christ. I assure you that all of you will realize, as we go on, that the name itself is not relevant to your progress."

My personal run-in with Paul occurred shortly after. Once again I was ready to "throw in the towel." We were told that the Course dictates that you must love and forgive every being that lives or has lived. I spoke up: "That's okay with me and I will do my very best to do so. However, I will never, as long as I live, love or forgive Hitler and the Germans of his generation who allowed him to be. Six million Jews were killed, and my father, grandparents, uncles, aunts, cousins, and childhood friends perished in concentration camps. I am entitled to my hate and I know of no Jew who does not share my conviction." Paul said, "You *have* to forgive them!" I retorted, "No way!" We argued back and forth for nearly three years. Paul finally appealed to my common sense. He made me understand that neither the Germans nor Hitler gave a damn whether I hated them or not—but that each thought of hate was destructive to myself only. Eventually, we compromised. I agreed that I would love and forgive the Germans and that I even would forgive Hitler, but that I would never love him.

I introduced many friends, and also my students, to the Course. One of them, Renée, had sought my personal advice. She was desperate and had no one else to whom she could turn. She had married a man she did not love because she was past thirty and her parents had talked her into it. He was a physician of renown, and very wealthy. He provided her with three children, each one a year apart...and not much else. He gave her neither help, money, nor respect, and he abused her verbally in front of the children. She was resentful and bitter and desperate to escape from him. But she would not leave her children and could not afford to hire a lawyer. She felt that she was irrevocably stuck. I introduced her to the Course. At first she was rebellious, but she agreed to learn and study and eventually apply it. The process did not happen overnight, but it did come about. She made the commitment to see her selfish, stingy, boorish husband as a child of God—an insecure, unhappy one who needed to boost his ego by making Renée feel inferior. When she changed her feelings from resentment, hate, and self-pity, to sympathy, acceptance, and love for him, he responded within a short time. The beast stopped growling and turned into a pussycat. Today, Renée's children are grown and live away from home. She and her husband are enjoying traveling and mutual pastimes and have grown very close.

One of the lessons in the Workbook reads: "To give is to receive." When we give love unconditionally with no expectation of return, it comes back to us in abundance. Also, the love within us expands and multiplies.

This is my synopsis of the Course in Miracles:

It deals with universal spiritual themes and reads like a revised, updated version of the New Testament. It emphasizes that God created man in God's image of spirit and perfection. Everything else—the body, the material world, the concepts of sin, guilt, fear, and evil—were created by the ego as man decided to separate from God: (The story of

Adam and Eve is only symbolic.) God is true love and is unaware that anything else exists. Jesus is not the only son of God, and he is not the only Christ. God plays no favorites: Each of us is a child of God, and everyone is part of the Christhood. We are all brothers and sisters, and Jesus is perhaps our older brother because he is more enlightened and therefore closer to God. As we all strive toward enlightenment, he is showing us the way. Our goal in human body form is to lead each other back to our original source—you may call it God, Universal Love, or Pure Consciousness.

The gist of the Course is love and forgiveness and letting go of fear. *Love* means to love unreservedly without discrimination or demands. *Forgiveness* does not mean to see sin or fault in others and then magnanimously pardon them, but to be free of judgment and to see only the perfection in the other. *Fear* is an illusion. F.D.R. said: "The only thing we have to fear is fear itself!" Evil actions, sin, anger, and guilt are all part of fear. Nothing and no one can hurt you when you replace fear with love. A *Miracle* is a change in perception or a healing between two or more people. Only when we can embrace an enemy and see him in love as a perfect child of God can we experience true happiness and oneness with God.

The principles of the Course are basically the same as those of early religions. The precepts of the Vedas and other ancient scriptures are nearly identical to the Course. The difference lies in the application. The three hundred sixty-five lessons of the Workbook are designed to return your mind to its pure state of childhood, before it was taught the ways of the world. It is a subtle but effective method of mind change, and it works for all who study and apply its teachings. The Course worked for me, although it took a long time to sink in. I am by no means a saint. I still sometimes lose my temper and give way to grievances, doubts, despair, and pangs of guilt. While I may have moments of resentment toward others, I am happy to say that I have overcome anger and hate. I learned to forgive when I realized that a criminal, a murderer, a Nazi—even a Hitler—is motivated by fear alone. I am no longer afraid, because I know that nothing and no one can harm me. Only good things can come to me, and I am protected at all times.

Jesus recognized the truths expressed in the Course while still on Earth and was therefore enlightened while he dwelt in the body. An enlightened being does not seek to sacrifice himself, but so loves humanity that he wishes to share and give of himself. He devotes his life toward creating a better world and continues to relay his message from the spirit world when he passes over. Jesus was not the only enlightened one in history nor is he the only one who can lead us to God. Buddha, Confucius, Moses, Lao Tzu, Mohammed, Gandhi, and many others—for instance, Martin Luther King—are on the same spiritual path.

I am now personally convinced that the true Jesus is one of our guides or avatars from the other dimension and that he was once a flesh-and-blood person. I have made my peace with him—and, yes, I love Jesus! I believe that he was born at the approximate time recorded in history, possibly in Nazareth or Bethlehem, and to parents named Josef and Mary (or Miriam in Hebrew).

I am certain, however, that the details surrounding his birth are pure fiction. He could have been a carpenter and/or a rabbinical student or a religious teacher. As a Jew of that era, he must have been married with children. We can assume that he was a charismatic preacher, railing against the injustices of the Roman leadership and the dissension among his own people, and that he helped and healed all those in need. As for his alleged magic powers, such as turning water into wine, he stated in the Course in Miracles: "It is not possible that a miraculous act takes place only once and does not happen again!" No doubt he was a rebel of his time, publicly condemning the money-lenders and irreverents of the Temple. He may have been nailed to the Cross, which was one of the methods of execution of that time. (According to one book, *Holy Blood, Holy Grail,* by Baigent, Leigh, and Lincoln, Jesus and his family escaped to France. Hidden archives and documented proof seem to have been discovered there that lead to the belief that his heirs settled in France.) In the Course, Jesus refers to the Crucifixion, saying: "Nothing is ever accomplished through suffering and pain—it is a useless journey!" And, he comments about the Resurrection: "It only emphasizes that death is an illusion and life is eternal!"

He chose Helen Schucman to deliver his message to our generation, but neither the giver nor the receiver of the Course were unique in their communicative effort. Libraries carry numerous books dictated through various methods from departed spirits to earthbound scribes. Helen was the perfect medium—not because she was spiritual or inspirational but because she was tenacious in carrying out all her assignments.

As to the subject of God, Jesus is as vague as the other Wise Ones who speak to us from the spirit world. All say that they are close to God and know him, but also admit that he/she is an abstract figure. In the Course material, Jesus refers to God as "He" or "the Father" "who has never been apart from us and who accepts us unconditionally." While God cannot be realized in form, his presence is with us at all times—to protect, hear, and guide us. The concept of God within is reflected in the majority of primeval religions. It is the core of Hinduism and almost all Eastern religions. It is ascribed to ancient Judaism, early Catholicism, and to the Jesus of the Bible, who is reported to have said, "I and the Father are one!" To equate yourself with God was considered blasphemous, and supposedly led to his execution. Intellectually, I see the God image as a divine presence or all-pervading intelligence—too abstract to comprehend with our finite minds. Emotionally, however, I think of God as "Him." (Feminists, forgive me.) I pray to him and consider him to be my personal God. I more than believe in him—I *know* that he exists. I called to him in my darkest hour of despair when I had nowhere else to turn. There was no bolt of lightning or crash of thunder, but I knew that I had been heard.

As to the Course in Miracles, it has come quite a way from its humble beginnings. It has developed into a worldwide organization and money-making enterprise. Various interpreters of the Course vie for recognition, and many books have been written about the subject. But no matter how the Course is presented, its principles remain profound and sound. "Love your neighbor as you love yourself" is revised to "Love yourself as you love your neighbor." It makes sense that you really can't love and give to others wholeheartedly until you first love and please yourself. The Course also teaches universal love, devoid of judgment and disregarding all differentiation of sex, religion, color, or social standing. The most difficult lesson to comprehend is the theory that all those who hurt, slight, assault, or even brutalize us are merely calling out for love. The Course has us see every living being as a spiritual child of God, conceived in his image. I feel that it represents true religion. Not everyone who studies it applies its precepts, as did Renée and others I know. Its simple message of love and forgiveness seems to be too difficult for many of the students to comprehend. They prefer instead to endlessly and intellectually try to dissect and argue it. Yet it works for all who make it part of their lives.

* * *

I am sure that true religions exist. I acknowledge Buddhism as one—even though the present Pope has denounced it as a nonreligion. Buddhism does not adhere to a deity, nor does it regard the world as created. It views all of nature as the spiritual essence of man. Buddhists believe in a cycle of rebirth or transmigration of the soul, with the goal of reaching *Nirvana.* Buddhism, which evolved from Hinduism, maintains that godly thought, rather than action or deed, determines the fate of humankind. Buddhist belief holds that it is not enough to be outwardly pure, rather that thoughts of greed, envy, and hate destroy individuals and all that surrounds them. Today, unfortunately, most sects of Hinduism and Buddhism practice their religiosity through worshipping statues, symbols, and images of gods and enlightened ones.

The Jains of India and the Theravada Buddhists, for example, still follow the precepts of the original teachings. I experienced it when I traveled with my husband through the countryside of Thailand. Every adult we met went out of his way to welcome and assist us, and the children came to us trustingly with goodness and love shining from their eyes.

Today's religionisms, especially those in the United States, seem to be on shaky ground. Their leaders are insecure, trying to keep their followers from deserting. The religious stances of today lean toward tolerance. The Catholic Church, as an example, is bending over backward to amend their anti-Semitic doctrines of the past and their one-time passive attitude toward the Holocaust and the state of Israel. However, while some of the flock have left the fold, a number of young people are returning to the bosom of the church or synagogue.

In the sixties and seventies, our youth wanted to know: "Are love and peace possible in today's world, which is overrun by materialism, greed, and selfishness?" Dissatisfied with Judeo-Christian traditions, they turned to Eastern religious practices for their answer. But today, the obsession with Eastern culture has subsided, and pilgrimages to India and other so-called holy places no longer are in vogue. Many young Christians have rediscovered Jesus, and mass rallies and demonstrations in his name are organized by university students and various other seekers. Crosses on neckchains and earrings and bracelets of rosary beads are the latest thing in jewelry and are worn by non-Christians as well. It makes me wonder whether the current pro-Jesus surge may soon peter out as just another fad. Other young idealists "searching" for meaning and truth, raised as nonpracticing Jews, are embracing Orthodox Judaism to the dismay of their families. Men are growing sidelocks and beards, married women are shaving their heads, and together they are producing a child per year and are emigrating to Israel.

Liberals insist that everyone has the right to practice their religious beliefs as they see fit, especially if it makes them happy and they do not harm others. Yes, I know people (or about them) who seem to be happy and completely fulfilled in their exclusive religious practices. They maintain that their children are raised in a close, family-oriented atmosphere, involved in the moral standards and rituals of their faith, and are unexposed to the temptations and dangers of outside society. They may be pious and pure, but in my opinion, these children also grow up isolated from the rest of the world—and, most likely, as lackluster individuals.

A sect of Southern Baptist fundamentalists, who worship venomous snakes and endure their poisonous bites, apparently hurt only themselves. But can you honestly say that the papacy, with its antiquated laws, is not harmful to women? It refuses to acknowledge their rights concerning if, when, and how to beget or not to beget, and it also encourages religious fanatics to execute abortionists. What about the Jewish religious extremists in Israel who are empowered by the government? By boycotting all negotiations with the Arab world they deny their long-suffering people their right to a peaceful existence.

Some optimists among us strive for the unification of all world religions. It is not utopian in thought, but it is unthinkable that it could happen in the foreseeable future. While Christians and Jews may eventually come to terms, other religions seem to remain unbending. Hindus prefer to stay exclusive, and the followers of Islam are united only in their intent to take over the world.

While we cannot change world religionism or political opinions, we, as individuals, can make a dent by opting for peace and unity among ourselves. I neither could nor would convince the ardent religionist that any kind of segregation is opposite to true religion and God's will. I can only reach those of you who are doubtful or dissatisfied with your present religious involvement.

I would like to appeal to your innate, God-given intelligence and common sense, as well as your rational and independent thought system. It will lead you to break away from all opinionated boundaries. You cannot deny that you were born innocent and pure—devoid of concepts of sin, evil, guilt, or fear.

We learned about these words and their implications from our parents, teachers, and our religious institutions. We were each taught to accept these ideas, emotions, and feelings as part of our character. Those in charge of us when we were small generally repeated what had been taught to them, and applied their threats to keep us in line. Our priests, preachers, and rabbis re-emphasized the same warnings in detail, further enlightening us about the consequences of sinning.

What did we learn in our houses of worship? Was it ever anything new? Or was it merely repeating words of wisdom that were said five thousand or two thousand years ago? Nothing new has been added, because nothing new has happened since. Neither the Jewish nor the Christian Messiah has made an appearance. Yet we are willing to repeat the same litany again and again, recite our prayers and catechisms, read our scriptures, and sing the same hymns over and over—like robots. Not only is it senseless to blindly believe, it is also wrong. As thinking people, we are duty-bound to exercise our own reasoning and judgment and to learn from our own experience. Why is it so difficult to break our ties with religionism? Do we truly believe that we are evil or bad and that we will be punished? Please do yourself a favor. Simply repeat this affirmation ten times in the morning as you get up and ten times at night before you go to sleep: "I am a good person and nothing adverse can come to me!" Say it with conviction and I promise you that it will work.

Do you need to belong and be accepted? That is, without a doubt, a natural human tendency—but do you have to be stuck to the familiar surroundings of your church or temple, follow the same services and rituals, and associate with the same people time and time again? Wouldn't it be fun to seek a different atmosphere and meet new people to socialize with? They might be of another denomination, culture, or color, but they could provide an interesting change. By listening and learning from authorities other than your own clergyman, you might expand your horizon and gain greater wisdom. Think of yourself as a spiritual rather than a religious follower, and seek companionship, as well as intellectual stimulation—perhaps in Unitarianism, Unity, Theosophy, Ethical Culture, and other nonreligionistic but morally and humanistically oriented groups. If you set an example in your home life as a moral person teaching spiritual precepts, your child will not suffer from the lack of a Sunday school education. This does not imply that you should deny your children their heritage, tradition and holiday fun time. In Israel, for instance, secular Jewry, which constitutes the majority of its population, celebrate each and every holiday as a historical rather than biblical ritual. The best times are had by children—most festivals are truly joyous occasions. (I still have a picture of my four year-old daughter, dressed in costume for the Purim celebration, looking pleased and adorable.) In my own intermarried family, both children and adults celebrate Christmas, Easter, Chanukah and Passover with equal enthusiasm. We also visit my Chinese friends on their New Year and join their festivities.

Religiosity works part-time only. You may feel virtuous and good about yourself while you attend your organized house of worship, but it is only a temporary fix. As soon as you leave, it wears off. True religion or spirituality is everlasting and ever-present. It is the way you cherish yourself and others as brothers and sisters and as holy children of God. If you are truly religious, you have love and respect for every person and you love and respect your environment. You will never harm anyone and you will never disrupt or destroy the balance of nature. True religion is about the way that you feel comfortable with yourself and appreciate and trust yourself. It is the knowledge that God is within you at all times, that God stands for good, and that only good can come your way. Nothing and no one can hurt, harm, or hate you if you refuse to acknowledge it and if you send love to all. "Love thine enemy" or "Turn the other cheek" are true words of wisdom.

Chapter Four

Meditation: My Mantra and Yours

The subject of meditation may not be as thrilling to discuss or as much fun to explore as some of the other topics in this book, such as psychic awareness or reincarnation. Yet, I consider this the most important chapter of all, and I ask for your undivided attention. I'm convinced that meditation is the foundation, the bulwark, and the springboard to our spiritual growth. As the first step on the spiritual path, it demands no stress, soul-searching, or intellectual musing, and it only requires a smidgen of discipline and dedication. I will teach you some meditation techniques later on in the chapter.

Basically, meditation is simple—as, in essence, are all great truths. However, to many people, the very word is steeped in mysticism, confusion, and especially, misinterpretation. The average Occidental believes the act of meditation to be a sacred ritual reserved for priests, monks, nuns, and saints, or for the hermit with his silent, uninterrupted lifestyle. The spiritual practice of meditation is also linked to the Yogis or Zen Buddhists, able to sit for hours without moving, either in the lotus position or on their heels. Many people associate meditation exclusively with Transcendental Meditation (also known as TM) with its mantras and mucho moolah in initiation fees, and they are apt to regard it as just another New Age fad.

Actually, meditation is as old as time itself. It has been traced back to Paleolithic and Neolithic history and has been recorded in the Vedas (the Hindu scriptures from around 1400–1200 B.C.). From earliest times, religious and philosophical sages have recognized the human need for spiritual renewal and have recommended that a part of each day be set aside to sit quietly and reflect inward. They advocated that the mind be diverted from materialistic interests to direct attention on the soul, thus affirming one's unity with the divine. The ancients also realized the practical values of meditation: its beneficial effects on physical and mental health as well as temperament and attitude. They understood mind relaxation's physiological impact. They also discovered that by devoting a short period of time to the suspension of mental activity in order to refresh body and mind, one could cope more efficiently with the challenges of daily tasks in often hostile environments. This was the essence of true religion, practiced at the highest level of spiritual communication and connectedness to God. It was built on knowing God through one's inner experience. It was neither intellectualized, pondered, nor questioned. Religion then had no name, but it was accepted as a natural part of our being. It was the knowledge that we are not alone. While we need to function and struggle to exist as individuals, we—as part of the Universe—are never forsaken.

I believe that sanctuaries such as altars, pagodas, and shrines originally were erected for individuals to sit in solitude, to discover the meaning of life in the innermost depths of the self. Sanctuaries still exist in many places of the world and people visit them for quiet reflection and meditation. With the advent of structured religions, attention was diverted from the individual sanctum to houses of worship such as temples, mosques, and churches. Meditation was replaced by prayer, and the divine self within was preempted by one remote divinity to worship and obey.

I am not negating the spiritual value that prayer holds when it is used to communicate with God or one's highest power and toward awareness of divine presence. But, although they are generally mentioned in one breath, prayer and meditation are not the same. To pray is either an expression of adoration or gratitude or a devout request or petition to a deity. This can be healing, and prayer can be extremely powerful if it is not one-sided but rather is carried through as a give and take. If you trust that you will receive what you ask for, and if you listen, answers will arrive.

Meditation is characterized as a turning within, to find the meaning of life in the interior rather than in outside forces. Essentially, meditation is a spiritual practice on a par with prayer to achieve God-realization or God-consciousness. The culmination of meditation, however, is self-realization that leads you to discover the highest truth—that God is in you and you are in God! The apex of meditation is that state of unity with cosmic consciousness when the body and the ordinary mind are transcended and the spirit becomes the all. The soul is liberated and released from the world of things as they seem, and the physical body is no longer of primary importance. Body, mind, and spirit unite with infinity. This state of being cannot be described unless it has been experienced. It is the attainment of absolute truth, transcending all that we refer to as reality or consciousness. The mind dissolves and returns to its original source of a never-ending cycle. It is called *Samadhi* in Yoga, *Nirvana* in Buddhism, *Satori* in Zen. It is the ultimate happening that can be reached in bodily form and it's the closest to enlightenment that a mortal can experience. I glimpsed it—but once—yet it is as vivid to me today as it was twenty years ago.

* * *

I did not consciously seek it, but apparently I was destined to meet Pir Vilayat Khan on one of his rare visits to the United States. He is a renowned Sufi master who lives in France, with a worldwide following. His aim is to spread universal love and discourage personal adoration. The meeting was held on Manhattan's West Side in a church so crowded with men, women, children, and babies that I felt lucky to fit into a tiny place on the bare floor. A very imposing figure, Pir Vilayat mesmerized me by his appearance and his aura, even though his heavy French accent made it impossible for me to understand what he was saying. But I did realize that he was going to lead us into meditation, and I, along with the others, became quiet and motionless.

At first, drifting toward sleep, I fought with my drowsiness, but all of a sudden—as if someone had jolted me—I became fully awake and conscious of my surroundings. I did not see the teacher but I heard his voice as if he were speaking only to me, telling me to let go. Although I was aware of the others, I felt myself floating in space, and experienced a sensation of bliss, peace, and ecstasy that cannot be described. I knew that I had reached *Samadhi* and I wished it to last forever. I believe that the meditation went on for an hour, but to me it seemed to be only one precious moment in eternity.

Because I had meditated for years and was familiar with the beneficial effects of meditation, I was fit for spiritual transcendence and welcomed it. However, most people *fear* unexplainable and, especially, esoteric encounters. Perhaps that is why TM became so successful. It appealed to those of the sixties and seventies who dared to venture away from the mainstream but were not yet ready for spiritual exploration. TM was presented as a nonsectarian and nonthreatening practice and was shrouded in scientific lingo and high-tech psychobabble. Its promises for physical and mental benefits were mind-boggling, complete with authentication from respectable researchers, physicians, and psychiatrists. Initially the fee for the course was seventy-five dollars; it increased to four hundred over the years. Two introductory lectures were offered free of charge: The first one presented the credentials of the Maharishi as the originator of the method in India, validated its extensive research program, and described the physical and mental transformations that the graduate would experience. The second part covered the technique of TM, stressing its superiority over other meditations and emphasizing the importance of the individual mantra.

These lectures were followed by a private session in which the trainees received their mantra.

The mantra, we were told, is individually selected by the Maharishi and transmitted to the teacher during initiation. Each mantra is chosen to coincide with the psychic vibrations of the particular student. No two mantras are alike, we were assured; they must never be revealed to another living person, lest they lose their power.

The speaker was powerful, compelling, and erudite, and also meticulously groomed and superbly tailored; yet, at the same time, he was mellow and sincere-sounding. I was willing to wager that he was a graduate of the Dale Carnegie Institute of Public Speaking.

Although previously I had made up my mind that TM was a promotional stunt, I promised myself that I would go through the course and be as open-minded as possible, because so many seemingly solid citizens among my acquaintances had claimed that it had transformed their lives. I did admit, however, that I was rankled about TM being such a success, and all my Yoga colleagues felt the same way. I had conscientiously trained in meditation at a variety of seminars, workshops, and retreats for many years. I'd studied most of the different meditation techniques—the Yogic ones, as well as Sufic, Zen Buddhist, Tibetan, Native and West Indian, and Christian methods. I had also received private instruction. But no one—whether an individual teacher, a society, organization, or group—had ever demanded monetary compensation. (Donations, of course, were always welcome!) For some time now, I myself had taught meditation to my students and their guests on a voluntary basis each Friday night. I considered it to be a spiritual practice, and I thought that receiving payment was as ludicrous as charging money for teaching someone to pray.

Because I had decided to receive a mantra, I had to force myself to listen to both lectures...and I was bored to the core. All the same, sitting in the audience surrounded by at least five hundred eager pre-meditators, I dutifully, and truthfully, completed my application and surrendered it with my check to one of the white-clad young women, who was one of more than two hundred staff members flitting about. She smiled at me benevolently and said I would hear from them. Four weeks later my check was returned with the explanation that Yoga teachers were not permitted to take the course.

I later learned that every applicant was carefully screened, and everyone in related fields of endeavor (especially therapists and psychiatrists) were rejected as prospective meditators. All the personnel, most emphatically the teachers, were trained to be suspicious of possible infiltrators, perpetrators, and imitators of the method—almost to the point of psychosis. They were sworn to secrecy and zealous guardianship of TM procedures and mantras. This was almost violently enforced at the time that "Levitation" or "Flying" was offered as a costly course.

I was both amused and annoyed by my rejection, but I remained determined to penetrate TM's inner sanctum. When I next found myself in Manhattan with enough time to suffer through another set of lectures, I reapplied. My residence and Yoga School in Long Island was one hour away and I doubted that I would be recognized. Using a friend's name and statistics, I filled out another questionnaire, with my occupation as "housewife," and included a bank check for one hundred twenty-five dollars (the going rate at the time). Lo and behold! I was cleared for membership in the club. Although I was requested to appear for four consecutive sessions, I showed up only for the first. My sole interest in all this rigmarole was to learn the nature of the mantra, to penetrate the secrecy surrounding it.

Finally assigned to my hour of private instruction and initiation, I was told to abstain from recreational drugs for fifteen days prior, and to bring fresh flowers, fresh fruit, and a white handkerchief as an offering to the guru. My teacher—another white-clad young woman with a beatific smile—locked us in a small room, took my gifts, and placed them in front of an altar, which was bedecked with flowers and portraits of the Maharishi. The room was permeated with an unpleasant smell of incense and kerosene from a small, metal-encased fire. Kneeling in front of the altar, the teacher bade me to take off my shoes and sit on the floor. She bowed to the picture of the guru and recited Sanskrit incantations; the room stank and was stiflingly hot, and *my* prayers were that my ordeal would soon end. To my dismay, she proceeded to throw rice into the flames, making the room smell even worse; then she apparently went into a trance. It had been explained to me beforehand that the ceremony was not a religious one—only a mere formality—but you could have fooled me! When I felt that I was about ready to choke, the teacher opened her eyes and whispered, "Your mantra is *Kerem*." She instructed me on how to repeat Kerem—silently with closed eyes and emphasis on the last syllable. Just as I was ready to bolt out of the room…I was released.

In later years it was revealed that everyone received a meaningless two-syllable Sanskrit word and that mantras were doled out according to the person's age. "Kerem" was bestowed to everyone between age forty and fifty. I have to admit that theirs was a conscientious organization; my Manhattan friend (rather than I) was besieged with telephone calls, letters, and literature for almost a year after my initiation. I felt that my money was well spent because I now considered myself qualified to teach the TM method to those who desired it. I, however, was able to accomplish it in five minutes flat—exclusive of rice ceremony and free of charge.

I am convinced that the TM structure fits into the category of a money-oriented religious cult. Its employees are on a par with all other guru devotees, disciples, or acolytes. Those in administrative or advisory positions receive payment, but all other workers in the organization are paid little or nothing at all. They serve out of love for their master and his ideal of spreading TM throughout the world, committed to devoting all their time and energy to the cause. The whole concept of TM is based on mantra concentration, which in Yoga is merely one infinitesimal part of meditation—it is neither profound nor exclusive.

It can't be denied, however, that the majority who tried TM, and especially those who stuck to it, benefited from its practice. For those who had never taken the time to just sit still and do nothing, it was a revelation. Extremely tense people found immediate relief from stress. Meditators reported lowering of blood pressure, reduced metabolic and heart rates, decreased anxiety and worry. Some achieved better general performance, with higher levels of energy, productivity, and well-being. Often it helped to restore mental balance where psychiatry and tranquilizers had failed. TM is undoubtedly a practical method, adaptable to a Western lifestyle.

The Maharishi International University in Iowa still exists and the organization's plush health spa and various other business enterprises are thriving. Although the TM course continues to be offered, it has lost its popularity—most likely because, along with other New Age methods, it was initiated as a money-making gimmick pitched to fad-conscious achievers. As such, it has been superseded by similar, newer techniques under different names. TM was successful because it was uncomplicated. But it is devoid of philosophical and spiritual depth and offers nothing on which to build and develop. In actuality, TM is not a meditation at all, but a structured mind relaxation. Accepted as such—together with biofeedback, hypnosis, relaxation response, and similar methods—it is an extremely valuable technique.

For people of spiritual background or training, meditation is a natural practice, easily integrated into their lifestyle as a daily routine. They maintain the practice because they have a need and desire for it and because it is pleasurable and meaningful. It is an important part of their daily life that they don't want to miss. They need no reminder to practice and it is never forced or regarded as a duty. But for the average person—involved in a continuous struggle to maintain a material existence, and whose waking hours are crammed with daily tasks and commitments—the very idea of structured meditation is regarded as a time-consuming interruption and a nuisance. Some may reluctantly attempt to meditate because it is something they've heard is "good for you" and that they think they ought to do. They may want to try it merely because their friends are doing it. "It's easy!" they are told by the experienced meditator. "All you have to do is sit down in a quiet place, close your eyes, and let go of all thoughts!" After a few attempts, even those with the best intentions and the fiercest determination give up the struggle. They decide that meditation is not at all easy; as a matter of fact it is the most frustrating project they have ever tackled. For the novice, to harness the mind, while conscious, is an almost impossible feat.

That is why I will teach you mind relaxation techniques in the next section of this chapter as a mere step in the larger learning of meditation, which is intended to lead you to spiritual awakening. Mind relaxation is the basis for successful meditation and also the requirement for a healthy and sound mind. I want to show you how to extend beyond the limitations that arise and how to move into the spiritual realm.

Being able to rest one's mind is, in fact, a physiological and psychological must for total well-being. While we rest the body when we sleep, the mind hardly ever rests; it actually works overtime, involved in dreams at a nonstop pace. During waking hours, the mind rambles on in a continuous flow of thoughts, relentlessly forcing us to think even when we don't want to. When I speak of the mind, I refer to the conscious level that dominates our everyday, ordinary existence. We allude to it as the rational mind, the one we are most familiar with, and believe it is in charge of our functioning on this Earth. We perceive it to be part of the physical body that inhabits our material world. It is the only mind that we can fathom. We also refer to it as intelligence, thoughts, psyche, or ego. It is the mind that we keep or lose, change, make up, "flip," "trip," or "blow" if we are so inclined. Think of it as a giant computer, a vast storehouse of information that we label as facts. Every thought, dream, and experience is recorded for posterity from the time of our birth to the present. Hypnotic regression has revealed that the memories of our past lives also have been stored. Any thought, no matter how puzzling, is fed into the big brain machine. This machine, crowded with daydreams, recollections from the past, and speculations about the future, has no release valve or stop button for us to press. Nor is it ever cleared or repaired. It stands to reason that the mind may be more sick than well because it is clogged up—by facts, data, impressions, opinions of others, and lots of trivia. The thoughts vie for priority.

Try to concentrate on one single thought right now! You will discover that it is impossible and that you are probably thinking ten thoughts simultaneously. Then test yourself to determine how many of your thoughts are purposeful and constructive! If you are truthful with yourself, you probably admit that a great number of your everyday thoughts are ineffectual, inane, and petty, or that you dwell on foolish daydreams. Negative thoughts such as greed, envy, or even a desire to harm another person also run through your mind at times. While thoughts rarely hurt someone else, they can damage one's own body and mind. Like poison to our system, they often cause us dissatisfaction, unhappiness, and physical as well as mental illness.

To quiet the mind without the aid of sleep seems to be the most difficult feat to accomplish, because the mind wants to work constantly and control us at all times. It can force us to think when we want to stop thinking; we allow ourselves to become the slaves of the mind. At times, thoughts become too much to bear and we anesthetize ourselves through alcohol or drugs, or we seek oblivion in other harmful diversions. We may be able to turn our thoughts elsewhere—but we can't deliberately turn them off. There *are* times, of course, when we involuntarily divert the mind from its ordinary pattern, especially when we devote our thoughts to our daily work schedule. We also rest the mind when we read an interesting book, watch a good performance, or are engaged in meaningful conversation. Total absorption in sports or other activities helps us to maintain our equilibrium, and our sanity.

These states of mind are fleeting, however, and produce no lasting value.

The ideal that we strive for is the voluntary cessation of thought, which can be accomplished only in meditation. All thought is suspended and the mind is freed from all distraction. It is neither a state of being unconscious nor is it a trance. It is the state of pure consciousness or superconsciousness—total awareness of one's spiritual nature and oneness with the universe. Most of us living in a world of pressure and turmoil think it is impossible to accomplish, yet a meditative state can be attained through diligent practice.

Mind relaxation is the way toward the goal—and in itself a spiritual practice. Through mind relaxation we reach our subconscious level of everyday mind, draw our attention away from day-to-day existence, and make contact with the powerful force within us all. The first step toward stilling the mind is to single-mindedly focus on one thought, one point, or one sound. This is a purely mechanical practice that I will teach you in the next section, but it is the beginning of mind mastery. You can learn to choose the thoughts that are pleasing and useful to you and eliminate those that cause you harm, unhappiness, and despair. As you work toward control of your mind, you can stop its endless chatter and experience peace and harmony within yourself and with your surroundings.

Other benefits will become evident in a relatively short time. Stress or tension can be eradicated, controlled or subdued. You can conquer all addictions and bad habits. You can prevent and cure physical and mental afflictions. Unproductive and unhealthy thoughts will diminish. Your ability to concentrate will increase. You will be able to focus your attention more intensely without being distracted, making it easier for you to accomplish your tasks. Your capacity for significant purpose and tranquillity can be realized once the powers of the mind are harnessed into beneficial channels.

You will have the strength to undertake and carry out what at one time you might have considered to be hopeless and impossible. Fears, uncertainty, and self-doubts will vanish as you become peaceful, tranquil, and still.

How To Meditate

One of the reasons why TM or similar success-oriented methods are not of permanent value is that they give little consideration to the wellness and comfort of the physical body. I have observed people, who claimed to be in deep meditation, huffing as they sat down and puffing as they got up, their noses running and their eyes watering. Perhaps they did experience some exultation as they meditated, but I doubt that it had a lasting effect.

Without regard to time limit, the prerequisite for purposeful meditation is to be able to sit in an upright position with the back, neck, shoulders, and head forming one straight line. Lying down or slouching defeats the purpose because it leads to dozing off or falling asleep. Total awareness and concentration, unhampered by physical discomfort, is the way toward successful meditation. Most Westerners are not prepared to sit erect and motionless for any length of time. The average American body is subject to poor posture, stiff shoulders and necks, and is prone to or is afflicted with arthritis, bursitis, tendinitis, and other "itises." Eastern meditators, as a whole, are trained to sit unsupported; they instinctively know how to prepare their bodies to prevent physical distraction. If we approach meditation with the knowledge and practice of physical principles, we pave the way toward stillness of the mind. When we prepare our bodies—and inadvertently, our mental wellness—through exercise, breathing, and good nutrition, we can effect a natural transition into the higher aspects of the mind. With the body in perfect health and attunement, meditation comes easily. Once we reach a meditative state by following a holistic path, we create a foundation for unlimited growth, because the body and mind form a single entity in a constant state of evolution.

I don't mean to imply that those in poor physical condition are unable to meditate or reach exultant states of revelation. It is possible even for those of ill health to achieve mental purification, but it may be extremely arduous and sometimes painful. There have always been people who achieved fulfillment despite physical handicaps: Helen Keller was one such person, and Beethoven composed some of his greatest music when he was deaf. But Hatha Yoga can be *the* perfect foundation for a lifelong practice of meditation. I am certain that there are other practices that serve well as methods of body attunement—such as the martial arts in preparation for Zen and other Eastern meditation—but I can vouch that the practice of Hatha Yoga can be *the* stepping-stone to spiritual transcendence and transformation. I realize that I can't convert everyone, but I will try my best to convince you. In Yoga, as we stretch our body in accompaniment with rhythmic breathing, we release muscular tension along with mental tension, and relaxation of body and mind follows naturally.

The majority of my Yoga students have enrolled in my classes for physical pursuits only—a strong, healthy, shapely body was their ultimate goal. They weren't even aware of meditation or other mental benefits. Yet, invariably, those who practiced diligently and progressed noticeably, expressed a desire to explore their mental capacities as well. I don't believe that meditation should ever be forced; it should come about naturally and should be pursued because it is sought. Along with all other self-disciplines, meditation will become a steady habit only if it's pleasurable. To establish it as an integral part of our daily life, we must welcome it, and give it preference over other activities. It may start out as a regimented practice and we might push ourselves into it at the beginning, but eventually we will experience a void if we miss even one single day of practice.

Most Yoga groups and organizations advise that meditation practice be performed daily at sunup and sundown for at least one hour each time. Zen Buddhism, perhaps the most rigidly enforced discipline of all, demands that the disciple spend several hours each day in utter silence. TM advocates twenty minutes of practice twice a day. If you can spare the time, I urge you to do so. But, being a practical person, I gear my own teachings, which are based on Yoga, to those who are involved in the hectic humdrum of everyday chores. I feel that even ten minutes of daily practice can fulfill our needs. As with Hatha Yoga, however, I stress that you be consistent and adhere to a schedule. It is the regularity of practice, rather than the length of time, that brings about the desired results.

Meditation is one of the self-disciplines that we include into our lifestyle—not because we have to, but because we choose to. It can be likened to a daily habit that we adopt just because it feels comfortable and right. We pursue it without a particular aim in mind. It can be equated with a hobby or talent that we cultivate just because it pleases us—without expecting awards and applause. The Japanese Sumi-e painter sometimes devotes his lifetime to the perfection of a single brush stroke. The great pianist Arthur Rubinstein said at age eighty-five: "Someday before I die, I hope to play Chopin's *Emperor Concerto* the way Chopin would have wanted me to play it." It means that true artists or performers strive for perfection but never reach the moment when they cry out, "I am perfect!" Nonetheless, by working toward perfection, they achieve much. Without actually attaining *Samadhi,* you too can reach unexpected heights and accomplish your goals.

I advise you to set aside at least ten minutes of your day for meditation, in addition to your practice of exercise and breathing. The time of day does not matter, but it is most effective if you keep to a consistent schedule. (I generally meditate after I finish my Yoga workout.) Please believe me when I impress upon you the fact that meditation practice is of vital importance to your overall well-being and functioning. In the beginning you may have to force yourself to incorporate it into your life as a vital part of your everyday existence. You may need to set your alarm clock ahead of your usual waking hour and also have a stopwatch handy to clock yourself for the ten minutes of doing nothing at all. This may be most difficult for you, especially when you begin to meditate; and you'll most likely say to yourself, "Why in the world am I sitting here like a lump, when there are a million things I need to do!" But be assured that if you refuse to get discouraged, it will get better and easier each time, and before long, meditation will become an experience you do not want to miss. You do not need to limit yourself to ten minutes, of course; whenever you have time to spare—for example, when you are on vacation—just let yourself go without regard to a schedule! You may also wish to join a meditation center and meditate in a group, or you may seek an individual mentor who can help lead you to your inner self.

When you practice at home, try to reserve a particular space for your meditation. It should be private and quiet, and you may want to keep away children and dogs, and take the phone off the hook. While silence does add to its quality, complete stillness is not essential for meditation. I know people who, for lack of time, find themselves meditating on buses, subways, or trains, and amidst all kinds of crowds. Eventually, inner tranquillity will compensate for outside disturbances. In summer, you may want to meditate outdoors. While you can meditate anywhere, it is at its best when practiced in beautiful surroundings. Anyone who has meditated in a meadow filled with spring flowers, or by a waterfall, will assure you that nothing is more conducive to inner stillness than the beauty of nature.

* * *

Let's go back to proper posture in preparation for meditation. If you are a practicing Yogi or physical fitness adherent, or someone who is naturally blessed with a strong back and flexible knees, by all means sit on the floor with your spine unsupported. Your legs could be crossed in the full lotus or half lotus or in tailor fashion. You could also sit in this way with a small pillow placed under your seat; this will elevate your back and make it easier to hold the position. You may prefer to lean against a wall or sit in a straight-backed chair with your feet on the floor—but do not slouch. If your back or legs are not comfortable, I suggest that you place a pillow behind your back. You can also purchase a comfortable meditation seat or bench. Inquire at your health food store or scan the ads in *Yoga, Zen* or *Fitness* magazines.

Let's say that you are aligned properly, sitting comfortably in perfectly silent surroundings, and have made all the necessary adjustments for being undisturbed. You have not meditated before or else you are a TM graduate, ready and eager to let your mantra work for you. You are set to relax your mind as you close your eyes. Your goal is to suspend thinking and eventually clear your mind of all thought. But as you begin to practice your particular technique, you discover that thoughts are rushing in from all directions. They have not the slightest intention of being shut out. They will actually scramble for your attention, overlapping each other—with each thought bombarding you, demanding that you give it preference. You may find yourself overwhelmed with frustration because you know no way to squelch, control, or subdue your thoughts. Perhaps you feel powerless, defeated, and discouraged. Realize that your thoughts are part of you and that you, in essence, are the sum and substance of your thoughts. Learn to acknowledge your thoughts free from impatience or judgment and grant them the right to intrude on you. Don't order them to leave you alone and disappear. Instead, tell them gently: "I have no time for you now, I have more important things on my mind. Please go away and come back later. I promise that I'll take care of you then!" Eventually they will abate and dissipate. Now you have discovered that meditation may be simple, but that it is definitely not easy.

One great help for mind relaxation, when you first begin and at every practice thereafter, is to start your session by releasing the tensions in your body. With eyes closed, mentally concentrate on the top of your head. Breathe in deeply and allow your breath to travel downward, flowing through your scalp, brain, back of your head, face, and neck. Direct your eyelids to become very heavy as they fall over your eyes. Direct your breath to your right shoulder and let the relaxation flow down your arm, into your hand, and out your fingertips. Repeat on the left. Now focus on the back of your neck. Inhale and visualize your breath moving through your spinal column and penetrating every part of your back—down to the last vertebra. Next, bring your attention to your collarbone. Breathe in and follow your breath moving down the front of your torso, through your sternum, chest, ribcage, waist, abdomen, pelvis, and pubis. Breathe into the right side of your groin. Send the relaxation down the length of your leg into your foot, and feel the breath moving out from your toes. Repeat with your left leg. Again, mentally seek the top of your head. Take in a full deep breath, and as you release it, visualize it as a silvery stream flowing downward and penetrating every part of your body.

In Yoga, the steps to meditation are concentration and contemplation. Before we can empty our mind of all thought, we must practice concentration. At this stage you learn to focus by directing your mind to a single thought. Contemplation is the next stage, when you are able to hold the image of an object or sound without allowing your mind to wander. You have achieved meditation when your mind becomes a continuous flow devoid of thought. When concentration becomes so intense that the continuous flow is absorbed and the past, present, and future merge, you have reached the state of true transcendental meditation.

There are many ways to practice concentration. Perhaps the easiest is to focus on an object. Gaze at a work of art—a picture or statue—or if you are outdoors, at a flower, twig, or tree. Any object that pleases your senses will do. Look steadily at the object for about three minutes. Don't let your gaze swerve or permit outside distractions to interfere. Now, close your eyes. Transfer your gaze to what the Yogis call the third eye, the area in the forehead between the eyebrows. Keep the image of the object in your mind as long as possible. Contemplate its color, shape, and substance. The immediate response may be quite vivid, but the image will soon fade and begin to melt away. Try to hold on to it and bring it back. At first this will be difficult, but with practice it becomes easier to achieve. When you no longer can recall the image, let it go completely, emptying your mind of all thought and impressions. After a while, you may perceive lights, colored reflections, even metaphysical abstractions (for example, kaleidoscopic-like patterns). Don't be afraid or try to repress them. Instead, sink into these visions and let yourself float with them. Concentrating on the flame of a candle in the dim light or darkness is also effective. Close your eyes, and hold the flicker of the flame in the third eye. Try to steady the flicker. When it recedes, order it back.

Another method of meditation is concentration on sound: It could be music, the sound of a bird, or even a fire siren. One of my favorite meditations is to concentrate on soft music: Bach, Haydn, Mozart—nothing with too much crescendo. Rock music or reggae just won't do. After a while, you will achieve awareness of every note and nuance. You'll learn to listen with every fiber of your body, becoming one with the sound.

* * *

We now come to mantras and facts and fallacies about them. The claim of TM that the mantra used in meditation must be attuned to the student's individual vibrations has, of course, been debunked. Sometimes a guru will give you a mantra that is presumably right for you. This does not mean that it cannot also be right for someone else. A personal mantra is not at all necessary for meditation. Any pleasing sound or word, or even an aphorism or a line of a favorite poem can be used. The desired effect results from persistent repetition at constant, regular intervals. Choose whatever mantra feels comfortable to you. In the beginning stay with just one. Close your eyes, prepare your body through relaxation and breathing, and say the mantra out loud to familiarize yourself with it. Now, repeat it silently in a rhythm that is suitable for you, concentrating on the area of the third eye. If a thought wants to interfere, allow it to pass through. If it is a pressing thought, deal with it and then send it away and return to your mantra.

A favorite Yoga meditation is the concentration on *Om*—the most sacred and profound Sanskrit word, traced back to Vedic times. It is said to have been the first sound produced in creation and the first sound a baby makes when it learns to speak. It seems likely that the Hebrew *Omen*, which became the Christian *Amen* and the Muslim *Amin*, was derived from Om. The Hindus use Om as an invocation and also to end their religious services. The Yogi completes his meditation with *Om Shanti* (peace) repeated three times. In its Sanskrit origin, Om consists of the three letters *a*, *u*, and *m*. Some scholars think they represent body, mind, and spirit, respectively. As a mantra in meditation, Om is repeated over and over either silently with the accent on the *m*, or as a hum. Holding the hum as long as possible creates vibrations that can be heard long after the sound subsides.

Another practice in concentration that you may want to experiment with is a favorite Zen meditation—focusing on the breath. Relax your body, close your eyes, and sit quietly. Breathe in through your nose on the count of one, and exhale on two; inhale on three, exhale on four; continue to the count of ten. Then start over. Many people find this to be a very pleasant and effective way to practice.

I urge you to experiment with different methods until you find one that works well for you. You may also enjoy guided meditation or guided imagery, often called visualization, a process in which an instructor or a tape recording leads you through all the stages. It is a wonderful way to relax and recharge your energy.

I offer you two examples of guided meditation: Prepare your body to relax, be quiet and comfortable, and let go. Imagine that you are on a secluded beach on a tropical island, one that you have visited or pictured. You are lying on the sand with the rays of the afternoon sun pleasantly warming your body. The sand feels warm and is caressing your skin. You can see the placid blue sky with its picturesque clouds above you, and the ocean beyond.

Palm trees are gently swaying in the slight breeze. The air is fragrant, fresh, and exhilarating. You listen to the sound of the waves swishing back and forth, and you hear the gulls and other birds chatting, chirping, and singing. You are all by yourself, but you are not alone—you are one with the sky, the sand, the ocean, and all of nature. You allow yourself to sink deeper into the softness of the sand and deeper into blissful relaxation.

Or, picture yourself hiking up a mountain, trying to reach the top (this time on a beautiful fall day). The air is crisp and fresh. You're wearing sturdy shoes and carrying a walking stick; and you are prepared to get to the top of the mountain today. The trees and shrubbery are in full fall color—the scenery is beautiful and peaceful, and you hear a brook gurgling nearby. You are climbing steadily, but the paths are becoming steeper while the top of the mountain seems far away. The thought enters your mind that you do not have to reach the mountain top today. Your legs are aching, it is getting cooler, and you consider turning back. But then you change your mind and decide to go on. You had promised yourself that you would reach the top, and you feel that you owe it to yourself to fulfill your goal. Once you make up your mind to proceed, climbing becomes so much easier. You continue to step strongly and firmly—before you know it, you have arrived at the top of the mountain. You yell with joy. Tears come to your eyes. You are so very happy! You have reached one plateau, and you know that you can also reach other plateaus and achieve whatever you set out do to. You continue to sit for awhile, contemplating your triumph and basking in the peace and quiet of the crisp mountain air—grateful for the gift you have bestowed on yourself.

When you start practicing, you may feel self-conscious even though you are completely alone. Remind yourself that meditation is essential for your becoming complete and whole. As you practice, do not get discouraged. While the beginning may be difficult, once you establish meditation as part of your daily routine, you will make progress each day, just as you have in your physical endeavors.

Do not begin with a preconceived goal in mind. Meditation is not a planned journey but an exploration into the unknown for the discovery of your true self. The journey is exciting because you will discover a whole new realm of experiences that you have never even dreamt about. You may not believe that you are ready for change, but I urge you to go with the flow and just let it happen. As you continue to meditate—maybe for no reason other than it has become part of your schedule—changes occur whether or not you seek them. You have already experienced the physiological and psychological benefits from your practice, and you appreciate these but have no further expectations. However, by sitting quietly and doing nothing you have set the process in motion; changes will continue to come about without strain or effort. Your thought system undergoes a transformation all by itself, and all of a sudden you will discover that you think differently than before.

All you had ever wanted was to be happy, but you looked for it in the wrong places and in the wrong tenses. Most of your thoughts dwelled in the past and flitted to the future and therefore were useless and unreal. When you recognize that the present is the one reality, you see yourself and your surroundings with different eyes. Happiness is in the "now" only and does not depend on circumstances, global conditions, or the standards set by society. *Happiness* is being in reality while residing in the illusionary world that we helped to create. We now know that what we strive for cannot be found on the outside—it is found only within ourselves. Meditation is not "being out of reality"—in fact it teaches us what reality is all about. Reality is *not* the aggrandized image of ourselves—the one we use to present ourselves and see ourselves as we wish to be or ought to be to coincide with our ideal of the perfect person. Nor is reality the outer world of striving and competition. Reality *is* the inner source of consciousness—our spiritual self. We realize that we are special, that our potential is without limitation, and that we can achieve all that we desire. We recognize that we have strengths within us that can move mountains if we wish. No longer do we need to depend on outside approval and appreciation, and acceptance from others no longer matters.

As you discover new horizons within you, you will let go of your old self—the one of self-doubt and unhappy thoughts that you hold onto because of fear, guilt, and lack of trust. You can expect to reach the innermost recesses of your true self and experience sensations of peace and joy beyond your wildest dreams. I believe meditation to be the true religion of humankind. It leads us to the infinite, to union with the divine, no matter what name we give it. By searching our essence, we seek the divine. Finding ourselves is discovery of the Universal Spirit. When we realize that the answer to existence lies within ourselves, we are able to lead meaningful lives. When we stop blaming our failures on Providence and learn to honestly evaluate our faults and appreciate our assets, we restore faith in the self.

Through meditation, we are able to free ourselves from preconceived concepts that we were taught because someone deemed them "good for us." As we open the third eye through meditation, we can penetrate the layers of falsehood and hypocrisy that have prevented us from knowing the truth about ourselves. Everyone is divine and can feel and experience their divinity by practicing inner reflection and meditation. Each of us can become strong and clear, so that we can lead ourselves through life with purpose and joy. And when the time comes, we are ready for a peaceful transition to the next existence.

Chapter Five

About Health and Healing: Do I Have A Witch Doctor For You!

One of the hazards we have to cope with while we are in the body is sickness, with its adjuncts of pain and suffering. Most people accept pain and not feeling well as a natural part of life, essential to existence, and see incurable disease as an act of God.

We blame physical sickness on genes, viruses, germs, environmental factors, or the incompetence of the medical profession. We hold unfavorable living conditions, business competition, hardships, and stress responsible for our mental illness and breakdowns.

Medical science is advancing at a rapid rate. We have a vaccination for many communicable diseases. A virus can be pinpointed and an antidote developed to kill it. An organ can be removed from one person and transplanted to save another person's life. Yet, with all the dramatic breakthroughs in medicine, the state of health in the world is a sorry one. Hospitals are filled to the brim with sufferers of chronic degenerative diseases, such as heart ailments, arthritis, diabetes, hypertension, and asthma. It is a rare person who, when asked, "How are you?" can truthfully answer that he or she is feeling well.

Most people are plagued by an array of minor-league ailments, colds and other respiratory disorders, allergies, obesity, nervous tension, digestive complaints, migraines, backaches, and insomnia. True, people are living longer, but for many it is an unhealthy old age. As a sickness-oriented society, we have become dependent on the world of medicine, medical societies, and "Our Doctor." He was the "Great White Father"; it was in his power to make us well and he could do no wrong. We would unhesitatingly ingest and inject every medication, antibiotic, and vaccine he presented. We wanted instant relief and the doctor complied. We have unquestioningly submitted to surgery, not daring to ask a second opinion.

The days of the good old family doctor, who patiently listened to you and took care of all your symptoms—and also made house calls—are gone forever. Most of today's medical training is geared to specialization, and students go directly into their chosen field after graduation. They don't learn how to be a really good doctor—one who is dedicated to the individual as a whole being. Our present system of medicine is structured to separate and segment body and mind. The body is fragmented into individual parts, and each organ, bone, and gland is designated to its particular expert. The mind is reserved for the psychiatrist to treat as a separate unit.

We can no longer view medicine as always compassionate and the medical profession as having only an ethical interest in preserving life. The fear of malpractice suits, for most physicians, is apt to outweigh the physician's altruistic motives. The majority of patients continue to follow doctor's orders to a T. They docilely fill their prescriptions, submit to triple bypasses, and undergo radiation and chemotherapy without seeking alternatives. But many others have discovered holistic health or alternative healing methods as the answer to their problems, to provide the cures that the medical profession has failed to provide.

All holistic healers have the following in common: They do not conform to allopathic or traditional medicine or treatment with drugs, and they don't dispense synthetic supplements. They generally do not condone drastic methods of intervention through surgery or radiation. They maintain that effective treatment considers the whole organism and discovers the root of the problem, instead of isolating parts of the body and treating only symptoms. Contrary to practitioners of orthodox medicine, they acknowledge the physical, mental, emotional, and spiritual nature of each being. They will generally take your complaints seriously and allow you to communicate at length. Holistic, or New Age healing methods, have multiplied, and new ones seem to crop up at a steady rate.

A large number of M.D.s have chosen to specialize in holistic practices. We now have holistic orthopedists, dentists, and oculists, in addition to the conventional holistic or alternative healers in the fields of chiropractic, osteopathy, acupuncture, iridology, homeopathy, to name just a few.

Chiropractic is the most firmly established and popular alternative form of treatment today, most likely because it is now compensated by many health insurance plans.

Chiropractors are taught that a misalignment of bones and vertebrae can lead to pains and aches, and also to a variety of other ailments, such as migraines, back pains, upset stomachs, and degenerative diseases. They have learned that the key to treating many problems is to carefully manipulate each vertebra of the spine back into position. A vertebral misalignment is referred to as subluxation and the manipulation of the spinal vertebrae is called an adjustment. Chiropractors believe that different segments of the spine connect to various parts of the nervous system. A problem with the knee, for instance, can indicate the need for realignment of a corresponding vertebra located where the knee's nerves originate.

At one time, chiropractors were consulted almost exclusively for specific problems related to spinal misalignment, such as a "slipped" or herniated disc, back and joint pain, pinched nerves, or whiplash injuries. But today, some chiropractors claim that they can heal every conceivable medical problem and disease from an ingrown toenail to hypertension. Osteopaths and physiatrists employ similar spinal adjustments in addition to rehabilitative measures. An osteopath is a licensed medical doctor and as such is authorized to prescribe medication. Physiatry is the latest medical profession to employ a variety of physical therapy methods.

Other popular alternative healing methods include deep-muscle therapy, Rolfing, reflexology, structural integration, polarity, naprapathy, craniosacral therapy, and Aston Patterning, among many others. Almost every method is described and advocated in books and has its share of faithful followers.

Chinese, Korean and Japanese healing methods are also sweeping the West and are sworn to by faithful adherents. Acupuncture, as a widespread holistic treatment modality, has come a long way from its beginnings in urban Chinatowns. It used to be regarded as a hidden, forbidden, mysterious oriental practice, performed in murky, dirty premises where patients were subject to infection from unsterilized needles. Today it has surfaced and become a legitimate medical adjunct. It has also turned into a "cure" for a staggering list of ailments, from arthritis to ulcers, from migraines to cancer, from addictions to mental disease, from deafness to blindness.

Using acupuncture to anaesthetize patients—a technique that American surgeons have not yet mastered—is mostly practiced in China. However, quite a few American dentists claim success in relieving painful procedures with the aid of acupuncture. Today, acupuncture is available as a quickie course for medical professionals and a significant number of M.D.s, dentists, and psychiatrists are wielding the needle. Acupuncture has become a lucrative practice on our Western shores.

Acupuncture is an ancient art of healing that originated in China and spread through the Orient. The theory is that all illnesses stem from an imbalance of *yin* and *yang,* the opposing poles of existence, which need to be balanced into one harmonious flow. According to traditional Chinese medicine, *chi* (or *qi,* as it is now referred to) is believed to pass through channels of electromagnetic energy in the human body. The fourteen channels are called meridians and supply energy to our cells, tissues, and organs. *Tsubos,* also referred to as pressure points, are points along the meridians where the energy flow may become blocked. Stimulating the body's more than three hundred sixty *tsubos* is thought to improve or balance the flow of *qi*. The technique of acupuncture involves the insertion of hair-fine needles just under the skin; at times they are twirled, heated or otherwise activated. This balances the energy flow so that the body can heal itself.

Acupuncture, an extremely intricate subject originally requiring an entire lifetime of study, was passed on among the Chinese from generation to generation. A three-year study is the minimum current requirement in China. Originally, acupuncture was not a symptomatic but a systemic treatment and more often used to prevent disease than to treat illness. In ancient times, sickness was regarded as a cardinal offense, and the Chinese physician was paid only when the patient stayed healthy.

Related to acupuncture is acupressure—probably most effective for relieving chronic pain, tension, arthritis, and asthma. The two practices share the same principles—based on the theory of *qi* and meridians—and the same roots in Chinese medicine. The difference lies in the procedure: one uses needles and the other applies finger pressure. Moxibustion is another Chinese (and Japanese) form of treatment for specific diseases. As in acupuncture, the treatment stimulates *qi* flow via the acupoints. Here, a small amount of a dried herb, called moxa (mugwort), is either placed on the skin and ignited to stimulate the energy or held above a specific area of pain. Not many Westerners are willing to submit to the discomfort and the odor. Its aroma is decidedly similar to marijuana.

Shiatsu, developed in Japan, is another stylized method for manipulation of *tsubos*. Pressure is exerted to all parts of the body with fingers and hands or with elbows, knees, and feet. It is basically a therapeutic massage that addresses a number of conditions, including insomnia, digestive problems, and lower back pain. Among other healing massage therapies from the Orient are Amma, Tui Na, and Do-in. They all claim to open the channels of the body, eliminate stagnation, and serve as remedies for a variety of medical problems.

Faith healing, spiritual healing, and psychic healing have been practiced throughout the ages in all parts of the world from earliest recorded history. Shamans and witch doctors have been, and still are, active in "primitive" societies; astrologers and alchemists, who were thought to be vested with the power to restore health, were sought out for healings in the Middle Ages. Yogis in the Himalayas, Buddhist monks, and early Christian priests were reputed to possess healing powers. They used amulets, sacred charms, talismans, divining rods, incantations, and magic spells, as well as herbs, roots, and potions. People either got better or they died. Scientific medical procedures employing sophisticated surgical and therapeutic techniques flourished in ancient Egypt, Greece, and Rome. Yet great physicians, such as Hippocrates (the Greek father of medicine) and Galen (a first-century physician of the Roman Empire), included astrology, numerology, divination, and other mystical arts in their practice.

Although alternative, holistic healing methods are slowly but steadily integrating into our sickness-oriented culture, nontraditional healing methods and healers are still rejected by most of the medical profession and a majority of the general public. They are considered to be scientifically unsound and therefore unacceptable. I, for one, shared this opinion for most of my life. In the thirties and forties, Los Angeles was a haven for kooky religious practices. They were held in various churches with names like Church of Mental Science, Church of Inner Peace, Church of Spiritual Being. When we had nothing better to do on a Sunday morning, my high-school buddy and I attended their services. It was free entertainment and it was a hoot. In New York, Radio City Music Hall and the Roxy Theatre were famous for their musical extravaganzas, and in L.A. the performances at evangelical churches were almost as lavish.

Aimee Semple McPherson, the famous evangelist who mysteriously disappeared in 1938, was the initiator of "showtime in church." Each church tried to outdo the other with features like larger orchestras, a chorus of two hundred or more vocalists, talented soloists, and luxurious costumes and decor. But the healing dramas that took place between musical numbers were the highlight of the show. Members of the audience were organized into precise lines and came up on stage, one by one or in groups. Assistants would place them in position and assist those in wheelchairs. The healer, man or woman, generally clad in white, flowing robes, touched either the forehead or the top of the head of the faithful. The orchestra built to a crescendo of rolling drums and crashing cymbals as the afflicted fell backward like hot potatoes. After a while, the stage and aisles of the church were covered with bodies, sometimes one on top of another. Writhing, moaning, weeping, and babbling—they could have been in ecstasy, trance, or convulsions. The audience went into a frenzy—screaming, crying, and laughing, waving their arms and legs and dancing in place. My friend and I were convinced that all of them were nuts and we always sneaked out before the collection plates were passed.

The grandeur may be gone, but evangelical healing performances still take place all over the United States, especially in rural areas of the Bible Belt. Medicine men and faith healers have always been part of the American scene, traveling in caravans, pitching their tents, and giving healing performances. Believers are sometimes healed and more often bilked out of their life savings. But faith healers are not confined to the fringe. Many mainline Christian churches especially in the United States, Australia and England, offer healing services and hold mass to pray for the sick. The head of the church usually conducts the services, but at times an accredited nonclerical healer may take his place.

Healing was a natural part of Early Christianity, though it was soon condemned by the religious hierarchy. It was revived in the nineteenth century and Episcopalian, Baptist, Methodist, and Pentecostal Churches are the most actively involved. They offer healing as proof that the miracles attributed to Jesus still exist in the modern world. Some of their services are lively, entertaining, and dramatic, and the audience helps by singing praises to the Lord and clapping hands; some enter trancelike states or speak in tongues.

The Christian Science Church, founded by Mary Baker Eddy is, perhaps, the most widespread and prominent religious organization devoted to healing. The curing of disease through prayer is regarded by them as a necessary element of salvation. Today, followers are not compelled by the Church to use spiritual healing exclusively, though most members still do. They claim that their healing power is the secret formula of Christ himself. Christian Science is unique in that each member is taught to heal and is involved in the healing process.

Many people make pilgrimages to miraculous centers of healing, such as Lourdes in France and St. Anne de Beauprais in Quebec and miracles of healings have been claimed for centuries. Especially those with incurable diseases, the crippled, and the maimed will undertake the strenuous journey, possibly as a last resort. They come in wheelchairs or on crutches which are displayed in various shrines to offer proof of the healings. Innumerable sufferers have gained help and some are entirely cured of a fatal or near-fatal disease. Healings at Lourdes are approved—or, often, disproved—by a special investigating committee of the Catholic Church. The claims must meet rigorous and demanding standards before being authenticated. Scientists try to prove that the alleged cures are neither perfect nor of lasting value, ignoring the fact that conventional medicine is imperfect as well.

The world of science also rejects the possibility of psychic healing. Many investigators have traveled to the Philippines to scrutinize the improbable claims of psychic surgery. Psychic surgery operates beyond the realm of the material world and clashes with all logic and intellectual comprehension. Operations of every kind are performed without the aid of scalpels, sutures, or anesthesia—surgeons use their hands only. No pain is involved, no scars are left, there is no aftermath of ill effects, and relief and partial and complete cures have been attested to for every kind of disease and affliction from back pain to cancer. (No deaths due to these procedures have ever been reported, but it can be argued that those who foolishly ignored emergency medical intervention may have been killed by their diseases.)

At times medical professionals and journalists who profess to be open minded are permitted to observe the surgical proceedings. What they see might look something like this: The patient lies flat on the table and the healer runs his hands along the body to diagnose and localize the problem. After ten or fifteen minutes of stroking the patient from head to toe, the healer digs into the body and blood oozes out along with globs of body parts that look like entrails, tissues, or masses. An assistant is standing by with a cup to catch the disgusting mess. The surgeon washes his bloody hands as the patient gets off the table to get dressed. A minimum of conversation is exchanged and seemingly no after-care instructions are prescribed.

Conflicting opinions abound. Some reporters insist that it is all a hoax and that the operation is a sleight of hand. They are convinced that the "blood" is catsup and that the globs and tumors removed are nothing but chicken innards. Others attest that, while quite a few of the Philippine healers may be con artists, there are those who are real. They admit that, while the operations make no sense, the results provide overwhelming evidence that the cures are indeed effective. (I personally know people who have been permitted to perform these operations under a healer's guidance. They swear that their hands penetrated the body, drew blood, and pulled out lumps.)

Today, psychic surgery is available in the United States as well, but it is illegal and therefore performed under cover. It is openly practiced in South America, especially in Brazil, where parapsychological happenings are accepted as everyday realities. Brazil's most famous psychic surgeon was one Arigo, known as The Healer with the Rusty Knife; he died in the seventies. No psychic healer's work has ever been as thoroughly confirmed and documented, by South and North American professionals alike. This simple, uneducated peasant saw as many as three hundred patients per day, diagnosed and treated them in minutes, and healed almost every known disease or ailment. Sometimes he wrote out prescriptions in an illegible scrawl on a plain piece of paper. Somehow they were translatable and able to be filled pharmaceutically. People from all countries came to consult him—famous statesmen, leading executives, aristocrats, doctors, and scientists. It is said that he cured fatal cancers with jackknives and razors, cataracts with scissors, and goiters with paring knives. He was observed removing an eye from its socket, cleaning it, and putting it back. While he worked, he apparently was in a trance and spoke with a German accent. He claimed to be controlled and directed by a German doctor who had died in the previous century and came to him in his dreams. Today, other like healers and surgeons practice in Brazil, but Arigo's achievements remain unforgotten.

Many Westerners pride themselves on their logic and skepticism. They won't believe what they don't understand, especially when it happens on foreign shores. What they want is proof about what they deem to be unfathomable, improbable, and downright preposterous. They need not look far. It was in America that the most amazing healer of our era practiced and cured through unconventional channels. His name was Edgar Cayce and he died in 1940. I find it incredible that so many people are unaware that he existed. He was a trance healer who was able to self-induce a hypnotic state and could almost always accurately diagnose and advise treatment for every conceivable illness or disease. Most of his clients were people he never saw. They wrote him letters describing their problems, which would be read to him while he was in a trance state.

Cayce was known as The Sleeping Prophet, and during his last years was called The Miracle Man of Virginia Beach. He never went past the ninth grade. He was a photographer by profession, a simple family man, and a devout Catholic. While in a trance, he seemed to possess an incredible knowledge of medicine, psychiatry, anatomy, chemistry, and pharmacology and many physicians turned to him with unsolvable cases. (A dear departed friend of mine, Dr. John Lalli, an osteopath, consulted him on a regular basis.) His healing methods were mostly unorthodox and his principles were undoubtedly the forerunners of our present concepts of holistic health. He perceived and prescribed for a person's total state—physical, mental, and emotional. He advised surgery and allopathic medication in extreme cases only. He favored herbal medicines, osteopathy, hydrotherapy, vitamin treatment, massage, and exercise as well as psychological guidance.

Cayce believed in the value of proper nutrition and is quoted as having said, "We are physically and mentally what we eat and think." Volumes have been recorded on the particular foods and herbs recommended for every kind of physical and mental disorder. Edgar Cayce's findings and cures cannot be regarded as the fabrication of a fanatic. The Edgar Cayce Foundation in Virginia Beach, under the auspices of his son, Hugh Lynn Cayce, has well-documented, stenographic records of more than thirty thousand cases that were correctly diagnosed in his lifetime. The medical files are open for examination by those with bona fide medical accreditation. I hope that more and more seekers will avail themselves of these facts.

I was the original Doubting Thomas, rejecting the possibility of faith, psychic, miracle, trance, or charismatic healing. Though I *knew* that I had healed myself through proper exercise, breathing, meditation, and nutrition, I attributed my healthy state to only the application of natural methods and sheer determination. I refused to accept that another person's power could penetrate and affect my physical state. When I met Harry Edwards in England shortly before his death in the late seventies, I changed my mind. He was the most famous healer of his time. He practiced the laying on of hands and, like Edgar Cayce, performed absentee healings by the thousands. He claimed that his guides were well-known deceased spirits, including those of Louis Pasteur and of Joseph Lister, who was a pioneer in the use of antiseptics to prevent surgical infections. Edwards used to draw enormous crowds when he gave demonstrations of his psychic cures all over Europe. He established a spiritual sanctuary in Surrey and was consulted by leading politicians and members of the Royal Family.

While traveling in England, I was troubled by an old skiing injury, a torn meniscus in my kneecap, and Doris Collins took me to see him. (You will hear more about her later on in the book.) Edwards was already very frail and no longer treated private patients. But because Doris was one of his former students and an old friend, he made an exception and saw me. When he touched my knee, I felt an intense heat radiating from his hands and penetrating deep into my bones, joints, and muscles. Within ten minutes after his treatment I was able to walk without pain for the first time in weeks.

Once I became fascinated with the subject of healing, I read the accounts of famous healers in history and attended the services of well-known healers in the United States. Kathleen Kuhlman was an acclaimed healer from Pittsburgh who held public healing sessions, generally in a church, accompanied by organ music and TV cameras. Her bearing was royal, she wore beautiful gowns, emoted eloquently, and put on a great show. While her act seemed contrived, her healings were nevertheless effective.

Olga Worrell of Baltimore was definitely more down-to-earth. As an acting minister of her church, she was probably the best known of American healers, chiefly because she was widely accepted by many in the conventional medical profession. Physicians would come to her for their own healings when their problems proved too much for their colleagues to analyze or cure. It is reported that both she and Kathleen Kuhlman healed cysts and tumors, as well as blood, cardiovascular, and joint diseases that had been diagnosed as incurable. Many in the medical profession admitted they were stupefied when afflictions that had been evidenced in X-rays and diagnostic tests simply disappeared.

I have met healers who have been charlatans and many incompetent ones who pretended to be healers. I believe that the most important factor in unconventional healing practices is that, although not everyone may be cured, no one is ever damaged or hurt unless, of course, they foolishly bypass emergency medical interventions. While miracle cures may occur, there is nothing miraculous about individual healing powers. Some healers are born with this special talent and some are more spiritually evolved than others. Some are unaware that they have the gift. But it is inherent in everyone. It can be developed and it is possible to train to be a healer. Many people sing, act, dance, and paint professionally, but not all are great. The same is true with healers.

There is no fundamental difference between faith, spiritual, psychic, or miracle healing. Essential to all healing is complete and unswerving faith in a God or higher power (or whatever one wishes to call it) and in oneself. Every healer I know or know of, including bona fide Philippine psychic surgeons, will evoke a higher power and the faith in himself to assist in the healing. There can be only one true motivation for a successful healer—to alleviate suffering and to help humankind. A dedicated healer does not heal for rewards, financial gain, or acclaim. Some, like Arigo, refuse to accept money, and others accept donations, but it seems that most true healers charge only a nominal sum to cover their living expenses.

True healers admit that their powers are transmitted from divine forces—God, Jesus, another deity, the spirit world, or an individual deceased spirit who directs the process of healing. Each healer is aware of the universal life force, the natural electromagnetic energy that carries consciousness as well as dynamic powers into the *chakras*, meridians, and cells of the body. It is called *qì* in Chinese, *ki* in Japanese and *prana* in Sanskrit, and it is within every being. The healer utilizes this force as a tool for restoring bodily functions. Generally, healing is done by touch of the hands. Some touch the forehead or the top of the head only; others run their hands over the afflicted body parts or the whole body. I have witnessed psychic or spiritual healings by people who do aura work. They balance the etheric or astral body by moving their hands along the outlines of the body without touching the skin. I have also experienced bio-energetic healing—an electric current sensation that emanates from the healer's hands and penetrates various body parts.

Once I was convinced that touch healing can be a genuine method for restoring and maintaining health, I aspired to be a healer. The New York New Age scene of the seventies offered healing courses galore. I chose those given by prominent healers, such as Lawrence LeShan, whose seminars were the most prestigious and sought after. I was taught how, where, and when to lay on hands along with meaningful prayers and incantations. The students practiced on each other and I would feel the warmth of their hands and the heat and tingling on my skin. But my own hands seemed to produce no effect on anyone else—they stayed cold. I convinced myself that I was a dud and resigned myself to my inability to heal. I decided to abandon the project.

Then I heard about Reiki from my friend Karen. "This is exactly what you are looking for!" she said excitedly. "A practical technique for healing yourself and others. Let's take the course together!"

Reiki sounded suspiciously like another of the New Age methods that are guarded in secrecy and available only for a price. But, rather than relying on my instincts, I succumbed to my still-present desire to become a healer and let Karen convince me to shell out three hundred dollars—the fee for the beginning course (exclusive of plane fare and hotel expenses). We had to travel to South Carolina to be initiated by a "master" and Karen continued to assure me that we were lucky to have been accepted.

We learned that *Reiki* is a Japanese word meaning "universal energy," and is an ancient healing "rediscovered" by a Dr. Mikao Usai in the 19th century. A Hawaiian woman, Mrs. Takata, acquired the method probably a hundred years after his death and instructed others in the knowledge. Reiki is claimed to relieve the body of all physical, emotional, and spiritual blockages and heal almost every illness and injury. It is a hands-on method called an attunement, that uses sacred symbols. The symbols, which are claimed to be derived from ancient Buddhist scriptures, are silently recited and mentally pictured as part of the treatment. As with TM mantras, they may never be revealed to someone who is not being trained in the process.

Although my initial hunch seemed to be correct, I nevertheless continued with the training. The second-degree course was a bargain at a mere five hundred dollars, and somehow I allowed myself to be talked into the third one as well. It set me back seven thousand dollars—but entitled me to a Reiki Master Degree. I stopped after that, but my friend saw it through. She took out a loan for another four thousand dollars and became qualified to be a Reiki instructor. She wholeheartedly believes in the method and still teaches first- and second-degree Reiki both in the United States and Europe. She assures me that she is happy in her work although her earnings are not that great. (The real money goes to the initiators of the original course, as is the case with other similar organizations.) I am not implying that Reiki is a fraud or that those who advocate it are not sincere. They truly believe their method to be a panacea and they do offer voluntary healing services whenever needed. And Reiki organizations other than the one whose courses we attended seem to charge much less for their trainings. (It seems logical to assume that their methods and symbols also may vary.)

I admit that Reiki worked for me, inasmuch that I finally accepted myself as a healer. When I decided to ignore the temperature of my hands, I simply started to heal. I practiced on young men with AIDS who no one else would touch. It was the early eighties, and the mere mention of AIDS threw most everyone into a panic—doctors and nurses included. I did not rely on my hands only, I also taught them Yoga exercises, breathing, meditation, visualization and helped change their eating habits. I am certain that I could have made a dent, especially for those in the early stages of the disease. But the experimental drugs that were flooding the market at the onset of AIDS won out. Everyone I was close to died within a short time.

I knew for certain that I could heal when a friend slipped on the ice and hurt her knee. I applied my hands for a length of time and the pain and swelling disappeared. Since then, I have healed other knees (including mine) and pain, bruises, and sprains in various body parts, and I have seen blood and blisters vanish under my hands.

Everyone can be a healer; we all have the ability to heal one another. The life force, or *qi, ki* or *prana,* is within each one of us, to tap into and transmit to someone else. All that is required is a pair of hands (hot, warm, or cold) and the desire to help and to heal. You probably will have to practice, however. The next time you encounter a person in need of healing—it can also be an animal or plant—ask for permission to lay your hands on the afflicted area. Sit quietly for about ten minutes with your eyes closed. You may either call on a higher force to assist you or confidently rely on your internal powers. Also, you could try rhythmic breathing, silently recite your mantra or picture your secret Reiki symbols. Don't expect results, just be assured that a loving touch can only help and never hurt. (I trust that you will call 911 when needed.) I also advise you not to concern yourself with problems and illnesses in an advanced stage. Trying to heal these may be frustrating and often are not successful. I personally don't trust in my ability to cure illness of long standing and rely on my powers to instant-heal only.

Not everyone responds to touch or other forms of faith healing. This does not necessarily mean that the healing is a failure or that the healer is inept. Many people are sick because, for various unconscious motivations, they choose to be sick. (It is an established fact that eighty-five percent of all illnesses are of psychosomatic origin.) *Psyche*—the mind and *soma*—the anatomical body, are intertwined and one influences the other.

Eastern thought and healing practices are aware of this relationship. Ayurvedic medicine, which originated in India, is based on the understanding that nothing can be experienced or conceived that does not influence the body and the mind of the individual to a lesser or greater degree. Ayurvedic treatment of disease is a combination of herbal medicines, Yoga exercises and breathing, and mind relaxations. In Chinese medicine, the emotions are considered to be seated not just in the brain, but are also dispersed into various organs. Each organ affects the others and the brain as well. Traditional Japanese medicine considers the importance of human relationships relative to each illness and endeavors to harmonize the two.

Orthodox medicine has little to offer for hypochondria, chronic complaints, and psychosomatic suffering. Medical students in this country are warned about these conditions, but generally are not taught how to cope with them. Conventional treatment is limited to sedatives, tranquilizers, and narcotics for who cannot be diagnosed. If nothing works, the patient is referred to a psychiatrist.

Psychosomatic symptoms and illnesses originate in the mind and are produced by the body. "As you think, so you are!" is a most appropriate proverb. Consciously, nobody wants to be sick, but living in a sickness-oriented society, we are programmed to be so from childhood on. Children are expected to be sick, and are pumped full with antibiotics, preventative medication, and shots and vaccines—even today when most communicable children's diseases have been eliminated. The threat of bacteria, germs, viruses, epidemics, and environmental pollution is hanging over our heads as part of "normal" existence. Most of the diseases of today's society are attributed to external tensions, which are deemed responsible for our physical and mental breakdowns, our disposition towards illness, and our inability to prevent or fight it. If we do admit to psychosomatic disease we blame tension or stress as the cause and never take responsibility for the fact that it is we ourselves who create them.

Other factors, such as grief, may enter into illness, but I feel that fear is the major underlying cause of psychosomatic illness: It creates the symptoms, the suffering, and pain. I can personally attest to it. After most of the fractures had healed (from my fall when I jumped from the burning building), I suffered from what was then called a nervous breakdown. I refused to accept that my mind was sick and that I needed psychiatric care. I insisted that I was physically ill and underwent a battery of tests to prove it. I fervently prayed for a "real" illness to show up—I was prepared to settle for cancer if necessary. When the tests came back negative I invented tangible symptoms. I created a raised temperature, unusual blood count, and pain in the right places to diagnose appendicitis, gall bladder problems, and gynecological irregularities. I found a slew of physicians willing to operate or explore. I would have been cut open many times if my husband had not held me back.

When he literally forced me to see a psychiatrist, I developed giant hives that broke out periodically and surfaced everywhere on my body. They did not subside until I was convinced that I would not go insane. (One of the reasons I was so compatible with my students was that I could easily empathize with them. When they complained to me about their physical problems I could truthfully say, "I know exactly what you are talking about—I had that too!")

Today the medical profession is apt to accept the body-mind connection in disease. Ulcers, colitis, and asthma are no longer the only diseases thought to be psychosomatic or psychogenic. Health care professionals are conceding that arthritis, diabetes, cardiovascular diseases, and many other ailments may also be of mental origin. Ironically, however, millions of dollars are still spent in the laboratory instead of investigating prevention in the mind. If we can assume that some diseases originate in the mind, is it not logical to suppose that almost all diseases are the result of destructive thinking?

Another cause for psychosomatic illness is the conviction that we are genetically disposed towards disease. We may be born with certain defects and ailments, we may develop them later in life, or we live in fear of contraction. "Does this disease run in your family?" is the most significant query of physicians as they analyze your medical problem. However, genetically inclined is generally karmically inclined. Sometimes we choose our parents with their particular heritage to take on a specific disease. Our purpose, for whatever reason, is to overcome the affliction in this lifetime, by rising above it or eliminating it. We can do so when we are willing to face reality and have no more need for the disorder. (This will be more clearly explained in another chapter.) But we may not be ready to let go of our mind's creations—even when they destroy us. That is why not all healings are effective.

All healing methods can help—whether they are induced by physicians, chiropractors, acupuncturists, faith healers, or psychic healers—but all are limited in their approach. They can change the symptoms of the disease and miracle cures do happen, but those are not necessarily permanent. Whatever abnormality or illness is manifested by the mind can reoccur. No one but the patients themselves can reach their inner depths to change the process that produced the disease in the first place. *There is no true healing unless the cause of the disease is removed.* A cancer, for instance, can only be subdued if the person is willing to locate the root of the growth and let it go. This root can be self-loathing, a deep resentment, or one of many emotions such as long-standing, unresolved anger, grief, or sadness. Successful cures can be effected by facing up to unreasonable fears, and ceasing to hold outside forces responsible for our ailments.

No cure can be lasting unless patients change their attitude toward sickness and health. We can prevent sickness and cure it with our system of thought—if we don't think sick or if we refuse to be sick. People who live meaningful lives and those who truly enjoy life are better able to cope with adversity. My mother was never sick, simply because she thought that it was a waste of time. She also refused to get old. At age eighty-two she volunteered at a hospital for the aged. She felt obligated to help the "old people." Once I, too, decided, at age forty, that being well was preferable, I refused to get sick again—and I rarely am.

Even those who are pronounced incurable often get better if they are determined to do so. Many stories are written and authenticated about those who completely recovered from a terminal illness, even advanced cancers, when all hope of cure was abandoned. Physicians seem to be baffled by the phenomenon and unable to offer a scientific explanation for "miracle cures." Norman Cousins, former editor of *Saturday Review*, writes in *Anatomy of an Illness* about his experience with an "incurable" disease. Drugs and other therapies proved useless. With the help of his doctor, he checked himself out of the hospital and moved into a hotel room with a television. With tapes of old comedy movies of Charlie Chaplin, the Three Stooges, the Marx Brothers, Abbott and Costello, and comic books, he laughed himself back to health. Laughter can help us shift from suffering, pain, and misery to mirth. Humor releases anger and fear, "massages" internal organs, releases endorphins, and strengthens the heart and the nervous system. Laughter and an optimistic outlook are excellent antidotes to illness.

Unconventional healers are considered bona fide in many parts of the world, especially Great Britain, where they are endorsed by the medical profession. Many physicians who run into a dead end refer their patients to them. Healers are also permitted to assist physicians in hospitals and administer last rites. In the United States, too, interest in this kind of healing has been aroused. Unorthodox healers are lecturing in medical schools and conduct workshops for doctors and students. Dolores Krieger, Professor of Nursing at New York University and an accredited healer, has successfully demonstrated that the laying on of hands, or Therapeutic Touch, by nurses and doctors can effect changes in body temperature and chemistry of the patient, resulting in remissions and cures. She has trained entire nursing staffs at many hospitals and her method is accredited by the medical profession.

Quite a few hospitals and cardiovascular clinics today offer classes and instruction in spiritual healing methods. Patients are taught meditation, visualization, T'ai Chi, Feldenkrais exercises, and other holistic practices—including Yoga. A number of practicing American physicians have changed or supplemented their traditional medical schooling by learning and incorporating holistically or spiritually oriented practices.

Among the so-called New Age M.D.s, some of the most noted are: Deepak Chopra, presenting Ayurvedic and Yogic principles of healing; Dean Ornish, stressing proper nutrition and meditation, especially in the area of heart disease; O.C. Simonton, who teaches meditation and visualization to patients with cancer; Irving Oyle, emphasizing psychosomatic aspects of disease and health; Bernie S. Siegel, who practices spiritual healing methods along with conventional surgery; and Dr. Andrew Weil, a best-selling author and acclaimed authority on alternative healing methods. All of them have written books that have been on the *New York Times* bestseller list.

While the complementary use of all healing arts may seem vague or improbable at present, it can definitely come about. But where do we stand at present and where do we go from here? We can first of all realize that good health is our birthright. We are all born spiritually whole. Even those with mental and physical imperfections possess the potential for wellness. We are created as a self-contained unit of natural resources and our system is designed to avoid sickness and fight illness—if we use it properly. We have existed and survived the Stone and Ice Ages, withstanding their dangers. We are able to live in the wilderness and remote regions of this Earth and be entirely self-sufficient. Tribes and civilizations in isolated areas of the world exist that are totally independent in their health maintenance and sickness prevention, living better, fuller, and longer lives than we do in the midst of our sophisticated science and technology. Yet we, too, as "civilized" human beings, can be in charge of our health if we comprehend the correlation of body, mind, and spirit and learn to rely on our inherent powers for survival and well-being.

We don't have to hold outside forces beyond our jurisdiction responsible for our ills and ails. None of these can affect us if our bodies and minds are kept pure and in spiritual alignment. We can stop blaming our background, genes, germs, viruses and bacteria, pollution, and weather conditions for our poor health, and recognize that these so-called disease-causing organisms can only affect us if we are receptive to them. We also must face the fact that we cannot abuse, neglect, or hurt our physical and emotional systems and get away with it. We need to realize that our body is the temple of the spirit and that its abuse or overuse defies the law of nature. AIDS is not a punishment from God, but it was initially spread and is still being perpetuated by sexual promiscuity. If we live on mostly junk food, overeat, and deliberately subject our bodies to cigarette smoke, alcohol, drugs, and harmful chemicals, we cannot expect to stay healthy. Excessive destructive thinking will also lead to our mental and spiritual deterioration. Holistic philosophy maintains that attitude is the sole factor in creating our state of mental, physical, and spiritual health, that it is our thought-system instead of external conditions and circumstances that determines the quality and course of our lives.

If we exercise regularly, breathe properly, eat healthily, drink pure water, and think pure thoughts—if we are attuned with and in harmony with our body and mind—we are unlikely to get sick. Yet sometimes we do. That is natural; animals get sick as well, as do plants and trees. *Yin* and *yang*, the positive and negative poles, action and reaction, are the balancing forces in human existence. Disease is nature's way of letting us know that we need to rebalance our systems.

Since we are not as self-sufficient as the Yogi in the mountains of India or the Hunza people who live in the valley of the Pakistani Himalayas, we do need healers. It is imperative that we exercise our common sense and choose the appropriate treatment when we need the help of healing professionals. It makes sense to consult a chiropractor when you have whiplash or a structural misalignment or to turn to acupuncture for relief from migraine or arthritic pain. But it would be downright foolish to refuse antibiotics or resist surgery in case of an acute infection or a burst appendix. The right medication given at the right time by the right healer can work wonders, and surgical procedures, when necessary, can save lives. On the other hand, when emergency measures are not indicated, I, for one, would first seek a faith healer, visit a witch doctor, or fly to the Philippines before I would risk exposing myself to medication, surgery, or radiation. The results of these procedures can be harmful and irrevocable.

Holistic, alternative healing methods by themselves may not provide the whole answer for wellness either. This approach deplores separation of body, mind, and spirit, yet it can become fragmented because of the large number of methods available. Each one is lauded as the real one that can help. Focusing on only manipulations, pressure-point stimulation, nutritional therapies, or centering techniques limits the possibilities for total healing. Many people are forced to mix and match treatments from different modalities to get the help they need, and get confused when they receive contradictory advice. Faith and spiritual healings, as well, are too limited in their approach to stand on their own but, incorporated into mainstream healing, could lead to truly miraculous, permanent cures.

Everyone and everything can be helpful—the physician, psychiatrist, holistic healer, the shaman, and the spiritual guru. All methods, systems, and ideologies can work if they are applied in the right way. There is some truth in everything, but no method or treatment is a panacea. There is no ultimate authority and no one has all the answers. *Real progress in health care can only occur when the medical, psychiatric, holistic, and spiritual methods of healing fully complement each other.* The concept may sound utopian at present, but I am quite certain that it *can* come about.

Here are a few commonsense reminders for choosing an unconventional healer:

- Be cautious about demands for excessive payment for treatment.
- Avoid healers who advise against all medical interference and tell you to trust only them.
- Don't believe healers who claim that the healing comes from them personally or that the healing depletes their energy.
- Don't be taken in by theatrics and gimmicks or convinced that crystals and other precious stones or special oils are essential for the healing. True healers rely on their connection to higher forces.
- Remember, unswerving and unquestioning faith in the healer is not required. You can be a skeptic and still be healed.

Finally, it's wise to recognize that although someone or something can lead you on the way, no one can be with you all the time, and eventually you yourself have to take over. No cure can be lasting unless you change your attitude toward health and illness. I believe that good rapport between the healer and the patient is the most essential factor in effecting the cure and that faith and confidence in the healer or doctor is an important factor in the success of any treatment.

Faith in oneself is the ultimate answer. I believe that each person has the ability to invent disease and to cure it. We have infinite powers within ourselves to channel in the right direction so that we, alone, can take charge of our health.

Chapter Six

Psychic Phenomena: Shop Wisely

Now that we've reached the millennium, the subject of psychic phenomena has emerged from the closet and developed into a timely "in" topic of speculation and conversation. While the very idea of mind-reading and prediction may still be unacceptable to scientists and skeptics, even people like Hillary Clinton and Nancy Reagan have consulted psychics or astrologers. (Abraham Lincoln, Franklin Pierce and Ronald Reagan were believers as well.) The British have long accepted that their royal families, past and present, have been advised by psychics, astrologers, and mediums.

In the forties and fifties, those who could afford it sought the solution to their emotional problems on the analyst's couch. In the sixties and seventies, the adventurous in our stress-and-strain-oriented society switched their allegiance from Sigmund Freud to Aldous Huxley and dived into the era of psychedelic highs. LSD, peyote, mescaline, and related drugs were said to lead to higher awareness and cosmic consciousness. These experiences were pursued by the young as well as the not-so-young who, perhaps, should have known better.

When "tripping" often proved to be damaging and even deadly, we decided to expand our drug-free minds via consciousness-raising gurus and groups, many of which had sprung up overnight. While some of us did receive answers in our quest for truth, others ended up more frustrated and puzzled—and poorer—than before. Undaunted, we plodded ahead, seeking someone or something to help us battle with the quandaries of our existence and find solutions to our problems.

Throughout the ages, psychics have been secretly accepted and outwardly rejected. As they began to surface to fill the void left by our previous advisory specialists, it became less risky to openly acclaim them as our new gurus. However, because in some circles there is still a considerable stigma attached to their work, many people who swear by them in private still refuse to publicly acknowledge the extensive influence psychics have on their lives.

The sophisticated of society have their personal psychics, astrologers and other spiritual advisors, whose names are well-guarded and shared only with best friends. Theater and film glitterati may have them flown in private planes to faraway locations and pay a great deal of money for a reading. But the average person of modest means can explore today's psychic supermarket for very little money. Psychics are available to the public via TV, radio, Internet and telephone. One session, it is advertised, can change your life and solve matters of love, romance, money, career and personal growth.

Psychics are employed or consulted by police departments to crack seemingly impossible cases, or to locate missing persons. It is an open secret that psychic investigations are being conducted by military and intelligence agencies, and it is implied that psychics are used to spy on enemy weaponry and strategies. Governments and private companies allegedly hire psychics to hunt for treasures and find appropriate locations for drilling oil wells and mining. Well-known psychics are also engaged in experimentation in psychic research at medical laboratories, hospitals, and universities.

Humanity has never been keen on decision making, and throughout the ages, advisors, seers, soothsayers, and fortune tellers have been consulted and exalted as wise men and women, prophets, and oracles. At times, they were accepted as members of royal households. Along with astrologers, they played an important role in ruling Europe. However, in the Middle Ages, when the Church came to power, all occult practices were condemned as the devil's work and the persecution and execution of so-called witches and other occultists lasted for several centuries. In the nineteenth century, mind-reading practices and spiritualism were revived in Britain and came to popularity in the United States at the end of that century.

Without a doubt, Great Britain has produced the greatest number of renowned psychics and spiritualists, among them D.D. Home, Ena Twigg, Eileen J. Garrett, Douglas Johnsohn, and Sybil Leek. America has also produced famous psychics, the most prominent of whom was Jeanne Dixon, who accurately predicted the assassination of John F. Kennedy. Edgar Cayce, the Sleeping Prophet, was not only a healer but also a brilliant psychic, who predicted many future events.

Psychics can also be referred to as clairvoyants, clairaudients, clairsentients and readers, but have been most commonly known through history as fortune tellers. Fortune telling became respectable in the United States in the thirties, when Dr. J.B. Rhine of Duke University and his colleagues began their extensive research into the mystic realm. Prediction of the future was termed ESP, or extrasensory perception, and as such, it became accepted as a credible subject.

Many psychics are also mediums who can contact the spirit world, and I have met those who can leave their bodies at will to travel to other dimensions and planets. Some have the ability to travel backward in time, project themselves into the future, and psychically tune in to the present. They can predict events before they happen, some as international in scope as a wars or earthquakes, others as trivial as finding lost objects or foretelling the outcome of a baseball game. They may reveal significant events in a person's future relating to marriage, childbirth, success in business, and state of health. Some who work for the police in kidnapping cases are able to sketch the face of abductors or locate the victims.

A psychic talent is often inherited; it is common for someone with this gift to be born to psychic parents. In many countries, clairvoyance is often regarded as a natural ability and practice and is taught to children as part of the cultural folklore. It is known that Gypsy children, for instance, are trained to read minds.

Most psychics perceive their talents as a God-given privilege, but there are those who are as astounded by the information they impart as those who receive it, and have no sense of how they acquired such powers. Many use and abuse these talents for the sole purpose of financial enrichment, but most of them feel that their psychic powers are a gift they are obliged to share.

During a reading, psychics may use a variety of methods to either impress the sitter or to help themselves reach a higher state of consciousness from which they can obtain the information they seek. Some read tea leaves, others gaze into crystal balls, yet others use playing cards or tarot cards. Ouija boards, pendulums, and like contrivances are also employed. Some read auras or see the future in your hand (palmistry) or in your face (physiognomy). Often they will merely talk with you and are able to pick up information vibrationally from you. It is quite common for psychics to be skilled in more than one method, and to combine several during a reading.

Many psychics do their readings while in a trance. Trance psychics are able to access the information they seek by shifting to a level of consciousness that is different from the ordinary waking state. Usually the information is provided by an entity from the spirit world, which speaks and gestures through the mind and body of the psychic. Trance psychics are usually unaware of what is being said when they are in trance, and have no recollection afterward of what transpired

Some of the departed spirits that people claim to have received messages from were well known in their time. They were not all as famous as Jesus, but generally have been distinguished by their achievements. Plato, Shakespeare, Voltaire, Albert Schweitzer, and Winston Churchill are among the many who have been reported to communicate through various mediums.

I personally experienced meeting Pedro Calderón de la Barca, the distinguished seventeenth-century Spanish poet and playwright. At the time I was in a state of utter desolation. My younger daughter had been catatonic for almost a year. I visited her in the hospital every day, but she would not acknowledge me or speak to anyone else. Her psychiatrist held little hope for her recovery.

One day after my yoga class, a longtime student of mine, Elisabeth, found me sitting at my desk, dissolved in tears. With some prodding, I shared my troubles with her, and she offered to help: "My son Kenny is six years old and he just started to walk," she confided in me. "It's a miracle because he was born with cerebral palsy. He was always a bright child but remained physically deformed. He looked like a spastic little ball, unable to move his fingers and toes. All the medical experts my husband and I consulted agreed that no cure was possible.

"One day, Juanita came into my life as a housekeeper. She was a recent immigrant from El Salvador who spoke no English. I, however, had studied in Mexico and am fluent in Spanish. She was a great help to me with Kenny and we became very close. One day, she mustered up her courage to tell me about Maria, her friend from El Salvador who had moved to Brooklyn. She told me that Maria is a psychic who is serving her master, Calderón de la Barca, who speaks through her and helps all who come to see her.

"Although I was reluctant and completely skeptical, I let Juanita persuade me to travel to Brooklyn for a reading with Maria. She is an uneducated woman who speaks in a peasant Salvadoran dialect. When she's in a trance, her appearance changes—she resembles a man—and her Spanish is old-worldly and cultured. Calderón told me that Kenny one day would walk on his own and become functioning and independent."

Elisabeth continued her story. "He told me that Kenny must be massaged twice a day with a particular oil and to bathe him once a day in a special solution. 'Juanita will help you,' he said. He also said that a foreign doctor would appear and perform an operation to cut Kenny's Achilles tendons, and this would straighten out his limbs. 'It will be painful and difficult and extremely expensive,' he warned me, 'but Kenny will be able to walk.' He also instructed me to light candles each night, burn incense, and recite certain prayers. After just three weeks of following all these instructions, I saw Kenny move his hands and feet for the first time. Two years later we heard about a specialist from South Africa, who subsequently performed a successful operation on Kenny's legs and arms."

"You are the first person I have told this to," Elisabeth confessed. "My husband and everyone else attributes Kenny's progress to modern science!" She offered to accompany me to the most dangerous part of Brooklyn, where I could meet Calderón. Since I knew no Spanish, I was grateful for her offer to go with me and translate.

The reading took place in a Botanica, a small store with statues of Jesus and the saints, religious artifacts, and incense and candles in the window. I believe that possibly hundreds of these Botanicas exist in the boroughs of New York that have a Hispanic population. Inside, people sit on benches, sometimes for hours, waiting for a reading with the medium. Maria's Botanica was filled to overflowing, but because of Juanita's friendship with her we were led right in. I did not understand what was said, but I was amazed at the transformation from Maria to Calderón.

He said to me through Elisabeth, "Your daughter will get better. She has the potential to recover completely, but *she* has to choose the direction she wishes to take. You have done for her everything that lies in your power, but now you must take care of yourself and follow your own path. Please free yourself from guilt—you are not responsible for your children!"

The very next day, my daughter emerged from her cocoon and started speaking and responding to treatment. With psychiatric guidance and medication she began to function. Elisabeth and I are still in touch. Kenny began walking on crutches after the operation and graduated to a cane. Today he walks with a slight limp, but unattended. He recently obtained his B.A. and is working toward a master's degree in political science. Both Juanita and Maria eventually returned to El Salvador.

More than anyone else, however, Doris Collins has had a profound effect on my life and I am grateful to her to this day. She began her career as a trance psychic with guides from the spirit world, but after years of bringing through information from others she was able to tune into her inner knowing and predict from her own consciousness. I first met her in London at the end of 1976. I had signed up for a week's tour with a Yoga group, which included sightseeing as well as various Yoga activities. It was a relatively inexpensive trip, unlike the kind of traveling I had done with my husband, but it happened at a time when I desperately needed a change of scenery. I had left my husband after thirty years of marriage because he was addicted to cocaine and bereft of morality. He treated me cruelly and flaunted his affairs with other women. Although I had no money of my own, I ignored the warnings of my family, friends, and lawyers because I had to leave him to preserve my sanity. My husband grudgingly agreed to pay for the trip, but insisted that we start divorce proceedings as soon as I returned.

Everyone in our Yoga group was signed up for a reading with Doris and assured me that this was a great privilege. She had been voted the number one psychic in England that year and apparently was world famous. I was in no mood for psychics—I'd recently had a disastrous experience with one—so I decided to cancel my appointment. But my roommate, who had already received her reading, persuaded me to go: "She is fabulous; she nearly blew me away with her insight. I insist that you stop moping and go to see her—she can only help you."

Sitting across from Doris in her hotel room, I was sorry that I surrendered. I was late and Doris, annoyed, told me that I was an extremely rude person. For five minutes we just glared at each other in mutual dislike. She then said, "You're an Aries, aren't you? I see the sign above your head." I nodded mutely. She became kinder as she continued, "Don't give him a divorce!" she said emphatically. "Your husband is a sick and lonely man, but the drugs have turned him into an animal. You were right to leave him because he is involved in illegalities with ruthless people and your life could be in danger. Even so, don't give in, no matter how threatening he may act. You may not understand the reasons now, but they will become clear in time." She said other things about my life and my children and everything was the truth.

I returned to New York, and my husband went into a rage when I canceled the appointment with the divorce lawyer. He continued to harass and threaten me when I refused to even discuss the divorce and went so far as to cancel all my charge accounts. I held on—on sheer faith only—and borrowed money from my mother and brother.

Exactly six months after I met Doris, my husband crashed in his plane while flying to the Bahamas. He was caught in a thunderstorm and missed the runway. Apparently, he was high on drugs at the time. I discovered that he had been in the process of changing his will to leave the bulk of his estate to his daughters and his girlfriend. My accountant told me that had the divorce gone through I would have been financially wiped out. Though I was spared this, for a while I faced destitution and possibly jail. At the time of his death, my husband was entangled in seemingly insurmountable complications. I had to fight off creditors, lawsuits, and threats to my life from drug dealers he had been in business with. When my situation was bleakest and I had nowhere to turn, Doris reappeared in my life.

She had come to the United States to read for some very important clients and somehow I managed to connect with her. "My dear," she said, "stop worrying. Everything will turn out well and in a year or two you will have a nice tidy sum. You won't have to worry about money for as long as you live. You must immediately dismiss your present lawyer; he has no interest in your well-being." I followed her advice and discovered that my lawyer, who was well known and had been involved with some of my husband's business dealings, had only taken my case to gain access to my files. He was acting on behalf of one his prominent clients, who had been one of my husband's cocaine-smuggling partners. All that Doris predicted came to pass.

I know that you want to hear more about psychic powers and the ability to predict the future, and about those who possess these talents. I promise that I will share more with you later in the chapter. Right now, however, I would like to discuss some other psychic phenomena to give you a more complete picture.

It was Dr. J.B. Rhine of Duke University who accomplished the difficult task of transforming the field of psychic phenomena, which was looked down upon by most people, into parapsychology, which made it respectable. The supernatural was more palatable to the public when it became the paranormal. Though parapsychology, or metaphysics, as it is also called, is still a controversial subject in scientific circles, it is today an accredited course in a number of universities. Parapsychology, or the study of psychic phenomena, can also be referred to as PSI. All these terms relate to psychic energy and the facilitation of psychic abilities that open and develop the spiritual aspects of the mind.

Astrology

In the public mind, astrology is placed in the same category as psychic or occult phenomena, but I disagree. Astrology is a science, along with other sciences such as medicine, chemistry, and astronomy, which were also at one time shrouded in superstition. The unwillingness of our current scientific society to accept astrology as a valid discipline does not make it less so. Astrology was acknowledged as a science by kings, statesmen, and sages in ancient times. It served as a guideline for the population, and astrologers were regarded as esteemed experts. They advised the masses on their decisions, indicating how they could more effectively conduct their daily lives as indicated by the positions of the stars and planets. Original astrology was also agriculturally oriented and it informed farmers when it was best to plant and harvest and what to produce.

There is vastly more to astrology than just knowing your zodiac sign and its basic character traits. Most people have no understanding of the origin of their sun sign and the enormous body of knowledge and complicated calculation that are the basis of astrological interpretation. Astrologers are neither psychics nor fortune tellers, though there are those who may also be gifted in this way, and a large number of psychics are knowledgeable about astrology. To accurately compile a chart requires statistical skill and concentration and cannot be accomplished casually. In this day and age, the work of drawing up a chart can be done by computer, but computer interpretations fall far short of what an experienced, insightful astrologer can see in someone's chart. It is unfortunate that astrology is known mostly through the superficial advice one reads in newspaper and magazine columns, which is meant primarily for entertainment and does not offer the deeper truths that astrology is capable of revealing.

UFOs

I also don't consider UFOlogy to fit within the subject of psychic phenomena. I see it as a natural phenomenon which is being hushed-up and suppressed by government authorities. It is understandable that in earlier years, UFO investigations were kept secret while evidence remained inconclusive. But it has been established that the Air Force *did* recover the wreckage of a flying saucer that went down in the area of Roswell, New Mexico, in the forties. Remains of extraterrestrials were found in the debris, and there are those who say that one or two were recovered alive. Many people flock to UFO conventions all over the country to attend lectures given by researchers in the field. The speakers, including present-day and retired military officers, are attempting to expose the government cover-up, claiming to have firsthand knowledge of the events in question.

A team of experts delegated by President Truman investigated the Roswell incident and inspected both the spacecraft and the travelers. Though nothing has been publicly confirmed, many assert that the extraterrestrials are of a race called the Grays, humanoid beings approximately four feet tall, with pear-shaped faces huge in contrast to their bodies, and enormous eyes devoid of lashes. Apparently they have no teeth, and their noses and mouths are but slits. These beings have only four fingers, which are considerably longer than those of humans.

This is also how they are described by abductees who reported having been captured by space people. A large number of men and women, usually of reproductive age, have come forth from all parts of the earth to tell of their experiences with extraterrestrials. They say that they have been taken, in some cases several times, aboard a spacecraft to a place that resembles a doctor's office or a hospital. They are told to strip and are submitted to various physical tests and procedures. Generally, samples of blood, semen, and other body fluids are extracted. The experiences are unpleasant, sometimes horrifying, but no one seems to be intentionally hurt. The creatures do not use language to communicate, explaining instead with their eyes. It is said that they are a race without emotions who in the course of their evolution became unable to propagate, and are attempting to obtain the needed genetic material from us to solve their problem.

Those who have been subjected to the experiments often seek help to understand what has happened to them, and a huge stigma has been attached to those who claim to have been abducted. Labeled as crazy, or simply as having a vivid imagination, many of these people have had to struggle with the impact abduction has had on their life. After many years of debate about whether abductions are real or imagined, Dr. John Mack, a professor of psychiatry at Harvard University, published a book in 1994 that gave credence to the claims of abductees, and brought the subject to the attention of academic and scientific circles, where discussion of the phenomenon was mostly dismissive. He was, however, successful in initiating expertly supervised group meetings throughout the U.S., where former victims could share and discuss their experiences.

For many centuries, UFOs have been sighted hovering above our planet as U-shaped lights or vehicles in the form of saucers, cigars or even the planet Saturn. It has been predicted that more and more will be visiting Earth in the near future, and that eventually an interplanetary meeting will be arranged. Is it not perfectly logical that a multitude of planets exist with populations of intelligent life more technologically advanced than ours and vastly ahead of us in space exploration? Though this idea may be difficult to accept, our future interaction with beings from other planets offers us a great deal to look forward to in expanding our understanding of the universe.

Crop Circles

I also don't categorize the appearance of Crop Circles as a supernatural or paranormal phenomenon. I place them in the same category as UFO's—alleged sightings devoid of acceptable explanations. Crop Circles of all sizes—ranging from five to one hundred fifty feet in circumference—of perfect symmetry and design—have been discovered or reported to have been seen all over the globe since the 17th century. They appear in singular form or as clusters in intricate patterns or formations, often with elaborate drawings within the circles. They show up in flattened wheat and corn fields, rice paddies, pine forests and mountain snow with the inside of the circle smooth and flat and the surrounding area intact. They are discovered by farmers, hikers, skiers and, since the last century, by crop dusters and other small-craft pilots. Pilots and passengers of low-flying planes have also reported viewing circles.

They apparently appear overnight. Some nearby residents report hearing loud, unexplainable noises; others hear no sound at all. Never has anyone been seen making the circles, nor has a single footprint been discovered that could prove an alleged hoaxter's presence.

Crop Circles have been investigated by astronomers, geologists, geographers and various other scientists, in addition to art historians and archeologists from all over the world—and, of course, hordes of "fraud busters."

Within the last decade, many sightings of Crop Circles have been reported from Canada. One of the more recent ones occurred in a deserted wheat field in the small community of Vanderhoof in British Columbia. Eleven circles of various sizes were discovered, interlinked in perfect precision and symmetry and shaped into one harmonious design. The area was flat and smooth amidst the abundance of unruly wheat crops. Scientists and experts from many countries came to investigate and evaluate. They concluded that the circles were authentic and concurred that, "they came from a force of concentrated energy"! Eva and her husband, who live in nearby Prince George, asked a pilot friend to fly them over the circles and were able to take clear and close-up photographs. When Eva recently visited mutual friends in New York, I saw the pictures and was thrilled to obtain firsthand information about the controversial subject.

I, personally, am certain that Crop Circles, along with UFO's, are the attempts of outer space intelligent beings to prove to us earthlings that they indeed exist. While it may seem improbable at present that contact with other planetarians can be established, I am certain that advanced technology from both sides will bring it about.

Spiritualism

Spiritualism definitely heads the list of PSI phenomena. It signifies the means of communication between the living and the spirit world. It is a most fascinating subject to explore and we will devote more time to it in the next chapter.

Psychometry

Psychometry is the paranormal faculty of obtaining information from touching or holding an object. Psychometry is based on the theory that everything that has ever existed has left a trace of itself in the ethers and can be transmitted to tangible objects. A psychometrist is able to hold a key chain, wallet, piece of jewelry, or written note, to name a few examples, and determine its origin by tuning in to the owner's vibrations. He may also be able to relate the person's age, profession, and other characteristics, as well as his past and future. A trained psychometrist may possess the extrasensory ability to extract virtually unlimited information from an inanimate object. Police often engage experts to track down missing persons. The psychometrist can tune in and receive vibrational clues that may lead to their whereabouts.

Psychokinesis

Psychokinesis signifies the power of the mind to move matter by intense concentration. It is the capacity to maneuver objects or alter their shape, composition, or motion without touching them. Even the outcome of a dice roll can be controlled in this way. Considerable testing has been done of these paranormal occurrences, which some people characterize as miracles.

The former Soviet Union was way ahead of the United States in demonstrating and proving the principles of PK (it was Dr. Rhine who shortened the name to PK) as a respectable science that surpasses the ordinary use of the mind. A number of American investigators have visited the former USSR to closely observe and film people with psychokinetic powers. With their hands resting in their laps, some moved bottle caps, ping-pong balls, matches, and coins from one end of a table to the other. Others rubbed their palms together to create static electricity and placed their hands near or above the object to be moved. This often produced rotation and spinning and even levitation of the object.

Telepathy

Telepathy can also be referred to as ESP or extrasensory perception. Experiments with these phenomena have been conducted at Duke University and in scientific and psychological institutions all over the world. Telepathic transmission is akin to telegraphic or telephonic transfer, but it is accomplished without the use of instruments. Thoughts are transmitted from one person to another and can even penetrate the dream state. Thought transference has been proven to occur across vast distances, even as far as around the Earth. Edgar Mitchell, the former astronaut, claimed to have sent telepathic messages from the moon to Earth.

Telepathy is more pronounced in some people than others but apparently is innate to all. Primitive humans used telepathy to signal dangers, and this ability is decidedly prevalent in children and animals. *The Hundredth Monkey* by Ken Keyes tells the story of the monkey whose root vegetable accidentally fell into the ocean. When he retrieved it, it tasted better than before, and subsequently all the monkeys on the island started washing their vegetables. This action became part of the universal consciousness, and the behavior was transmitted to monkeys on other islands. Eventually all monkeys with access to sea water acquired the same habit. (I can't vouch for its truth, but it is undoubtedly a great story!)

Precognition

Precognition refers to the specific knowledge of future events that most often occurs in the dream state. The events unfold in dreams or visions because they cannot be accepted while the seer is in an everyday state of mind. Precognition transcends the time barrier. The sinking of the Titanic, for instance, was predicted fourteen years before it took place. It also said that Abraham Lincoln dreamed about his assassination many years before it happened. I have also heard that the 1994 earthquake in Kobe was predicted by many people.

Precognition is often associated with noises or other signals that warn that a dangerous situation is about to occur. An ordinary sleeper, dreaming of a disaster such as a fire or a car accident, will regard it as an unpleasant nightmare and go back to sleep. Precognitive dreamers, however, clearly recognize the event as an actual future happening. They are aware that they can possibly prevent it by alerting either the authorities or the individuals who might be involved.

Carla, one of my students, told me of her incredible precognitive experience. She woke up in the middle of the night after witnessing in her dream the wreckage of a small plane, consumed by flames. Her husband was in Canada on a business venture, flying from place to place. She tried frantically to get in touch with him all night and the next day but could not locate him. He called her that afternoon, his voice shaking. The two-engine plane that he was supposed to have taken had crashed and everyone aboard had died. A last-minute change of plans had saved his life.

Dowsing

Dowsing is a method of locating underground water, oil, precious minerals, or other materials through the use of a divining rod. The rod may be in the form of a twig, stick, or even a coat hanger, which will dip, tap, or rotate of its own accord directly over the spot of the find. Today, divining rods are manufactured and dowsers are often employed by big business for offshore drilling, landscape analysis, or archaeological discoveries. Since these methods often prove to be profitable, it does not seem to matter that they may be scientifically unexplainable.

Dowsing, or divination, is an ancient art of tapping for a variety of uses, from discovering buried treasures to diagnosing and healing medical problems. A pendulum is also considered to be a dowsing instrument. Pendulum power and dowsing are generally linked under the heading of radiasthesia or radionics.

Nonbelievers have come up with a long list of explanations for the phenomenon of dowsing. They theorize that dowsing rods and pendulums respond to the magnetic force emitted from under the earth and from the hand. Or that the mind and body are linked by an electromagnetic field, which generates signals in the form of tiny electric shocks. Some feel that rods and pendulums respond to an unconscious muscular reaction, or that radiation is produced which activates nerve impulses. I prefer to think that dowsers respond to their own psychic vibrations, which guide them to the area of exploration; the rod is but a tool. So is a pendulum, which responds to our spiritual impulses, and I will teach you how to use one later in this chapter.

Astral Projection

Astral Projection is also called out-of-body experience or OBE. It is the adventure of leaving the physical body and traveling to another time, location, or dimension. It is the awareness of the astral body detaching from the physical one, voluntarily or involuntarily, and it can happen in many different states of consciousness.

Our astral body is attached to the physical body by a cord—some say it is a silver one—that detaches itself when we die. (Since we enter the world attached to the umbilical cord, this makes good sense.) The astral body was referred to in ancient Egypt as the *ka;* as the Shining Body in the *Tibetan Book of the Dead;* and as the Other Body in various Oriental texts. A psychic can see the astral body as one of the layers of the aura that surrounds the individual.

Most out-of-body experiences are reported by those about to die, as a near-death episode, but many occurrences are not confined to these moments. Some people can temporarily break away from the physical plane even when not close to death. When they return from their travels they sometimes relate their experiences, which go beyond our everyday concepts of time and space. OBE may take place spontaneously, in sleep, at the brink of sleep, during meditation, or in altered states of consciousness. I believe that sleepwalking can be likened to an OBE. OBEs can also be induced through hypnosis, auto-suggestion, or in laboratory experiments with polygraphs, biofeedback machines, or other apparatus.

Those who tell of their astral projections say that the body consciousness and preconception of the "I" is transcended, but no two experiences are alike. Some observe their physical self sitting on a chair or couch, listening to a family discussion while their astral body floats above the scene. Others visit the homes of relatives, friends, or strangers in various locations. Some can travel at the speed of light to distant cities, countries, and even other planets. Sometimes witnesses report seeing *doppelgangers,* or doubles, of the travelers. It is an experience that can occur once in a lifetime or frequently. It is usually joyful and thrilling, promising greater awareness in one's life The skeptic refers to it as a dream or coincidence. Psychiatrists may label it hysteria, hallucination, or autoerotic longing. Others, such as Dr. J.B. Rhine, some physicists, and psychoanalysts like Carl Jung have joined with parapsychologists to take part in the expanding research and documentation of the ever-increasing evidence of OBE occurrences.

Possession

Possession generally refers to spirit possession, the invasion of a person's body and mind by an earthbound or disembodied spirit. (This is an entity that has physically died but has not accepted the transformation, and is trying to cling to life by assuming the body of a living being.) The victims usually experience drastic, unexplainable personality changes, and often turn to psychiatry for help. They are apt to be told that they suffer hallucinatory, psychotic, or schizophrenic episodes.

Psychic investigations have revealed that many "incurable" patients in mental hospitals are actually suffering from spirit possession. Medieval Christian theology believed in spirit possession and appointed exorcists to cast out devils, demons, and evil spirits. Modern exorcism employs psychics or spiritualists who are experienced in dealing with the reluctant entities. They are able to convince the spirits to vacate the bodies of the living and accept their residence in the spirit world.

Voodoo, Santeria and similar West Indian, East Indian, South American and African practices are geared to thought possession—transferring thoughts and intention (most often hostile ones) to the mind of the enemy. We are generally familiar with their practice of sticking pins into the strategic areas of a doll that bears the image of the victim. It has been discovered that this can produce physical harm, even death.

* * *

I need to emphasize that both spirit and human possession can only affect those who dwell in a negative or self-destructive frame of mind.

In regard to all psychic phenomena, there always have been and still exist those who appoint themselves to save humanity from the fraudulent practices of the paranormal. Their whole purpose in life seems to center around debunking, discrediting, and assaulting psychics, mediums, and the whole field of PSI. They are on an anti-psychic crusade to expose all who claim to possess psychic powers.

The most ardent defrauders are professional magicians who insist that psychic phenomena are nothing but magic tricks. The Great Houdini spent most of his lifetime trying to prove that he could duplicate feats that are claimed to be metaphysical in nature, such as levitation, materialization, and telepathy. Today, The Amazing Randi, who is a truly amazing magician, is hell-bent on proving that all psychic phenomena are scams, quackery, or deception. At one time he received funding and support from the scientific community to promote his exposés. His personal vendetta seemed to be with Uri Geller, the famous Israeli psychokinetist and telepathist. Geller was observed making objects move or fly through the air through the power of his mind. He caused broken clocks and watches to start ticking again and was able to halt a cable car midway in its course. His specialty was bending all kinds of eating utensils by merely stroking them. Randi would publicly prove how most of Geller's feats could be accomplished by sleight of hand. "Uri Geller is nothing but a conjurer, an illusionist, and a deceiver!" he would state for newspapers and television.

It is, of course, true that the realm of psychic phenomena is rife with charlatans and is often practiced as a deliberate deception. I have personally come across all kinds of trickery by spiritualists, mentalists, and psychometrists. A pro can definitely fool the public if he so desires, but I am convinced that many magicians and mind readers (definitely *not* The Amazing Randi) also possess psychic or spiritual mastery, or both. This was said about Houdini, despite his skepticism, and Dunninger, the famous mentalist. The Amazing Kreskin, a well-known present-day mentalist, admits to being blessed with ESP, and Doug Henning, a talented magician who recently passed away, relied on his spiritual powers as well. He and his wife engaged in daily meditation.

Because of my intrinsically suspicious nature, I never rely on hearsay, only on what I experience as the truth. Once I attended a PK party, one of the New Age goings-on in New York in the eighties. The parties were initiated by Uri Geller and taught by those who had studied with him. I felt pretty silly, sitting among a group of strangers, all of us clutching our allotment of forks and spoons. But since I had already paid for the privilege of bending cutlery, I obediently followed the instructions. We were told to close our eyes and focus on a point of concentration in the forehead, grab the fork or spoon at each end, mentally command it to bend, mentally release the command, and let go. It worked! I felt the forks and spoons becoming pliable and was able to bend them into desired shapes. It definitely was a high! While I saw no earthshaking value to bending silverware, I had to admit that with mind over matter, it is possible to achieve anything.

I also doubted very much that I could leave my body other than in a dream, hypnotic state, meditation, or at death. But I was curious enough to try that as well. I "learned" how to do it during a four-day seminar in Virginia, which was conceived and led by Dr. Robert Monroe, author and expert on clinical death experiences. (Was it expensive? You better believe it was!) We spent our time listening to lectures and retreating to our individual cubbyholes equipped with dark curtains. There we sat for a designated time, earphoned and plugged into various electronic equipment, awaiting our body propulsion. Afterward we would "share" our experiences with the rest of the group. Most of them seemed to have experienced "trips" and "flights," but it was *nada* for me. However, on the last day, as I sat in my cubbyhole, feeling ridiculous and bereft of all expectation, I felt myself propelled out of my seat. I pierced through the ceiling and then the roof. I, or my consciousness, was flying above the building, viewing the beauties of the countryside. I was totally conscious, exhilarated, and devoid of fear. I knew I would get back. The OBE most likely lasted for less than a minute, but I knew that it was real. I would like to stress something here that seems to be a psychological reality. Whenever we pay good money for a course or an undertaking, we somehow manage to make it work! (This definitely holds true for TM!)

Another episode of psychic powers that I was exposed to was not as pleasant—in fact it was dreadful! I classify it as possession, a phenomenon I had held in disdain. I negated the possibility of spirit possession and I was certain that horror movies, such as *The Exorcist,* were geared to a brainless public. I also did not believe in voodoo and other similar practices; I thought it impossible that another person or persons could invade my space with their thoughts or designs. With this incident I experienced a rude awakening, one I was unable to deny.

It happened shortly after I returned from London and found myself abandoned and maligned by my husband. My future looked bleak, to say the least. I previously had met Yogi Amrit Desai when I visited his *ashram* in Pennsylvania to learn about his specialty, Kripalu Yoga. I was my old skeptical self when I encountered his spacious retreat run by at least five hundred white-clad devotees. I had heard that he was a commercial artist by profession, and I sarcastically deduced that he had entered the guru business because it was so much more profitable. Yet he was unlike the other gurus I had met. He had a wife and child and seemed to be devoted to both. He spoke excellent English. He was charming, warm, and personable and he catered to me as a colleague. He was also extremely handsome in his well-tailored saffron garb, and had long, black hair and soulful eyes.

Greatly in need of a spiritual boost, I decided to attend the one-day seminar he conducted in New York City. He told the group, about twenty attendees, that he had the power to bestow Shaktipat (or Kundalini awakening) upon us. He said that he could not disclose how it was done, but that some of us would experience it in some way. Everyone else was enchanted with him, but I didn't believe a word he said. I felt once again, as I had with Swami Muktananda, that I was immune to guru magic.

Two days later, while pushing my shopping cart down the aisle at the supermarket, I experienced a jolt that shook my body from head to toe. Overwhelmed by a surge of sexual impulses, like a cat in heat, I considered raping the pimply grocery clerk. Not even at the height of orgasm had I ever experienced anything like this. I somehow drove home and called my most intimate women friends, confessed my dilemma, and pleaded for help. (To the dismay of my former shrinks, I had never masturbated.) My friends were most sympathetic and suggested a number of methods. I tried them all, but nothing worked. In desperation, I considered going to a bar to pick up a man. I even fantasized about calling my husband and pleading with him to take pity on me, but I squelched both impulses. The agony was unbearable and I feared that I might lose my mind.

At eleven o'clock that night, when I was at the end of my wits, it finally dawned on me what had happened. I put in a call to Yogi Desai in Pennsylvania, but since all his calls were screened by his disciples, I never expected to speak to him. But he got on the phone as if he been waiting for my call.

"Yogi, baby, what did you do to me?" I gasped. The s.o.b. knew exactly what I was talking about.

"Please calm down," he replied in dulcet tones, "opening the lower *chakra* will lead you to spiritual awakening, your rightful path."

"But what do I do *now*?" I screamed at him.

"Drink some warm milk, eat a few almonds, do your most powerful breathing exercises, and meditate," was his advice. "You'll feel better in the morning," he assured me.

I did what he told me to do, somehow got to sleep and *did* improve the next day. (Soon after, I also found a lover to help me along.)

Yogi Desai apparently continued his dangerous game for many years. He reigned above criticism as one of the most revered and richest gurus in the West. His fabulous Kripalu Center in Massachusetts became a world-renowned spa. A few years ago, the Yogi was ousted from his Center in disgrace, allegedly for having affairs with guests, but I knew there was more to this than met the eye. Eventually, quite a few women came forth and reported that he had done his Kundalini *schtick* on them. Not all had been as fortunate as I, and some had suffered severe mental and emotional damage.

I can only describe Yogi Desai's powers as a skill that is apparently more easily attainable in the Indian culture. What we in the West regard as the mystical and occult seems to be accepted in India as a way of life. Snake charming and lying on a bed of nails are part of the street scene and future predictions are easily taken in stride. Visitors to India who consult seers report that they have incredible insight into past and future. Sri Sathya Sai Baba, the famous materialist, amazes the crowds that witness his astonishing feats. He literally pulls things out of the air—holy ash and holy oil, watches, jewelry, and other trinkets, even chairs and tables. Scientific investigators and magicians from all over the globe who try to expose his tricks have yet to come up with a logical explanation. (I was not surprised when I learned that he was caught cheating!)

* * *

We will now return to the subject of psychics, those among the vast realm of PSI practitioners to whom we most frequently turn with regard to our personal lives. Let me remind you again that a person's ability to see the future and experience flashes of insight is neither mysterious nor eerie and definitely is not unusual. Along with the capacity to heal, it is a natural talent or aptitude, as one might have in mathematics or music. Yet to be a professional in the field—that is, compensated for psychic services—sometimes requires a certain amount of flair or showmanship, a bit of exaggeration, and some deception. Even the most sincere soothsayer tends to improvise when it is called for.

A few years ago, a famous psychic came to New York from England by popular request. He was renowned as a trance medium who channeled guides from the spirit world, who spoke through him in various accents. I had signed up for my session six months in advance, prepaid (a hefty sum) for my reading, and was envied by those unable to receive one.

The famed one turned out to be a youngish man, ordinary looking but flamboyantly attired, his demeanor impersonal and polite. He bade me sit opposite him, instructed me about his method of transformation while in trance, and questioned me as to my purpose for the reading. I told him, truthfully, that I needed direction on how to proceed with my life and gave him no further information about myself. He leaned back in his chair, closed his eyes, fluttered his lashes, breathed deeply, and about three minutes elapsed before the first of one of his guides made himself heard.

Altogether three guides came forth; each spoke in a different voice, timbre, inflection, and archaic British accent. As each of the seemingly elder gentlemen took his proper turn, they spouted cosmic and New Age wisdom. I "learned" about God-consciousness, the Bible, Jesus, Buddha, Mohammed, karma and reincarnation, and was told that I had lived at least one hundred times prior to this life, once as a member of Spanish royalty. As to my present life and how to improve it, I was advised that exercise would help me: "Look into Yoga," I was told," it is gentle, and suited to those like you who are no longer young. It would also be good for you to learn meditation and proper breathing; it will help to open your spiritual centers." He admirably aroused himself from his "trance," making appropriate noises and gestures of "coming-to," and smiled at me expectantly, as if awaiting applause. I was positive that his was no trance. Although his imitations were jolly good, I felt that I had wasted money and time.

This man is still famous and much in demand and people swear by his prophecies. I suggest that he could have had an off-day when he saw me. The truth is, however, than many a psychic can put on a good act.

There are also those who are genuinely psychic and genuinely greedy as well. I encountered one such specimen when I was in the deepest depths of despair and frustration. My older daughter seemed to have disappeared from the face of the Earth. We had only a note from her that read: "I want no contact with you ever again! Don't try to find me, it will do no good." Neither my husband or I nor any of her friends could explain her behavior.

The next day I found myself on an errand on Lexington Avenue in Manhattan, pushing through the crowds of shoppers, when a boy thrust a flyer into my hand. It read: MRS. EMMA, WORLD FAMOUS PSYCHIC. SHE HAS THE ANSWERS TO ALL YOUR PROBLEMS. SEE HER AT ONCE IF YOU NEED HELP! My first impulse was to throw the paper away. I had never before consulted a psychic and had only a vague idea what they were about. I knew I didn't trust them, but I *did* need help. I located her address and amazed myself by climbing up four rickety flights of stairs to confront the World Famous Psychic. She was a rather young, dark-complexioned women of either Hispanic, West Indian, or Gypsy origin, wearing large hoop earrings, a long, flowered, dirty skirt, and a wrinkled tacky silk blouse. She looked exactly the way I had pictured a mind-reader to be.

The room was almost bare of furniture and as messy as she. Something was cooking on the stove and it smelled as vile as witch's brew. I was ready to bolt, but she literally forced me into a chair and squeezed herself close to me. "How can I help you?" she asked, and I blurted out, "I must find out what happened to my daughter!"

She closed her eyes and heaved a deep sigh. Then she shuddered and crossed herself and spoke in a voice different from her own. "I can clearly see your daughter," she intoned, and accurately described her. "She is surrounded by evil. She is enslaved by godless people who want to keep her away from you. They are alienating her from you through wicked ways and there is almost no hope that she will ever come back to you." She verified the cult surroundings that my daughter had fallen prey to.

When she opened her eyes, it was obvious that she had come out of a trance and had no recollection of what she had said. But she was quick to notice the sheer horror on my face; she was also quick to notice my jewelry. "Don't despair, darling!" she assured me. "I can help you, but you must do what I tell you. When you get home, take a raw egg and place it in a white handkerchief along with four twenty-dollar bills. Wrap it all tightly and place it under your bed. Bring it to me when you come to see me in five days, and I will meanwhile pray for you and light candles."

To this day, I cannot believe that I obeyed her; I must have been slightly insane, devoid of all logic and reasoning. When I returned, I had the distinct feeling that she didn't know who I was, but she spotted the handkerchief. "Is the money in there?" she asked. I nodded. She made me sit down and watch as she placed the bundle on a piece of newspaper on the floor. She stepped on it with her high heel and mashed the contents around with the bottom of her shoe. She then opened the handkerchief. There among the mess of broken egg and soiled money was a little black object that resembled a devil's head. She let out an ear-piercing scream and commanded, "Cross yourself quickly, it's the devil himself!" That's when she lost me—apparently she didn't know I wasn't a Christian. I left her the money and quickly escaped. But a week later we discovered our daughter's involvement with the cult.

There exist many Mrs. Emmas who are innately psychic. Some are definitely legitimate, but the majority of those distributing handbills or advertising in sleazy publications follow their true calling—that of a con artist.

For a relatively small sum they promise you love, health, fortune, and the solutions to all your problems. Once you enter their premises, they try to strip you of your resources with egg tricks and other scare tactics or promises of great wealth. Although the police have an eye on them and once in a while there may be an arrest, psychic frauds exist today as they always have—possibly in greater numbers to meet the growing demand. There is a vast group of "professional" seekers who devote much of their time and money exploring the occult. Many gullible people will take no action without first consulting a horoscope or a crystal ball.

Every respectable astrologer or clairvoyant will tell you that he or she is fallible. Predictions may be accurate only eighty percent of the time. It is as sensible to consult a psychic advisor in times of turmoil and indecision as it is to seek psychotherapeutic or other counsel, but discrimination is mandatory and especially important when you are distressed, and therefore vulnerable.

"But how do I choose a reliable psychic?" you want to know. This can be quite a problem, because, aside from those who set out to bilk you, there are many pseudo-psychics who are convinced that their powers are authentic. Even if their motives are pure, many suffer from delusions of grandeur, misleading others in turn. You don't need to be distrustful, but do be cautious about those who use elaborate gimmicks or gadgets and those operating in trance who apply theatrics and exaggerated accents. (I also wish to remind you not to treat a psychic consultation as a lark.) It is always best to seek advice from psychics who have been recommended by someone you respect.

True psychics are generally spiritual people, who attribute their powers to a higher source. They will usually start the reading with a short meditation or prayer, thanking God or the higher forces for allowing them to be a vehicle that can help others.

Another word of caution: Never blindly accept what is predicted, no matter how much you wish for it. Don't disregard your own sense of what is right and replace it with information that doesn't click with you. Know also that no true clairvoyant, prophet, or seer, even one with the capacity of a Nostradamus, can control what they predict. What they "see" in the universe or in you is already there. They have no magic powers to make things occur for you or prevent them from happening, nor can they change future events. All they can do is alert and forewarn you. You are the one to choose whether or not to heed the advice and you are the *only one* with the power to change your destiny.

I want to stress something I said earlier: Psychic powers are not supernatural; ESP, instincts, intuitions, and hunches are natural functions of the mind. Most great inventions, such as Einstein's theories or Edison's light bulb, resulted from flashes of insight. The difference between an ordinary person and a genius is that, in addition to having a superior intellect, the latter relies on his intuition. This distinction also applies to the difference between a professional mind reader and a layperson. A genuine psychic trusts and acts upon the first impression that comes to mind, whereas most of us dissect it, intellectualize it, or chew it to death. However, we all possess ESP. Every one of us has insights, instinctive reactions, and predictive impulses which, if acted upon, would prove to be correct. How often do you say, "I was just going to say that." "You took the words out of my mouth!" "I thought exactly what you were thinking."? How often do you *know* that someone is going to phone you, pay an unexpected visit, or return their loan? Does it happen that you can predict the outcome of a game, a winning number on the roulette table (usually when you have no money on it!), or find a parking place just where you need one?

We all experience precognitive dreams or déjà vu. Attempting a rational explanation, we term the events coincidence. We are programmed not to trust our intuitions out of fear of saying the wrong thing or making the wrong decision. Children are innately psychic, but they are not believed, and are usually told not to make up stories or assured that their imagination is running overboard.

If you desire to learn how to trust your innate psychic ability, I can steer you to those who will assist you. But it is required that you accept and *know* (it's not enough to believe) that everyone on Earth is blessed with guides from the spirit world. They are your personal, generally self-appointed entities who are with you at birth, await you as you depart for other dimensions, and assist you during your lifetime. You may have one or more, depending on your situation, and they may change over the course of your lifetime. Your guides can be former relatives or friends or complete strangers. An inspired psychic can often tell you their names or something about them, and you yourself may find means of your own to discover their identity.

The guides are advanced spirits who are continuing on their path of advancement as a soul in the spirit world, and in that form have chosen to assist those on Earth. You cannot see them but you can learn to sense them around you. They are most eager to connect with you and there are ways of communication open to you.

A direct method of contact is via a pendulum. You can fashion one yourself or purchase a crystal one in any New Age bookstore or curio store. Try several for size and choose the one that feels best in your hand. To start, sit by a table or a desk and rest your forearm on the edge. Hold the string or the bead between your thumb and forefinger, allowing the attached pendulum to dangle freely. Instruct the pendulum to rotate to the right to signal yes and to left for no, or you can reverse the signals. Before you begin asking questions, state firmly that you want the pendulum to tell you the absolute truth and affirm that none of your preconceived ideas will interfere with the accuracy of the answers. Otherwise your subconscious mind is apt to take over and control the proceedings.

Thank your guides for being with you. Take a few deep breaths and ask your question, either out loud or silently. Start with insignificant matters, and as you drop your prejudices and increase your confidence, use the pendulum to explore more important issues and experiment with real life situations. It may take some practice before you feel secure that the pendulum actually rotates on its own with no help other than your concentration.

Be the only one who uses your pendulum. If you desire more specific responses than yes and no, draw a large circle on a piece of paper or cardboard and divide it into wedge-like segments. If, for instance, you wish to take a trip and are undecided about where to go, write the name of a location in each section. The pendulum will move in whatever direction you instruct it to—up and down, sideways, or diagonally—to indicate which place would be best for you. You can also fashion an alphabetic chart and practice becoming adept at receiving lengthier messages. According to scientific interpretation, it is your inner intelligence communicating through the nervous system that creates the movement of the pendulum, but I know better! This is a phenomenon created through one's connection to the spirit world.

Here is an alternate, simple method for receiving strictly yes-and-no answers: Place the thumb and forefinger of either hand together to form a circle. Thread the forefinger of your other hand underneath, connect with the thumb, and lock both circles. Tell your guides that you want thumb and finger to stay locked to indicate yes and to open for no, or the opposite if you wish. This comes in handy if, for instance, you are lost in the woods. I am an ardent hiker without a sense of direction, so it often happens to me. I might ask, "Am I on the right path?" If I forcibly pull my fingers and they stay locked, I know that I am. If, however, they open easily, I need further instructions.

Another method of divination for answers from a higher authority is the *I Ching*. It is derived from an ancient Chinese oracle system and philosophical text based on the understanding of *yin* and *yang*. Many Westerners are familiar with it as a way of receiving answers by throwing coins or sticks (originally yarrow sticks) and getting profound messages from the way they fall. It is, however, extremely difficult to interpret the messages; to reach anything other than the most superficial level of interpretation can require a lifetime of study. This method is perhaps best left for those who are steeped in the culture in which it was created, or for those scholars who can delve into such studies. Since I fit neither category, I regret that I do not have further information on this method.

A popular entertainment for two or more people who have nothing better to do on a rainy evening is the Ouija board. The most psychic individual in a group can be chosen to be the channel for answers from a higher dimension. You can buy commercially produced boards, which have printed on them the letters of the alphabet, zero and the numbers one through nine, and the words "yes" and "no." The board comes with a planchette, which is of a size and shape so that two people can place their fingers on it. As the guidance comes through, the planchette moves from letter to letter to spell out messages. Even skeptics admit that it moves of its own accord. (You can also operate the Ouija board by yourself.)

Many lay people and metaphysical experts condemn amateur attempts to communicate with the spirit world. They warn of evil spirits that are likely to confuse and even harm you. It is true that some discarnate spirits may try to scramble the answers, especially if you treat spirit communication as entertainment. But these are disembodied, confused, and sometimes mischievous souls who want to latch on to the living.

Don't believe what you see in horror movies. Confused spirits are neither dangerous nor evil. I personally don't acknowledge evil. Like the devil, it is merely an invention of Western biblical teachings. The very word "evil" or even the word "bad" is nonexistent in most Oriental languages. I believe in *yin* and *yang,* the positive and negative forces within all of us, and that being good or godly has no opposite.

The sure-fire way to reach your spirit guides is through meditation. It requires no gadgets or tools and is the most direct method of connecting with those who are truly there for you. It is available to all, but comes easiest to those who include meditation in their daily routine.

Prepare yourself by sitting quietly in an undisturbed atmosphere and enter your subconscious level through deep breathing and body relaxation. When you have cleared yourself of all outside intrusions, center your mind on a mantra—or use some other meditation practice—to bring you to a place of silence and openness. Then speak either audibly or silently: "I wish to speak to my guide who is with me and comes to me from God" (or whatever name you call your higher power). Listen for the answer. It may be a while coming and, like everything else, requires practice and patience.

Meditation, practiced regularly, is also your road to independence. Because, regardless of your success with spirit communication, there will come a day when your guides won't answer when you call them. The pendulum stops moving, the fingers won't stay locked, and the planchette refuses to budge. This is likely to occur when you abuse your guide's assistance or regard psychic communication as frivolous fun. But, regardless of whether you are a non-serious or a serious seeker, your guides will one day no longer be there. They may return at a later time, but they will let you know that now you are on your own. The message is, "We are always with you and will absolutely respond to an emergency call, but it's time that you take over and get used to making your own decisions. Rely on your own instincts and intuition and take responsibility for yourself. You need to grow up and progress on your own!"

This is not easy to accept; I know because it happened to me. All of a sudden, I was forced to trust myself—not halfheartedly but implicitly—and it was a hard nut to crack. All of us try to avoid being in charge and mapping the course of our lives. We pretend to be helpless, yet when push comes to shove we somehow manage to stand on our own two feet. Each person possesses psychic abilities, which can be developed if he chooses. We all have positive experiences with intuition, and intuition is a definite indicator of psychic ability. Sixth sense, or ESP, is a natural power within us all; it just needs to be nurtured.

Meditation is the key to psychic development. Eventually you will be able to sit and without any will or effort your psychic abilities will develop on their own and direct you clearly to your goals. Right now it may require some work for you to increase your psychic potential. Practice by concentrating on the third eye; it is your psychic receptor for seeing and creating visions that can materialize. If you mentally draw in exact detail a future project or outcome that you desire, chances are that it will happen according to you plan.

You can also tune in to your solar plexus, the area in back of the navel referred to as the *hara* by the Japanese. It is the seat of your psychic impressions, which you can learn to trust. A knot, or tightening, or "butterflies" in the stomach indicates your "gut" feelings, and if you respond to them you will not go wrong. They will warn you of dangers and alert you how to cope with situations and people in the most effective way.

Practice tuning in to each of your *chakras*; they are the psychic centers of your consciousness, which you can learn to open on your own without any qualms.

Experiment with psychometry and telepathy and give in to hunches and first impressions. Explore anything and everything that appeals to you into the world of psychic phenomena. No harm will come to you as long as you do this responsibly and with respect for your innate wisdom.

As we break loose from societal restrictions and structures, we enter the real world of unlimited possibilities. It is almost certain that we can look forward to a psychic generation that has an expanded mind capable of transcending all physical restrictions. People will be in touch with themselves and with each other, trusting themselves and having proper discernment about those in their world. They will be aware that existence has reason and substance and have the ability to predict the future of humankind.

Chapter Seven

Mediumship and Channeling: I'm Four Thousand Years Old, But I Don't Look It

Perhaps by now you have accepted, or are on the way to accepting—or at least have an inkling!—that we do not really die or cease to exist. If you are still finding it difficult to release your structured belief systems, I hope that you can let go of them by the end of this chapter. There is no death—honestly—it's only the body that disintegrates, and the body is merely a composite of bones, flesh, muscles, organs, and blood.

It grew from a fertilized egg just as a tree or a flower grows from a seed, and everything that grows has a purpose. The tree provides us with shade and with oxygen, the flower offers its beauty and fragrance, and the body is the shelter that envelops the soul. The body is comforting and handy to have around and it serves us to carry out our mission on Earth. Whether or not we have completed what we set out to do, when we depart from this planet we simply shed the body the way we take off our clothes before going to sleep. The yogi says, "We give up the body."

The real us, however—the soul, spirit, psyche, personality, or "I"—continues to exist in the world that is our true home rather than in the world of illusion we have created here on Earth. When we leave the body, we are returning to our rightful residence. The spirit world is our eternal world, existing before physical manifestation came into being, and surviving all form and matter.

There are those among us who have accomplished all their objectives, wound up their affairs, and fulfilled their commitments on Earth. They are coming home to stay and will have to roam no more. They are blissfully happy and remain in that state throughout eternity.

At the other extreme are those souls who misused the opportunity to learn their lessons and have become a problem to themselves and others. They have physically died, but either don't know this or don't want to acknowledge it. They may have died unexpectedly, tragically, violently by accident or suicide, or else in a stupor caused by alcohol or drugs.

These are the truly lost souls—confused, rattled, discombobulated—the ones we refer to as earthbound or disembodied spirits. Some of them manage to attach themselves to the living, most likely to someone in a weakened or negative state of mind. One can compare them to parasites, who live vicariously through the body they inhabit.

Other spirits may roam freely, flitting about from person to person, in search of opportunities to mess up lives. They especially like to interfere with those among the living who seek communication with the spirit world. But the real troublemakers are the bizarre phenomena known as ghosts or poltergeists, who seem to have nothing better to do than haunt and harass. They have made the transition into death but are stuck among the living without the benefit of a physical body. They either install themselves in domiciles (British castles seem to be a favorite haunting ground) or else refuse to budge from their former surroundings.

Most ghosts died in a ghastly way but have no recollection of the occurrence. They continue to remain in their familiar environment because they feel they belong there. Some don't leave because they think they have no place else to go. Unfinished business—such as inheritances that have gone to someone unintended—can tie a ghost to its earthly abode. Powerful emotions, such as anguish or guilt experienced just prior to death, can also inhibit the ghost from vacating the premises. Often, they are unaware that time has passed, so we hear of ghosts who have occupied old houses for generations.

Some ghosts appear as apparitions—luminous, transparent, and often lifelike—moving about and generally scaring the hell out of those who see them. Not all ghosts are offensive or ornery, however; some are submissive and well-mannered. We hear about residents of haunted abodes who have made friends with their resident ghosts and coexist in harmony. It does, of course, become sticky when a home is for sale. No owner wants to admit to the presence of ghosts—what could be worse for real-estate values than a haunted house?

Even more upsetting than the apparitions, which most often come and go about quietly, are the poltergeists or noisemakers. They are without form and make their presence known through raps, knocks, rattles, and by banging doors and windows and throwing things around. They may shatter mirrors, cause paintings to fall off the walls, move objects or make them disappear, or pull bedding off of people as they sleep. Apparently the only ones who can deal with troublesome ghosts, visible or not, are churchmen or shamans trained as exorcists, or professional exorcists, or de-ghosters (or ghost busters if you prefer).

Hans Holzer, a psychic researcher, was well known for this as were Ena Twigg and Eileen Garret, famous clairvoyants and trance mediums. They visited haunted dwellings all over the globe, battling ghosts and convincing them to stop haunting. Robert A. Monroe, author of *Journeys Out of the Body*, is also in great demand as an exorcist and is often called upon to de-haunt sailing vessels and cargo ships, especially old ones. When I attended a seminar of his in Virginia, he regaled us with his fascinating experiences. He was able to contact the ghosts of sailors who had been shipwrecked, some centuries ago. One of them believed himself to still be in the ocean, holding on to a raft. Bob Monroe convinced him that he had indeed died and that it was time to "get out of the water."

The majority of souls who die are neither the enlightened ones who have fulfilled their goals and met their agreements, nor the befuddled ones who remain on earth. Most proceed through the standard route of transition, much of which we have learned about from those who have had near-death experiences. I will discuss this further in Chapter Eight.

Some accept the fact of physical death better than others. Many are still confused, dazed, numb, sick, violent or rebellious, especially those who died suddenly and were unprepared or are angry because their life was interrupted. Others refuse to accept the transition to the spirit world because it doesn't coincide with what they expected heaven to be.

Every kind of help is available to those unable to adjust to their new surroundings. It may take years before they can face their situation, but since time in the spirit world is nonexistent, the gap between death and its acceptance is of no consequence. Eventually everyone recovers from traumas, mental ills, and fears, and is able to progress. All are destined to reach the divine perfection that is their true destiny.

The souls that enter the spirit world in a relatively peaceful state of mind proceed to the next phase without further delay. They continue on the way to spiritual consciousness and are aware that the spirit world is indeed utopia, paradise, heaven. They find themselves immersed in beauty, light, and love, and experience a sense of happiness, fulfillment, and belonging that defies all description. All have only one desire—to remain in this magnificent realm forever and ever—but the majority are made to realize that they have to earn that right and that the road to purification is a tedious one. It is difficult for them to comprehend and accept that, although they are finally home, there are still obstacles blocking them from permanently residing on that plane. More lessons need to be absorbed, and to learn these they must return to the earth plane again and again until they are completed. Each individual, depending on his or her current level of spiritual development, takes a different route and amount of time to reach the state of completion that will make another incarnation on Earth unnecessary. Those who made sincere efforts to progress during their lifetime are definitely ahead of the game.

We need to understand that while discarnate spirits are physically dead, the emotions, habits, and patterns of thought of the individual basically have not changed. When people die, they do not suddenly alter in character and thought and automatically become saintly or benevolent. However, they are more detached from the limitations of the ego and have a clearer understanding of the nature of their earthly existence. Released from the physical body and the material level of mind, they do become wiser, more aware, and more sensitive than before death. In the human body, they were primarily concerned with personal gratification; while they may have loved others and been sympathetic to their needs, their ego got in the way of unbiased understanding.

Now that they are out of the body and freed from most hang-ups, egotism, and other restrictions, they are able to fully attune to the ones they left behind. They can then review their past life and see how amends might be made for any unhappiness, sadness, or hurt they caused while on Earth and, indeed, they are eager to do so. They realize that the forgiveness of others is essential to unblock their own path to redemption. It is also important for the departed to inform the living that they are "alive and well" and that there is no need for grief. Prolonged grieving by those on Earth for their loved ones presents another barrier to spiritual progress.

Most of those in the spirit world with ties to the living are eager to establish contact, but not all have the means to do it directly. For some it is possible to assume their etheric body and visit the living as an apparition. They appear visually to many as ghostlike, transparent images or lifelike projections—proof that death is but a myth. Others are able to make their presence known through generating sounds or smells.

Seeing apparitions and receiving communication from the spirit world are not exclusively reserved for occultists and spiritualists; ordinary people can experience these phenomena as well. Some are startled and frightened by such events, or believe them to be hallucinations, but most of those who receive the visitations are happy and peaceful—assured that there is no death.

The majority of departed souls, however, cannot establish contact of their own accord, so they depend on those on Earth to take the initial steps. Spirit communication is generally initiated through a medium, an intermediary between the living and the dead. Mediums can be referred to as spiritists or sensitives and are also associated with other practices that pertain to psychic phenomena. Some are born with the talent of mediumship; others develop it through various spiritual practices or with the help of advanced teachers.

Spirit communication can be traced back to ancient times, and practically all cultures and religions dabbled in prophecies and revelations from the beyond. Communication between the earth plane and the world of spirit has occurred from earliest recorded history. The Akkadians, Egyptians, Persians, Greeks, Hebrews, and many cultures of the Far East incorporated spiritualist phenomena into their beliefs.

In the mid-nineteenth century, mediumship was widely practiced in Europe and a period called the Era of Modern Spiritualism began in the United States. (Spiritualism and spirituality should not be confused; they are not the same. Spirituality is a general term that refers to the seeking of higher consciousness by any number of different means. Spiritualism is a specific movement considered by its adherents to be a philosophy, a religion, and a science based on the reality of the continuation of life after death. In short, a Spiritualist is one who believes in communication between the earth plane and the spirit world by means of mediumship, and attempts to act in accordance with the highest teachings of such communication.) The National Spiritualist Association of Churches has a Declaration of

Principles that defines the beliefs of Spiritualism, circulates publications about its work, and ordains and licenses ministers, healers, mediums, teachers, and missionaries after a rigorous training. One can, of course, be in accord with the basic beliefs of the Spiritualist religion and not be a member of any organization. Many people consider themselves spiritualists though they have no formal affiliation.

Though many Christians have been drawn to Spiritualism and have been trained in mediumship, it is not a Christian religion at all. In fact, so many people brought their beliefs from other religions to Spiritualism, that it became necessary to define Spiritualism as separate from any particular religion. It is interesting to note here that original Christianity *did* teach that the body takes on successive bodies until it perfects its course. The Apostle Paul claimed that we each have a spiritual body and a physical body. But, as time went on and the priesthood gained more control, they asserted that they alone had the power to predict the future, heal the sick, and employ the arts of divination.

In the early days of Modern Spiritualism, a great number of mortals who grieved for their loved ones and eagerly awaited messages from the departed were attracted to meetings and sittings, also referred to as "seances" (from the French). These often took place in what were called home circles, at which people were grouped together, sometimes around a large table, and instructed to hold hands, be silent, and go within. The room was kept in semi-darkness and all doors were tightly shut.

The medium would enter a trance and an entity from the spirit world, known as a spirit control, would begin to speak through the medium in various voices and accents, relating messages for the bereaved. The conversation might have gone something like this:

"I sense a visitor from the spirit world who wishes to contact her dear sister. If there is a Mary present, please speak up!"

Invariably someone would cry out, "I am Mary and my sister Helen passed over many years ago!"

"She is Helen indeed," the medium would continue, "and she tells me that she is well. Your parents and Uncle Harry are also here and say hello. They all want you to know that they love you and they urge you not to worry about them."

The exchange of chitchat was generally pleasant and insignificant. Many sitters came away elated and grateful and were generous in their contributions. Not everyone in a sitting would receive messages—sometimes only one or two came through—but the dedicated seekers continued in their pursuit from sitting to sitting.

The physical phenomena of table tipping or rapping were also in vogue as a form of spirit communication. Sitters were asked to lightly place their hands on top of the table and ask questions. Knocks, raps, thumps, and other sounds would "spell" out the answers. Lightweight tables were also prone to levitate, move in circular motion, or hop about, indicating that spirits were present.

Especially popular during this time were trumpet seances, conducted by specialized "trumpet mediums." Tiny trumpets would float about in a darkened room, apparently by their own power, glowing mysteriously and hovering eerily above the heads of the audience. The voices of the dead came through clearly in a properly spiritual tone. The spirits either addressed individual sitters, giving names of departed ones, or communicated universal messages to those assembled.

Some mediums were famous and in great demand for their ability to materialize those discarnate spirits who returned to Earth to inform the living of their presence. These spirits often appeared in diaphanous, undulating, ghostly forms shrouded in ectoplasm. Ectoplasm, according to the dictionary, is the firm outer layer of the cytoplasm of a unicellular organism or a plant cell. To the Spiritualist, ectoplasm is a spiritual substance that exudes from the body of the medium during a trance. It is said to be the same matter used by discarnate spirits to appear in tangible form. Ectoplasm has been known to flow from the body of the medium and pour onto the floor, then take on a pillar-like shape that can raise a table off the floor.

While seances and other such practices no longer seem to flourish as they once did, they are by no means extinct. Spiritualists continue their attempt to bridge the gap between science and Spiritualism by conducting experiments to demonstrate the validity of spiritualist phenomena, and those who are merely curious or sincerely interested can always find mediums or attend a summer camp where sittings are held.

In the eighties, while I was on my spiritual treadmill, I was "dying" to attend a seance but was unable to locate one in the New York area. I finally came across an article about Camp Silver Belle in Ephrata, Pennsylvania, which had been founded in the twenties by one Ethel Post Parrish. (Silver Belle, an Indian maiden, had been her spirit guide.) It was heralded as a spiritual retreat for believers and I read that seances, open to the public, were held on Saturday nights during the summer. I coerced my friend Jane to come along—a good friend indeed—because, although she was convinced I was nuts, she was afraid to let me travel there by myself.

We drove up late one Friday evening. It had been difficult to find the town and almost impossible to get directions to the camp. The staid Pennsylvania Dutch burghers made it quite clear that Silver Belle was a thorn in their side, to say the least. We managed to find the office still open and the youngish woman in charge eyed us with disapproval: "Shorts are not allowed to be worn on the premises. This is a religious institution and tomorrow you must dress decently," she said sternly. We sensed that she would have liked to send us back where we came from, but since we had registered and prepaid by mail, she reluctantly showed us to our room.

The main house was large, impressive in structure, and well kept, apparently built at the beginning of the century. The grounds were spacious and manicured, but our billets in a ramshackle structure were sparse and not very clean. At breakfast, "decently" attired in slacks and t-shirts, we encountered the other campers—about sixty of them, consisting of couples and single ladies, mostly elderly. We discovered that we were still out of sync with the dress code: The men wore suits, starched shirts, and ties, and the women were attired in old-fashioned, long-skirted dresses, obviously purchased in thrift shops. They looked bizarre and weird to us, and apparently Jane and I made the same impression on them.

We were the only outsiders present and our friendly hellos were met by silence and suspicious stares. Although many activities, such as tarot card-reading classes and lectures on esoteric topics, were offered to fill up the day, we decided to flee the hostile atmosphere and explore the countryside instead.

Following instructions, we showed up for the seance promptly at eight p.m. and left our shoes outside the tent. We were ushered to our seats on one of the benches that lined the sides; they were quickly filled to capacity. The audience sat quietly, looking eager yet solemn. The tent smelled of incense and was steeped in candlelight.

The medium entered at eight-thirty sharp and took her place in a comfortable armchair placed near the center of the tent. Her name was Miss Dorothy and she apparently enjoyed great popularity. Everyone beamed at her as she addressed the group: "All of you are, of course, aware that we never know who of the enlightened ones chooses to respond. We may not get an answer for everyone tonight, but I urge all of you to be patient and still."

Soft, spiritual-sounding music was played as Miss Dorothy closed her eyes and almost immediately seemed to enter a trance. The candles went out and the tent was immersed in complete darkness. All of a sudden, a glowing image appeared in the center of the tent. It looked like the ghostly outline of a tall male figure, surrounded by a halo of a vaporous, white, iridescent substance.

Everyone gasped in awe and someone whispered, "It's Brother Eliezer!" The apparition started to glide about the tent and spoke in a low but audible voice: "I greet my brothers and sisters and am happy to see so many familiar faces. I bring you messages from the dear departed and hope that each of you will benefit tonight." He seemed to be a very generous spirit and we watched him communicate with everyone present, throwing out tidbits like: "Your Aunt Mabel sends you birthday greetings" or "Your father thinks that you made the right decision." He even addressed Jane and me with such profound biblical sayings as: "Remember that you and the Father are one!" and "God listens to you at all times!" He was a fountain of trivial information, and his performance lasted for at least two hours.

As soon as we were able to leave, Jane and I bolted from the tent, ran to our room, and exploded with laughter. We were certain that this was, without a doubt, the most ridiculous spectacle we had ever witnessed and that all the "believers" were fruitcakes indeed. We agreed, however, that the alleged ectoplasm looked very real and we couldn't figure out how it was done.

I discovered the answer a few years later, when I came across a book called *The Psychic Mafia* by M. Lamar Keene. I learned that the "ectoplasm" consists of yards and yards of chiffon or gauze. Both fabrics are so fine that they can be rolled into a small ball that can be hidden in the clothing of the "apparition" or in a body cavity. It is truly amazing how genuinely eerie effects can be created by cleverly draping fabric around the body. I don't wish to imply that genuine ectoplasm and its materialization do not exist. I have heard from reliable sources that the phenomenon can be real and that the substance actually can emerge from the pores of a spiritually advanced medium.

The writer of *The Psychic Mafia* also exposes other hoaxes and trickery. For example, he reports that files are compiled with names and detailed information on seance regulars and these files are circulated among various seance groups. Many a medium has become very wealthy by milking a gullible public, but I am not suggesting that all seances are faked. I have heard and read that people whose judgment I trust have experienced true communication with discarnate entities and I am sure that it is possible. And I have had my own experiences in this area, which I will tell you about a little later. But I, for one, can not comprehend that table tipping, rapping, floating trumpets, and other outlandish phenomena would be required to contact the spirit world.

Many bona fide mediums have existed and exist now who are blessed with uncanny powers and remarkable abilities for uniting those on Earth with other dimensions. Such gifted mediums as Ena Twigg, Arthur Ford, Eileen Garret, D.D. Home and many others of their caliber did not need gimmicks. They had been thoroughly researched and investigated by psychic as well as scientific experts and have proven to be impeccably honest and capable in their efforts at direct spirit communication.

As time passes, the forms of spirit communication evolve—for example, spirits can now record their messages directly onto tape, something that would have been impossible in the last century—and the more bizarre physical phenomena and demonstrations are slowly giving way to direct communication without the need for props.

I have personally encountered quite a few present-day spiritualists who are completely sincere and right on target. But I definitely consider Doris Collins to be, by far, the most psychically evolved personality and an outstanding intermediary. My opinion is shared by many who have met her, not only in her home country, England, but in other countries all over the globe. She has read, predicted, and acted as a medium for members of the British royal family, and for international TV, stage and screen stars. Peter Sellers, the famous British actor, was her devoted admirer and regularly consulted with her, and Liza Minelli, James Coburn, and Liv Ullman have traveled to England to seek her advice. Many outstanding members of the British and Australian entertainment world are her loyal clients and friends. Her personal audience with the Dalai Lama was widely publicized.

Her psychic capabilities were already evident when she was very young; she was able to visualize and communicate with her grandparents and others who had passed away, and was explicit about what she heard and saw. When others commented that the child was weird, her mother replied, "No, Doris is just different!" In a way, she is still different, even from other mediums: she seems to have a hotline to the spirit world. She does not need to be in trance and, except for reciting a short prayer, she does no other preparation—she zooms right in.

I compare her to an overseas telephone operator who effortlessly carries on a two-way conversation, knowing exactly when to plug in and when to get off the line. As soon as a reading is over, it is erased from her mind. However, Doris is experienced and discerning enough to screen out what she doesn't want you to know. When she sees imminent death or disaster, she keeps it to herself unless it is important and appropriate to inform or warn you about it. She has spent her lifetime developing her remarkable gifts to heal, help, and give comfort to all she has touched.

I had never considered the possibility of after-death survival and used to dismiss all such assertions as utter nonsense. When, during my first session with Doris in London she said to me, "I have your father with me from the spirit world," I almost fell off my chair. I stared at her with disbelief as she told me his name and described the way he had looked when alive. But, when she said, "He tells me that a number was branded on his forearm and insists on giving it to me. Do you know what he is talking about?" I broke down completely. I was shaking and crying as I explained to Doris that my father had died in Auschwitz, where all inmates had been tattooed for identification. "He tells me that he died a most horrible death," Doris continued," but I will spare you the details." She seemed to be shaken up, but composed herself quickly.

Doris then said, "He is letting me know that he asks your forgiveness for his brutality. He says that he didn't know how to be a good father, but that he did love you very much. He claims that he was also a very bad husband and asks you to please tell your mother to forgive him if she can do so. He wants you to realize that he is with you at all times and that he is doing all he can to protect you." I remembered instances, such as my escape from the fire, when I had been close to death and almost mysteriously had been saved.

My husband's mother, who had died the same way as my father, came through to Doris and said to me, "I want to thank you for taking care of Eric for all these years. You were a wonderful wife to him. He was basically a good boy but impetuous and difficult to control and I always worried about him. I still worry about what will happen to him now."

My grandparents and my favorite uncle also spoke to me through Doris. They told me of their love for me and assured me that they were at peace. All three had perished in concentration camps.

By now I was crying uncontrollably and Doris was sympathetic, but she mentioned that my time was up. Back in my room I found my roommate, who had also made contact with her departed father. Together we cried and marveled about what had taken place. There was no doubt in my mind that Doris was a true medium and that I had actually spoken to my father. Years of therapy had not abated my hatred for him, but now I felt released from hate, doubt, and fear. I gained new hope that my then-current predicament would get resolved and that eventually I might be able to lead a meaningful life.

Throughout the difficult years that followed, somehow Doris was always there for me whenever I needed her. She had previously traveled to California each year to lecture, but now came to New York instead. She stayed with me, lectured at my Yoga Center and gave readings to my students, friends and anyone in need of advice and guidance. From year to year the waiting list for private sessions with Doris grew, and to this day, whenever I visit Long Island, I invariably meet someone who asks about her.

She reestablished contact with my father shortly after my husband Eric was killed. "He is very sick and extremely confused," said my father, "and we have him in the hospital. I and many others are looking after him and in time he will straighten out." Two years later my father told me through Doris, "He is coming around now; he is coherent and remembers his past life. But he refuses to speak to you; he is still mad at you. He wanted you to be penniless and now you got everything." Since I knew how stubborn Eric had been on Earth, I didn't expect him to change his mind soon. But not even a year had passed when Doris made the connection with Eric and he seemed to be fine as well as repentant: "I had turned into a beast and I sincerely regret it. You were my true love and I will always love you."

In later conversations he advised me on business matters. One time I was visiting Doris in London and had been considering selling some property. When she put me in touch with Eric he cautioned me, "Don't sell now. Hold on to the property because it will increase in value." I listened to him because he had always been a good businessman, and I didn't regret it.

I learned through these experiences that those in the spirit world *do* change for the better but that their essential characteristics remain for the time being. My father, although he is now benign, still comes through as a European chauvinist. He never inquired about my girls but once told me, "I have my grandson here with me and you would be proud of him!" Doris was puzzled and so was I, until I remembered what I had relegated to my subconscious years before. I had been eight and a half months pregnant at the time I was caught in the fire. The baby was stillborn and I had been told that it was a boy. (Although I am a pro-abortion advocate, I admit that since then I have had misgivings about interrupting the path of a being. I have questioned many in the spirit world about the time that the soul enters a human being—whether this takes place at conception, during the embryonic or fetal state, or at birth. I have not as yet been able to receive a definite answer.)

The connection with the world of the spirit can be established by anyone, regardless of the person's moral or intellectual abilities. Some people may regard it as an esoteric or mysterious undertaking, but it is in actuality just another form of personal contact. It is truly comparable to modern telecommunication techniques such as telephone, telegraph, television, modem, email or fax, all of which seemed incomprehensible until the capacity to grasp the principles of their operation was developed.

Channeling is a more contemporary term than mediumship, but the methods are basically the same: a medium can be said to be a channel, and a channel may act as a medium. Those with the ability can also be called guides or controls. All of these mediators can establish contact with the spirit world via a trance state or by listening to an inner voice. This is the most popular mode of communication, but other systems or tools such as the Ouija board, pendulum, or *I Ching* are also employed. Mediumship, however, usually focuses on contact with a familiar, comparatively recently departed one, whereas channelers tend to tune in to more highly evolved spirits who are available to offer information and guidance relevant to both individuals and groups.

The messages that come through channels are generally profound and indicative of a higher level of consciousness. Many are surprised that conversations with a loved one in the spirit world can be exhilarating and uplifting, but is often limited to trivia and banalities. We imagine that those on the other side have somehow dropped their materialism, have become spiritually imbued, and are ready to spout words of wisdom. Instead, they are likely to make comments like, "You are wearing my favorite dress!" or advise you, "If you are looking for grandmother's watch, you will find it in a shoe box in the attic."

In contrast, the channeled entity often seems to be steeped in spirituality, sometimes advanced to such a degree that the complexity of their ideas may preclude comprehension by a mortal. Often these entities explain that they are simplifying their messages because we are not capable of grasping the multidimensionality of their viewpoint. As in *A Course in Miracles,* the channeled material may require an interpreter or mediator to help "step down" the message so that it is easily understandable to most people.

Answers to questions posed through channels can be direct and personal, but often tend to be hypothetical and symbolic in concept. They usually relate to the problems and concerns of large groups of people or, indeed, the entire world. As we entered this millennium, many entities sent messages through various channels to warn and advise us about what we need to do to stem the tide of destruction that is threatening the life of this planet. They remind us that they cannot interfere directly, but they have an overview of our situation and want to aid us in every way they can.

Channeling is as old as humankind itself. In Greek history, those who purportedly received messages from the gods were called oracles. It has been said that with the rise of patriarchy as the dominant religious mode, the feminine, receptive way of receiving messages from the divine realms fell into disfavor, and in some cases became punishable by torture or death. Channeling rose from obscurity during the Spiritualist Era, which began in the late 1840s, but still lay relatively dormant until it was revived along with other occult arts in the 1960s, during the so-called dawning of the Age of Aquarius.

Edgar Cayce was relatively unknown when he passed away in 1945, but now his work—and the writings about him—have become part of the popular literature. With his gifts of healing and clairvoyance, he came to be known as The Sleeping Prophet, which is also the title of a book about his life, written by Jess Stearns. He regularly established contact with the spirit world while in a self-induced hypnotic state. His readings were recorded by his wife and microfilmed by his son for psychic research and archival purposes. Many people today still refer to and follow the advice given in the many thousands of readings he conducted.

Cayce was a unique channel in that he was able to establish direct contact with the spirit world without the aid of a guide, or control, or any devices. Apparently the information came through his own consciousness from previous incarnations. He repeatedly elaborated on his belief in karma and reincarnation, and referred to the civilizations of Atlantis and Lemuria, first mentioned by Plato. Atlantis was a continent that allegedly sank into the Atlantic Ocean; Lemuria was another large continent that supposedly was submerged in the Pacific Ocean about twenty-six thousand years ago.

One of Edgar Cayce's quotations stresses that each soul manifested on the material plane makes known to all others through the thoughts it projects what it believes its relation to Creative Forces to be. He was aware of the deep interconnectedness of all being and all beingness, and considered himself a deeply religious man.

Ruth Montgomery was another outstanding example of contemporary channeling. She worked as a syndicated columnist for political affairs in Washington, D.C. and simultaneously functioned as a medium. Her first books on the subject of the afterlife, published in the sixties, were channeled from her own experiences, but in the seventies she acted as a channel for the deceased Arthur Ford, a fellow medium and close friend. He spoke to her from the spirit world through two different spirits, one named Fletcher and the other a so-called control named Lily.

Later books were dictated to her directly by Ford. He shared his experiences in the afterlife, offering detailed explanations and facts about death and rebirth, karma and reincarnation. He also mentioned Atlantis and Lemuria and referred to them as preexistent civilizations of high cultural standards and advanced technology. Atlantis was said to have self-destructed through misuse of technical experimentation.

Ford conveyed his understanding in this way: "All souls have one continuous existence through an infinite number of lives. God exists as the totality of all souls, living or dead, and all matter of energy. There is no heaven, hell or purgatory, except of the soul's own making. The purpose of existence in both life and death is the continuous process of learning and self-evaluation toward the goal of all-encompassing, purely selfless love in a constant quest for the ultimate spiritual achievement—the oneness with God."

Jane Roberts also came to fame in the sixties as an exceptional channeler and produced a number of books that dealt with the revelations she received while in trance state. The Seth Books, or Seth Material, have been undoubtedly the most widely distributed and read books of this kind during the New Age. They brought channeling to a new audience, and channeling began to enjoy broader public attention than it ever had.

Jane Roberts was a published novelist and poet unfamiliar with the subject of psychic phenomena. She and her husband were frivolously experimenting with the Ouija board one day, and were profoundly startled when the Seth personality came through, offering amazing disclosures about the afterlife.

Nothing in Jane's background had prepared her for her journey into the psychic realm, and she initially tried to rationalize to her husband and herself that Seth was only a projection of her subconscious mind. Once Seth convinced her of the reality of his existence, she became the vehicle for his voice from the other dimension. With practice, she was able to enter a trance, and her husband took notes and transcribed the information that came through. Through books, workshops, and study groups they proceeded to inform people about subjects such as ESP, the afterlife, the meanings of dreams, and reincarnation.

Seth demonstrated that we are not dependent on physical matter for our existence; we continue to exist outside of time and space as part of the universal consciousness. He emphasized that each of us creates our own desires and belief systems from which we design our own reality.

In reference to God, Seth says, "What you call God is the sum of all consciousness, and yet the whole is more than the sum of its parts. God is more than the sum of all personalities, and yet all personalities are what He is. The responsibility for your life and your world is indeed yours. It has not been forced upon you by some outside agency.

You form your own dreams, and you form your physical reality. The world is what you are. It is the physical materialization of the inner selves which have formed it."

Edgar Cayce, Ruth Montgomery, and Jane Roberts have entered the spirit world, and while their books are still widely read, they have been superseded by a new wave of channeled material. It was during the eighties that the spiritual market became flooded by "Ramtha" books, Ramtha material, and Ramtha seminars. Ramtha was on most everyone's lips and the Ramtha character became known as the most flamboyant and charismatic entity that ever descended upon us from the beyond. The most awesome fact about him was his formidable age—he claimed to be thirty-five thousand years old.

J.Z. Knight is the name of the woman who channeled Ramtha and created his popularity and fame. She also did well for herself in the process. Knight was an attractive Washington housewife who had a strictly Christian upbringing and was totally unfamiliar with metaphysics. One evening, she encountered a tall male apparition standing in her kitchen. She relates that he smiled at her radiantly, introduced himself as Ramtha, the Enlightened One, and convinced her to act as his channel.

He claimed that she was his beloved daughter from another lifetime and that it was their destiny to be together again. He apparently taught her how to enter a deep trance and leave her body, which he then took over with his personality and energy. It is said that she "becomes" Ramtha while in a trance; her features take on a masculine quality, she emulates his gestures, adopts his mannerisms, and speaks with a deep male voice in an archaic, stylized dialect.

Ramtha refers to himself as a spiritual and political leader and relates that he lived but one life in a physical body. He apparently was a descendant of people from Lemuria and lived in a part of Atlantis that had been saved from destruction. In later life, he seems to have traveled to the area now known as India. There he became renowned as a warrior king and died in battle, killed by the sword.

He devoted his afterlife to searching for the unknown God until he realized that he himself was God. His message to humanity is that each of us must realize our own divinity, or Godhood, as the intelligence and life force that flows through us all.

During his seminars, he brings forth universal information on spiritual matters, but also counsels the audience and responds to individual inquiries. He addresses each person as "master" because he stresses that all of us are our own master, teacher, savior, and our own God.

In his words: "I am here to tell you that you are loved, even beyond your understanding of love, for you have never been seen as anything other than a god-figure, struggling to understand itself. And from every experience in all your lives, you have earned knowledge and wisdom; you have given to the world and you have added to the virtue of unfolding life."

All his messages and advice are, without a doubt, beautiful and profound, and it is certainly laudable that those who are striving toward enlightenment wish to avail themselves of his teachings. But it cannot be denied that "Ramthaism" turned into a cult. With the aid of extensive PR, the seminars, held in the state of Washington, became the New Age rage—many left families and jobs and surrendered possessions to worship at the feet of Ramtha/J.Z. Knight and acclaim them as their gurus.

She is the most financially successful channel alive today and admits to having earned millions through Ramtha's teachings. She owns a publishing house that produces brochures, videotapes, and audiocassettes, which circulate throughout world. Knight has invested in horse farms and other companies and has allegedly coerced her disciples to invest with her. All of her seminars are filled to capacity at four hundred dollars per head, and are booked for months in advance.

At one time I sought to experience her personal discourse with Ramtha, so when a one-day seminar in New York City was announced, I reserved promptly and mailed in my check. There must have been at least three hundred of us—men, women, and children—who showed up at the Holiday Inn at La Guardia Airport that Sunday morning. Some had traveled great distances to attend the event, and luggage and baby paraphernalia were piled up in the hotel corridors.

The session was scheduled for ten in the morning, but noon came and went and no one appeared. Rumors went wild about a possible accident. Everyone was agitated, children were screaming, but I along with most others, decided to stick it out. At one o'clock a young man appeared and tried to calm down the crowd by announcing, "J.Z. unfortunately was unable to come today, but she promises to be with you next month. Your tickets will still be valid then."

When I (apparently the only one among the pilgrims) asked him to return my four hundred dollars, he advised me to write to their headquarters in Washington. It took nearly a year of phone calls, correspondence, and finally a threatening letter from an attorney, before my money was returned.

I am positive that Ramtha is truly enlightened, but I am also convinced that his go-between is nowhere near it. I again wish to stress that spiritual endeavor does not guarantee spiritual clarity. It seems that channeling is more popular than ever. New books on the subject and extensive channeled material appear at a steady rate, and names such as Lazaris, Emmanuel, Michael, and Mafu are familiarly thrown about in New Age circles. Channeling workshops, seminars, classes, and lectures evidently provide a nice income for those who channel, because tuition and fees are rather high.

When I resided in Northern California, which offers a multitude of spiritual action, I attended a one-day workshop where I met Lazaris. He is channeled by Jach Pursel of Florida, a businessman who had learned to meditate and go deep within. One day his wife, Peny, heard him speak in a strangely accented voice that apparently came through him from another dimension. She asked questions and received answers, which she wrote down (in later sessions the questions and answers were taped). The entity identified himself as Lazaris and proclaimed that he had never lived on Earth or anywhere else in physical form.

Lazaris refers to himself as an entity that is part of a spirit group existing on many planes simultaneously. He explains that other beings also inhabit these levels, and we as humans are able to contact them and exchange energy and information with them. This is known as blending, and it is a process that generally happens at the end of each seminar. All those in attendance are invited to become silent and encounter Lazaris in this way.

During the session I attended, Lazaris first led us into relaxation and meditation through guided imagery, and afterward answered questions from the audience. All fifty of us in the group (in those days the groups were relatively small; nowadays it is common for six or seven hundred people to attend a weekend seminar), had been instructed to prepare our question, but only a few of us were favored by a reply. I personally concluded that no one present actually received a direct answer. While Lazaris uttered beautiful spiritual truisms and dwelled in philosophical generalities, he spoke in parables as far as I was concerned. I wrote off my one hundred twenty-five-dollar contribution to experience, but promised myself that I would go a'channeling no more.

Another popular entity that is being channeled is named "Michael." A woman named Jessica Lansing was the original contact. She, like Jane Roberts, was playing around with the Ouija board with her husband just for fun when they encountered their astral guru. The Michael material is still much in demand.

Michael teaches that each person belongs to a group of one thousand souls that remain connected with each other even when not on Earth. Michael says that he is part of a collective of individual consciousnesses, no longer separate from each other, that have been offering their combined knowledge and experience to aid and instruct humankind for the past two thousand years. They give themselves a single name so as not to confuse their students. (Michael was the first of his group of a thousand to "cycle off" the planet, meaning that he completed all his earthly lessons and no longer needs to return here.) He refers to channeling as a method by which the false personality is set aside, so that extended growth and contact with one's essence can occur.

Michael seems to be the most easily accessible source of information from the spirit world; hundreds of people claim to channel the Michael entity. Interestingly, none of them are trance channels. Michael uses the personality of the individual channeler to enhance the messages he sends through them, so you probably would have a very different experience with readings given by various Michael channels. But they all claim to be able to reveal information about your "soul age" and type so you can see more clearly where you are in your evolution and what issues remain to be worked with.

One channeled entity, who apparently is more "down to earth," is "Emmanuel." I personally can relate better to him than to those who offer mostly abstract musings. He is channeled by a woman named Pat Rodegast, who first saw him as a "golden vision" during meditation. Unfamiliar with psychic phenomena, she thought she was hallucinating. It was not until she joined a spiritual community that her fears were dispelled. Pat learned to tune in to Emmanuel while in meditation, but later she was able to hear his voice at will. As is the case with Doris Collins, she does not need to be in trance when she communicates with the spiritual dimension. Emmanuel apparently *did* exist in bodily form and he told Pat that the two of them had been together in past lifetimes, and that they will again be reunited when she leaves her body.

I find his teachings to be close to *A Course In Miracles* in that he maintains that we co-created the world with God and we must accept responsibility for our actions. He also dispels the myths of darkness, Satan, and evil, and regards sins as errors that need to be corrected. According to Emmanuel, fear, guilt, anger, despair, and pain are self-inflicted and lead to spiritual growth and progress when they are overcome.

He also discusses current topics of human interest, such as politics, sexuality, abortion, diseases (such as cancer and AIDS), and nuclear power. In *The Emmanuel Book,* Pat Rodegast demonstrates that Emmanuel is not only wise but commonsensical and humorous as well. Here are some of the answers to questions raised in her seminars:

Q. Is there a cosmic significance to the strange weather we are having?
A. Do not read disaster into natural phenomena. The earth is very wise; she is simply balancing her ecology.

Q. Why are some bodies healthy and others ill and diseased?
A. Some people choose genetic factors as they would buy a house with a southern exposure or a swimming pool.

Q. Is there a cure for all illness?
A. I would say yes, if you would be wise enough to consider death a cure.

Q. What does it feel like to be dying?
A. It is akin to having been in a dark, stuffy room where people are talking and smoking and you suddenly see a door that allows you to exit into fresh air and sunlight.

I know very little about "Mafu," a spirit entity who seems to be popular in Southern California. He is channeled by Penny Torres—a housewife married to a policeman—who was raised as a devout Catholic. Mafu, like Ramtha, calls himself the Enlightened One, and claims that he was last on Earth in first-century Greece. While Torres' channeling sessions and presentations are widely attended, her critics accuse her of either consciously or unconsciously imitating J.Z. Knight and her Ramtha.

It is my opinion that all channeled material that appears in writings or is presented in seminars is very much of a similar nature. The entities that come forth have different names, sexes, personalities; some were flesh and blood individuals in the past and others were spirit only. Some claim that they can contact angels, archangels, and other entities that have a non-human form. Regardless of their nature, all come forward to relay important messages that they hope will awaken us to the truth. They may communicate in different languages, accents, and manners, but what they speak about is universal.

All mention the existence of inhabited planets besides Earth and the previous existence of others that have disappeared or been destroyed. All refer to Lemuria and Atlantis. They let us know that Earth is a learning ground, and our lives here provide an opportunity to correct errors from the past. They speak of karma as a mode of learning about these mistakes, and as a way of discovering how to take responsibility for them so we can transform unconscious patterns into conscious behavior. Each reminds us that our world is an illusion and that our lives are a continuum of birth and death, incarnation and reincarnation. They reassure us that death is merely a transition into another dimension and is neither ominous nor to be feared.

All questions about God are answered in metaphors, and though all agree that God exists, no one seems to have encountered God in form. They all speak of the divine within us, the god force as all-encompassing universal consciousness, and God-realization as the ultimate fulfillment.

There is no mention of the devil, though sometimes Lucifer is named as one of the archangels who created the universe. Jesus, or the Christ, is seen as the embodiment of love, light, and divine consciousness, and we are as much a part of God as he is. Everyone agrees that love is the universal connection between all beings and entities, and paves the way to everlasting peace and bliss. And everyone maintains that meditation is the direct route to spiritual attainment.

Nothing negative can be said about the entities who are channeled, or the individuals who act as channels unless they deliberately exploit their followers. It is the seekers themselves who, becoming zealous devotees of a particular medium or channel, are apt to turn a spiritual undertaking into another New Age fad or even a cult. It is sadly true that divided camps exist that cling to and single-mindedly follow the teachings of a particular channel. Therein lies the danger of guru adherence, blind obedience, and unquestioned loyalty, all of which detract from self-growth and self-reliance.

It is possible that not everyone has the capacity to channel a highly evolved spirit whose words of wisdom may benefit all humanity. But it is certain that each of us who desires to do so has the innate ability to get in touch with the spirit world in our own way. All the methods I mentioned previously for contacting your guides are applicable: the pendulum, *I Ching,* Ouija board, and of course, meditation.

To successfully establish communication with departed ones through meditation requires patience, dedication, and preparation. To accelerate the process, you might want to look into hypnosis or biofeedback. Relaxation and breathing techniques, practiced diligently, will certainly help you on the way. Visualization or mental imagery—using your imagination to create what you wish to accomplish—can also be a powerful aid to reaching your goal.

I have been able to contact my loved ones while in deep meditation, either intentionally or when they came to me of their own volition. I speak to them internally and they answer me in the same way. I generally use this method of communication when I am in doubt and need to be assured of their presence. But when I wish to receive direct answers to specific questions, I find automatic writing most helpful. It is a truly effective technique and I would like to acquaint you with it. I learned about it from books by Ruth Montgomery and decided to try it after my mother had passed away.

Ruth Montgomery "wrote" automatically by using a typewriter. She channeled Arthur Ford and Fletcher by gently placing her fingers on the keys, and within a few minutes, the machine would take off at its own rapid pace.

Jane Roberts also wrote her last Seth books in this fashion. It is a method that seems to come easily to professional writers who are used to writing directly on their typewriter, word processor, or computer.

Conventional authors of the past such as Robert Louis Stevenson and William Thackeray felt that some of their writings came to them from an unknown source. They acknowledged that sometimes their books were dictated to them by an unseen power. Contemporary novelists and other writers sometimes also report that their creative inspiration comes to them from a spontaneous unconscious force rather than from conscious thought. Something seems to flow through their hands and make them move automatically.

When I tried my first experiment with automatic writing, Doris Collins was unavailable and I was eager to get in touch with my mother. Mother had been unable to comprehend my involvement with spiritual matters; when I tried to explain to her what happens to us after we die, she shook her head in disbelief. Doris also tried to tell her about the afterlife, but although mother adored her and loved to exchange recipes with her, she did not believe Doris' explanations either. We both understood her reluctance—mother was raised a devout Jew and was certain that her religion represented the truth. She was, however, the only one in my family who listened to me and took my advice. When I extracted her promise that, regardless of her doubt, she would get in touch with me if she died before me, I knew that I could trust her to do so. I was also certain that her transition into the spirit world would proceed smoothly, without a hitch. She had been a positive, warm, and wonderful person throughout her life, had never harmed a living being, and gave comfort and help to those in need.

I hopefully placed my fingers on my typewriter several times but nothing happened. I gave up and took to the pen instead. (Some people prefer writing with a sharp pencil and others use crayons, but a pen works best for me, providing that it feels comfortable and light to the touch.) My darling mother eventually came through to me as I had hoped for, and I can speak to her whenever I wish or when I need her support.

She reports that she is very happy where she is—together with her parents and siblings—and describes the spirit world in glowing terms. She advises me on things she knows about, but for more specialized answers I consult my guides.

How did I know that I was indeed talking to my mother? I tested her with questions that only she could have known the answers to, as well as with certain idiomatic German expressions that we had used exclusively between us. I still write to her and my father in German, mostly to keep up my own practice. I know that I can reach them in English or any other language because communication in the spirit world is by thought rather than by spoken word.

I have wished that I could receive voluminous messages from the spirit world, but must admit that my talents lie elsewhere. I have friends who are able to channel endlessly, receiving messages for themselves and for others from various sources. Some can even get in touch with other planets and other planes of existence. My younger daughter, who didn't always function all that well in life, is extremely spiritually advanced. In one of her better periods, she channeled a guide named Lexicon, and wrote pages and pages of beautifully worded profound wisdom and sage advice that he shared with her. He told her that she could get completely well in this lifetime if she so desired.

It is best to let go of any expectation of success when you begin your experiences with automatic writing. Do it just for the fun of it—and I can assure you that it will indeed be fun once you see results. For some people, the pen may start writing on the first attempt. Others may have to be patient and concentrate before anything moves. Choose a quiet period of your day or evening when you can be by yourself without being interrupted. Place a clean sheet of lined paper or a notebook in front of you and lightly poise your pen or pencil on a line. Prepare yourself through meditation and breathing to enter a light trance state. When you are ready, slowly open your eyes until they come into semi-focus. Write or address a question to anyone you wish to contact. Then sit quietly and await the action. It may or may not happen right away and sometimes the fingers holding the pen will only tingle. Eventually you will observe the pen move on its own accord. Usually it will begin by drawing doodles, dots, dashes, scribbles and squiggles, and unintelligible scrawls.

Don't try to control whatever comes forth. Please realize that mischievous, confused, and troublesome entities are apt to interfere with your attempts to reach the spirit world, for whatever reason they choose to do so. Let them have their way for a while, but stop them when you've had enough of their antics. Politely, but firmly, tell them to scram. Be explicit, and say or write something to the effect of, "I wish to speak to my higher powers *only* and I insist that all interference stop at once!"

When the pen starts to write legibly, ask, "Are you from God? My higher powers? The spirit world?" Wait for a yes or no. Continue your questioning if the answer is yes; if no, choose another time to proceed further. Try to find out who you are talking to but don't insist—learn to judge your correspondence by the quality of the answers. Through your efforts you may receive yeses or nos, words, sentences, or paragraphs. The penmanship may look like your own or may be totally different, and words and sentences may seem to run together. All the writings I receive appear in interlocking words and the *i*'s have no dots. I often don't know what is being written until the pen stops moving and I have separated each word by a vertical line. I hear from others, however, that their messages come through clear and legible. If at first you are unsure that the pen is writing on its own rather than by your impulses, here is how to test it: Place your pen on a line and close your eyes while it is writing. Check whether the pen stops at the end of the line or skips to the next line neatly and/or continues writing on its own. You can expect to be surprised as well as convinced.

* * *

I urge you to make the effort to contact the departed by whatever method is comfortable for you. Know that they are most eagerly waiting to hear from you and that a communication that will benefit and serve both sides can be established. Try to visualize and believe that those on the other side are still close to you and care about you, and wish wholeheartedly to help you. It is, of course, understandable that you initially mourn them and miss their presence, but try not to extend your grief. It may be difficult to fathom, but it is true that those in the spirit world are as real as you are. They are different in that they are without a physical body and earthly senses, but their perception and intelligence remain the same as before. Once you unthink what you were taught—that life and death are separate states that cannot be bridged and the spirit world cannot be comprehended or penetrated—you will feel relieved, released, and unafraid.

An important issue we need to confront—one that is terrifying to all humankind—is the possible destruction of our planet. We have been forewarned throughout history by prophets, oracles, and seers that we must change our ways or face oblivion, but the threat of planetary annihilation seems most ominous at present. The channeled material reaching us today is more voluminous and pressing than ever before. The enlightened ones from the spirit world are doing everything in their power to awaken us to the dangers that lie ahead if we continue to pursue our path to either nuclear or ecological destruction. It is no coincidence that they all speak of Lemuria and Atlantis, civilizations that once prospered and then disappeared.

There is hope, however, that we have a chance to avert disaster if we replace abject materialism and greed with spiritual ways. Many among us are trying earnestly to save the planet and lead its inhabitants to cosmic consciousness.

It may not be too late; we may yet succeed. Individually we can strive to better ourselves, secure in the knowledge that we will be around for eternity. Most of us have formerly lived on other planets, and if this one goes *kaput,* there is always another one to reincarnate to before we return to the eternal world of spirit. Other planetarians are among us now to prepare us and to pave the way in case of emergency. This is not an excuse, however, to avoid responsible action to avert disaster.

You may feel that it is morbid to ponder the danger of a total wipe-out. I don't agree; I think it is morbid to keep things hushed up and make believe they will go away. It is dangerous to stick our heads in the sand and bury our fears in the subconscious. I also feel that it is unrealistic to worry about what lies outside our individual jurisdiction and waste precious time in speculation about what may be inevitable. But it is up to each of us to determine the effect of our consciousness and behavior as citizens of this planet.

I stress the importance of squarely facing up to both the inevitability of your physical death *at any moment* and the possibility of wide scale destruction. It is only then that you can fulfill the most important purpose of your present existence—to relish life and enjoy your part in it, as you come to discover the true nature of your being.

Chapter Eight

Death and Dying: "No Such Thing!" Shirley MacLaine Says

In the Judeo-Christian tradition, death is undoubtedly the most unpleasant, unpalatable, and unmentionable subject for discussion—except possibly for undertakers and funeral directors. While many societies of the world accept death as a natural occurrence, we in the Western civilized, technical sphere still live in the Dark Ages. Most of us think of death as a mystery, a curse, a punishment, or an evil and picture it as the Grim Reaper. We hush it up, cloak it in secrecy, and try to sweep it under the rug. We pretend that if we ignore it, it will disappear. We feel that being in contact with death makes us more vulnerable to the possibility of our own death, and brings us face to face with our own mortality. We never fully believe that we are going to die; it seems to happen only to someone else.

While the subject of life after death is popularized in movies, TV, and books, it is apt to invite ridicule rather than support belief. High-powered entertainment and literary critics tend to review all material that smacks of the occult with a chuckle or a sneer, and governmental authorities try to squash any reference to, or rumor of, "abnormal" happenings. The clergy maintains that death is an act of God, and its circumstances and timing should remain an unquestioned issue of faith. They wish death to be confined to the rituals and formalities of prescribed funeral procedures.

For pure scientists there exists no reality other than *the material world*, and individuals are regarded as merely living organisms with organs of perception. They believe that the destruction of the body and brain signals the finality of human life. The physician is trained to suppress, delay, and conquer death—the absolute enemy that must be fought to the end.

A large proportion of medical research funds is allocated to developing lifesaving machinery such as pacemakers, artificial organs and body part replacements, oxygen tanks, monitors, and emergency resuscitation equipment. Often patients and their families are deceived about the imminence of death and are instilled with false hopes.

There seems to be an unwritten law or conspiracy in the Western world of physics and technology that supports *ignorance of our spiritual nature and a negation of immortality.* Our rational three-dimensional minds are able to comprehend the intricacies of space travel, nuclear power, quantum physics, and computer science, but in relation to ourselves we can't seem to think beyond the physical body. Since we can't scientifically explain the function of the soul, we doubt its existence. It seems incredible and incomprehensible that so many among us choose to believe theories that propose that *creation came out of nothingness*, or see Darwin's evolutionary theories, which deal with only the physical development of species, as being more rational than the concept of *eternal human existence.*

Many non-Western cultures have a much easier time dealing with the subject of death. They may shroud it in mystery and superstition and ritualize it to the nth degree, but most have a context that makes it more acceptable. In some societies, death is even celebrated as a joyous occasion, for they believe that the soul has just passed into a blissful afterlife. Reunion with loved ones, the presence of angels and gods, liberation from the strains of life, or a step up the cosmic ladder are much-desired expectations for many. Funerals are often glorious celebrations, with dancing, singing, eating, drinking, and gaiety. In some regions, the mourning rituals provide entertainment and stimulation for families, friends, and the entire village or neighborhood.

My husband and I once got caught up in a funeral procession when we were exploring the mountains of southern Italy. It was stupendous. Six ebony-black-lacquered and intricately carved funeral coaches, decorated with lavish floral designs, were each drawn by four black horses. The first hearse contained the coffin, which displayed the corpse in its elaborate finery. At the front of the procession walked the officiating priests, followed by two priests swinging censers, and then the altar boys, all in their respective robes. We were surrounded by wafting incense, incantations, and chanting. Behind the cavalcade were the "wailing women," clad in black floor-length gowns, with faces veiled; they were sobbing, moaning, and lamenting. We gathered that they were not relatives but professionals hired for the occasion.

Following the wailers were the townspeople, dressed in traditional costume—men, women, and children, all keeping in step. My husband and I had parked our car and joined the crowd on their way to the cemetery. Although we were beckoned to come inside, we did not wish to intrude. We listened outside the gate to the wailing women, who now went into their act fully by letting out ear-piercing screams and howls.

Apparently the funeral was a huge success. Someone explained to us in broken English that the deceased was not a particularly wealthy man but he, like everyone else in the area, had put aside a good part of his life savings so his demise could be properly celebrated. For these simple mountain folks, marking one's death was seemingly more meaningful than life, a lavish funeral being the prestigious culmination of one's stay on Earth.

Within our culture, more often than not, we prefer to grieve for the dead and to surrender to sadness and morbidity while heaping blame upon ourselves for what we did or didn't do to them or for them when they were alive. We often treat the dying elderly as immature children, keep them in ignorance, and rob them of their dignity through lies and deceit. In many cases we prefer to commit them to hospitals or nursing homes so they can die antiseptically and out of the way. We try to allay our guilt with expensive coffins, expansive eulogies, and elaborate funeral rituals.

But it is also a fact that many among our present generation have changed their perception about death and dying and have learned to acknowledge death as a normal part of life. Viewing it as a natural occurrence can definitely erase its threatening aspects. Open-mindedness and intelligent reasoning also lead us to realize that our true essence does not dwell in the grave. The practice of cremation within Eastern religious culture is based on this certainty as well as the belief that it is easier for a soul to let go of its attachment to earthly life if the physical vehicle it inhabited is consumed by fire. Even in Western cultures, more and more are voicing their preference for cremation rather than burial.

One can also have pets cremated. Many people find this a comforting, practical way to say good-bye to their beloved pets.

While I was still in a traditional marriage, adhering to traditional values, I never considered cremation to be a proper send-off for myself or my family. My husband, Eric, would sometimes threaten me in jest: "If you ever let some rabbi who never knew me officiate at my funeral, I'll come back to haunt you!" But when he crashed his plane in the Bahamas, where he had flown on a drug-buying trip, I made the quick decision to have him cremated on the spot to avoid examination and possible exhumation by authorities or insurance people. (I was positive that he had been high as well!) The ashes were flown to me in New York in a cardboard box, where they remained on a bookshelf for two years. I just didn't know what to do with them. One day, good friends who own a cemetery on Long Island came to visit and inquired about my husband's remains. They were appalled when I showed them the box and suggested tactfully that a small plot in their cemetery (free of charge) would be a more appropriate burial place.

I invited no rabbi to the ceremony, only those family and friends who remembered my husband without resentment. A mere handful attended, but each one said something to him directly. Afterward, we went to my home and opened the best bottles of the rare French wines Eric had been so proud to collect. While we drank, we toasted him, told anecdotes, and had a fine time. My husband told me later through Doris Collins, "It was a fun funeral and I truly enjoyed it!"

Thanatology (the word was coined in the nineteenth century) is the science that deals with the physical process and theoretical facets of dying, including the psychological mechanisms of coping with death. An acclaimed pioneer in bringing death out of the closet is Elisabeth Kübler-Ross, a Swiss-born physician and psychiatrist. She dared to defy the medical profession with her unorthodox theories and views on a subject that was rarely aired. Her book, *On Death and Dying,* emphasizes the importance of open, honest communication with the dying, stressing that most dying persons are in need of close personal contact and psychotherapeutic help. She gives evidence that those who are able to discuss their death process openly and without qualms can await their demise more peacefully. They, in turn, can teach important lessons to the survivors about how to cope with the loss and how to release anxiety about their own death.

Her courageous efforts caused a dramatic change in the attitudes toward death held by many health professionals. This change has led to the revival of hospices, which are a much more humane place than hospitals for accommodating the needs of the dying. It is interesting to note that what is considered the old hospice movement originated during the time of the Crusades, when an order of knights created resting places for sick and wounded soldiers. The modern hospice movement in the West started in England in the 1950s. Of course, there has also been a tradition of hospices in Eastern cultures. Hindu and early Buddhist cultures emphasized training for the care of the sick and dying.

While Kübler-Ross incited the interest of open-minded physicians and psychiatrists, she also stirred up controversy among the more conservative members of the medical profession. One of them was her husband of many years, who ended up divorcing her. Elisabeth (I call her that because she told me to do so) conducted training seminars for physicians, nurses, students, and ministers, sharing her experience in psychotherapeutic work with terminally ill patients. In later years, her seminars became geared to nonprofessionals with severe physical and emotional problems, and used consciousness-raising, transpersonal therapy, meditation and other approaches for self-help.

Being a workshopaholic, I attended several of hers in California, New York, and Virginia. I was impressed with her work and also with her as a person—warm, witty, and wonderful—who truly devoted her life to helping others. At that time she did not elaborate on esoteric subjects or dwell on the afterlife; she was still too much of a scientist and a Swiss pragmatist.

She has radically changed her views since that time. This may have come about when she suffered a heart attack and decided to survive. She no longer regards death as an issue of importance, nor does she consider it the end of life. *She preaches immortality and is convinced that consciousness outlives the demise of the physical being.*

Shirley MacLaine has helped alert a horde of unbelievers to the possibilities of life after death. Her book, *Out on a Limb,* converted many skeptics who would not have been caught dead in the metaphysical section of a library—to a belief in the afterworld. Her book was bought, read, and to a great extent accepted only because she was a renowned show-business personality. She is fully aware that she was fated to become famous so that she could make an impact on people and help them awaken to their true essence. Her book has been criticized as glib and lacking in metaphysical depth, but I am convinced that she has provided a great service to mankind.

Almost all Eastern and ancient religions, as well as primitive cultures, such as the Australian Aborigine and the Maori of New Zealand, take for granted that death is not the cessation of life but the beginning of a new and different stage of existence. Most ancient civilizations held the same doctrine, which was first recorded in the *Egyptian Book of the Dead* in 1300 B.C. The book speaks about the process of dying, *the passage of the soul from the body,* and a luminous light that points the way to ecstasy. The book also mentions the eventual evaluation of the soul's past lives by a tribunal of judges.

The *Tibetan Book of the Dead* (or *Bardo Thödol* in Tibetan), is a guidebook to train and prepare people to meet death and *exist in the afterlife in as conscious a state as possible.* The book recommends that these teachings be committed to memory and understood as deeply as possible: *"It should be proclaimed in the ears of all living persons; it should be read over the pillows of all persons who are ill; it should be read at the side of all corpses; it should be spread."* The whole aim of the teaching is to aid individuals *to awaken into true reality,* freed from all illusions, so that they can reach the state of *nirvana,* which is beyond all paradises, heavens, hells, purgatories or worlds of physical incarnation.

This eighth-century text describes a series of states, called *bardos,* that the individual passes through when the soul departs from the body and during its time between incarnations. Other cultures refer to the bardos by different names, and their cosmologies indicate different versions of what takes place in the state between death and rebirth. Some see the afterlife as a dwelling filled with light and delight, others as a sorrowful exile or a site of horror and pain.

The ancient Egyptians spoke of the life between lives as a continuous state of pleasure during which one awaits reincarnation into a new body. They also made sure that their dead were well equipped for that period by burying food, cooking utensils, and weapons along with the dead. In this and other societies of that time, servants of royalty and others of prominence were slain and buried along with their masters to serve them in the afterlife. Hebrews of old, on the other hand, pictured the hereafter as a place of misery, turmoil, and self-recrimination for one's earthly sins, where one lingers without end in sight.

All Eastern religions conceived of the existence after death as a sort of holding pattern, followed by rebirth into a new body. Hinduism, Buddhism, and Zoroastrianism have never swayed from that belief. Modern Christianity, Judaism, and Islam, which question the existence of reincarnation, originally thought otherwise. Early biblical writings refer to rebirth and Jesus is reported to have said, "Every soul comes into the world strengthened by the defeats of its previous life."

The concept of reincarnation was actually part of the Christian religion until the fourth century A.D., when it was attacked by the reigning emperor in conjunction with the hierarchy of the Catholic Church. It was condemned as a "monstrous" notion. The writings of the Essenes, an early, progressive Hebrew sect, indicated that *rebirth was the logical procedure for people to become closer to God* and atone for sins. The Kabbalah, a Jewish tradition of mysticism (*Kabbalah* translates as "a chain of inner transmission of the secrets of esotericism"), states that "the body, which no longer serves you, goes, and the soul goes on and on." A sect of Hassidim maintains that "all great teachers return to Earth in different bodies to continue their work."

Many in the West still cling to superstitions regarding death and are preoccupied with the search for ways to *increase our life span.* We seek miracle drugs, operations, and freezing techniques, devoting money, time, and effort so we can live longer. Yet we accomplish nothing more than squelching progress and growth and increasing fear. On the other hand are New Age and New Thought advocates who forge ahead and continue to confront us with bona fide evidence of eternal existence. They have already convinced a good number of our population, and even hard-core skeptics and cynics are willing to lend an ear.

Once the word *death* (and what it has been taken to mean: oblivion and unconsciousness), ceases to be terrifying, we can face those who are dying without prejudice and fear. We may not be able to divorce people (especially the older ones) from their traditional or religious beliefs, nor should we try to convince them that "there really is no death; you are merely going on a journey." But if we ourselves are certain that this is so, we can be more patient, solicitous, and sympathetic.

Sometimes the dying will hang on to life because they think that their loved ones may not be ready to let them go. You can help by encouraging them to depart. Speak to them, even if you feel they are unable to understand, and let them know how much you love them and feel loved by them. Assure them that the love will continue forever. Thank them for having come into your life and indicate that they will always be with you. You can do this even when a person is in deep coma. There are many recorded cases of people who have clung to life for days, weeks, months, or even years, hooked up to life-support machines and unable to regain consciousness, who finally let go when a beloved one told them it was okay to leave.

It can be sad to sit with the dying, but it can also be a beautiful experience, especially when they die peacefully in their own bed at home. Some who have observed the actual moment of death have seen the soul leave the body in the form of a white light or cloud. This has been verified through Kirlian photography, developed in Russia in the thirties. Kirlian photographs can show an aura or energy field around the dying person and successive shots can picture the stages of separation of the various spirit bodies from the physical body.

Many who sit by a deathbed observe the facial expression of the dying person change from pain and fear into a radiant smile. Others report a similarity in final words as the person begins to move toward the other side: "Here is John!" or "Father is beckoning to me!" referring to a loved one who passed away previously. This is proof to the believer that no one dies alone, that a spirit guide is always present to lead you through the process.

Unfortunately, not everyone crosses over tranquilly, in a familiar environment, surrounded by loved ones. In general, hospitals are a dreadful place to die. For six weeks I had to witness my mother lying strapped to her bed, connected to "life-saving" apparatus, with tubes in her nose and throat. My pleas to the staff to let her die in dignity fell on deaf ears. I had been pressured into consenting to an operation that I knew would be useless and would only prolong her agony. I suffered with her while she lay dying, and was released along with her by her death. I could not be with her when she closed her eyes for the last time, but I was certain that she, too, was not alone.

Those who are glad to leave Earth most likely adjust to the spirit world within a short time. The ones who are suffering or just tired of life usually don't regret shedding their troublesome physical body. They easily slip into their eternal cloak, freed from the burden of ailing flesh and other barriers to well-being. The etheric body is always healthy and whole; those who were ill, maimed, or crippled on Earth are now in perfect form, with all their body parts intact. The signs of age are erased as well: No one looks really old and no one looks particularly young, including those who died as children or even as babies.

Some who die while of relatively sound mind get to "attend" their own funeral. They may still be bewildered, not realizing that they are no longer in a body. They try to tell the mourners to stop the proceedings: "Look at me!" they may shout, but no one can hear them. But most of them enjoy the fuss that is being made over them and listening to what people have to say about them. Many find it possible to read the minds of the mourners.

Once aware that they are not coming back, the departed can begin to settle down in the spirit world and get used to their new surroundings. Most are surprised to enter a familiar atmosphere of streets, houses, gardens, museums, and parks. Others see farmland, woods and mountains, streams and lakes, birds and flowers. Many report encountering scenes of incredible beauty and harmony.

Albert Brooks produced, directed, and acted in a clever and witty film called *Defending Your Life,* costarring Meryl Streep. The new arrivals to the spirit world from Earth, each clad in white flowing gowns, are whisked off in streamlined buses to a city center and assigned to various hotels. Some are designated to luxury suites in four-star hotels; others have to contend with one room in a lower-quality hotel. But all lodgings are adequate and the service is always efficient and courteous. Entertainment and restaurants are bountiful and everything is free of charge. (I especially liked the idea that one could indulge in delicious, calorie-laden food without worrying about gaining weight.) Socializing with other souls is accepted and one can make dates for dinner. Who knows—the other side could be like that! We generally encounter and experience whatever we picture the afterworld to be while we're still on Earth. Those who long for heavenly scenes of fluffy white clouds, the Pearly Gates, and Edenic settings may get their wish. Yet everything we see as reality in the spirit world is real in thought only.

It is most likely that everyone is greeted by relatives and friends from past lives and by their beloved pets who have died. The reunions are always joyous and never awkward because one faces only those one truly wishes to see. After the initial greetings, the newcomers are introduced to souls experienced in the ways of the spirit world, who advise them how to proceed in their new home and acquaint them with the prevailing laws and customs. All new souls are entitled to remain for as long as they like in whatever idyllic atmosphere they created. They can move without restrictions, explore the countryside, sightsee in different environments. Some may wish to rest and do nothing at all. Everyone in the spirit world is freed from all worry and no longer has material needs such as housing, clothing, food, or drink.

Some who pass over still feel themselves drawn to material pursuits, such as business deals and money-making. They will continue these activities (in spirit form, of course) until they understand that earthly goals no longer matter. It may take aeons, but eventually every soul realizes, or is helped to realize, that it is time to move on and progress, and that the true purpose of the soul is to reach spiritual enlightenment, or union with God. Those who are ready to proceed will have an abundance of help to point them in the right directions.

Schools are available to suit all levels of intellect, and those who may at first shy away from them soon become aware that their senses and their ability to learn are sharper than they were on Earth. Every subject of interest is taught and one can also learn how to remember and how to forget. Consciousness-raising and meditation classes, and private counseling are available.

Those entering the new dimension without resistance, especially if they know what to expect, will, of course, adapt more easily than those who came in ignorance. People who insist that there is nothing beyond the grave and think everything in the spirit world is an illusion will, of course, be perplexed or even rebellious. Those who die filled with resentment, anger, hate, or bitterness will have a most difficult time. They may remain in that state of rebellion and emotional turmoil until they awaken to the truth or are led on the way. Those who die suddenly and unprepared—usually victims of accident, murder, or war—are usually shocked to find out where they are, but it won't take them long to adjust. They are helped to realize that there are no accidents and that their time was up.

You, yourself, decide when to be born and when to leave; this is a corollary of the law of cause and effect. When children, or even babies, die—as tragic as it is for the parents and as senseless as it seems—there is always a reason. They came to Earth on a mission and completed what they set out to do—to open hearts and teach love.

Suicides have the most arduous time adjusting and are the truly unfortunate ones in the spirit world. Suicide is definitely not the best way to go—it's a cop-out from life. It forces you to repeat what you didn't finish when you had the chance. The problem that you sought to avoid by destroying the body is manifold now—you have to go back to first grade and start all over again.

Is it a "sin" to take your life or that of another? When, if ever, is deliberately ending one's life a justifiable act? These are complex questions. You may feel one way about a healthy, successful man in the prime of life who shoots himself in despair because his wife has left him, and another way about an eighty-two-year-old woman who takes an overdose to end years of horrible suffering from an incurable disease. What about people who "pull the plug" on a beloved family member who has been in a coma for months with no hope for recovery? And what can we say about physicians like Dr. Jack Kevorkian, who has many times acceded to patients' requests to hasten the moment of death? Are these actions murder or mercy? Where is the line between a compassionate ending to suffering and mere escape? These issues are so complicated that we cannot make definitive judgments (although judges and juries are asked to do so all the time), but we can at least say this: Everyone has to face the consequences of whatever action and decision is made.

I personally believe that there exists an unwritten law that prohibits the *willful, negative* destruction of any living thing and that it is the offenders who suffer the greatest torment. They are the ones who have to live with the guilt and shame of their own making. But even murderers can, in time, learn to forgive themselves and atone for their crimes. Toward the end of this chapter we will discuss ways to come to terms with past actions that have harmed others.

One can no longer attribute the descriptions of the afterlife, or the accounts of what takes place after death to figments of the imagination, hallucination, mere speculation, or hocus-pocus. It has also become possible to contradict the common argument, "Nobody has ever returned to tell us about it." A wealth of material on the subject has now been amassed, not by kooks or science-fiction writers, but by respected members of the medical and psychiatric profession. They have presented, to an often disbelieving public, findings based on personal contact with those who have died and returned to life.

Most scientists have admitted that their experiences with this realm at first disturbed and confounded them and went against their scientific and logical grain. But once recovered from the initial shock, they felt morally obliged to spread the word. Dr. Raymond Moody was perhaps the first physician to make an impact in this field with his book *Life After Life.* In it, he recorded the encounters of various colleagues with patients who lived to tell. In this book, Dr. Moody also introduced the term "NDE," which stands for near-death experience.

Those who research and write about near-death experiences unanimously attest that almost all who return from the edge of death emerge with a significantly broadened perspective. It seems their physical and emotional systems undergo a regeneration process that has a profound effect on their attitudes toward life and death. Those who return are released from fear, because they now know the unknown. Back in their earth body, they are imbued with new views and values that make every part of life more meaningful from then on. The spiritual awakening or expansion they experienced gives them true peace of mind, and they can help others accept death as the normal, natural process it is. Many find their intellect and perceptiveness increased after their NDE, and others discover new or heightened psychic abilities. They are able to read people's minds, communicate telepathically, or predict future events and "see" them as they unfold.

Children who have had near-death experiences benefit richly. They have many years ahead of them and the capacity to mold those years to their desires. Without the hindrance of fear, life can be enormously enjoyable, adventurous, and creative, and is never wasted.

It is an indisputable fact that people who have physically died have been revived and fully recovered. They met all the requirements of clinical death—stoppage of breath, cessation of pulse and heartbeat, dilation of pupils, loss of color, and change in body temperature; nevertheless they came back to life. The doctors did their duty of pronouncing them dead, and the patients dared to defy them by responding to resuscitation methods. Due to advances in medical techniques and lifesaving machinery, thousands of people are being brought back from death. Many are unaware of what took place, but just as many can remember all of it.

Near-death experiences can be had by anyone, whether through an accident, heart attack, an adverse reaction to medication, or any other life-threatening event. Each experience is different and the reactions are varied, but most who come back to life have a story to tell.

While NDE and OBE are bona fide abbreviations, I feel that they are too glib to apply to experiences that can be so deeply spiritual in nature. In addition, it can be confusing to differentiate between the two. In fact, all near-death experiences are a kind of out-of-body experience; however, certain elements characteristic of near-death experiences do not occur in out-of-body experiences. Following are two examples of out-of-body experiences that were mistaken for near-death experiences by the people undergoing the experiences. They later realized that they had been merely unconscious.

A man involved in a car or motorcycle crash picks himself up and walks away from the scene. As far as he can determine, he is unharmed, he feels fine. He is amazed to see people crowding around an unconscious form on the ground. He steps nearer and discovers that the body, covered with blood and obviously injured, is his own. He tries to make himself heard: "Stop making all that fuss!" he tells the bystanders. "I'm fine!" But no one pays any attention to him. He watches helplessly as his body is carried off on a stretcher and whisked away by an ambulance. He is definitely annoyed as he races along to the hospital. The next morning he awakens in the recovery room.

A young woman who is an excellent swimmer feels herself drowning. She has gone for a swim in the ocean and gotten caught in an undertow. At first she treads water frantically, flailing her arms to get back to the surface, but realizes that it is useless. The blood is rushing to her head, her eardrums are bursting, and her body is sinking deeper and deeper. She decides to let go and at once feels calm and peaceful as she listens to her conscious mind: "I admit that it was foolish to venture into strange waters all by myself, but how fortunate I am to be able to die in this beautiful ocean!"

She is vaguely aware, but experiences no physical sensations as her body is pulled out of the water into a motorboat by two men who have witnessed the entire scene. They bring her to land, stretch her out on the sand, and one applies mouth-to-mouth resuscitation as the other pounds on her chest. She coughs up the water from her lungs and recovers fully.

Many people who leave their body temporarily refer to the process as "floating out of it." Some float on a cloud, others through space. The majority of those reporting near-death experiences say they float to the ceiling over a hospital bed, emergency room stretcher, or in their own bed at home. They report being upside-down with their back securely attached to the ceiling, feeling very comfortable in their unusual position. A middle-aged lady who suffered a cardiac arrest reported: "The last thing I remember as I passed out in my home is telling my husband, 'I can't breathe—I'm going to die!' I can't recall being in the ambulancc or arriving at the emergency room. I came back to consciousness when I found myself clinging to the ceiling, viewing my body lying securely strapped to the table below. I was wearing a green hospital gown, my eyes were closed, my hair was disheveled, and my face was greenish. I looked terrible and was disgusted with myself for presenting such a sorry picture because I always take pride in being well-groomed.

"My hearing was extraordinarily acute. I could understand what was going on in other rooms in the hospital and I heard my husband's voice speaking to my daughter and son-in-law in the hallway. They sounded terribly upset and my daughter was sobbing. I longed to tell them not to grieve, that I was really okay, but I knew that no one could hear me—especially not the doctor and nurses, who were crowded around my body, looking concerned. I recognized my personal physician despite his mask and appreciated that he had come. All of a sudden, everyone below me jumped into action. I heard one doctor say he couldn't find a pulse and a nurse screaming, 'Oh, God—she's dying!' I watched machinery being wheeled in and saw myself being attached to it. Shocks were placed on my chest and my body was about to jump off the table. I desperately tried to tell them, 'Don't go through all that trouble—I'm just fine!'

"And I really was. I felt myself floating away from the ceiling and drifting between two worlds: one that I was familiar with, and one that I was curious about. But they insisted on bringing me back with their sophisticated gadgets and I reluctantly gave in and opened my eyes."

In these and similar cases, different reactions to being revived from the rim of death have been reported. Some people are happy to return, others are upset or resentful and reluctant to come back to life. They all, however, knew themselves to be dead and were unafraid.

People with near-death experiences present different accounts of what they experienced when they left the physical realm. Most commonly describe what is referred to as the "tunnel ride." This is the experience that distinguishes near-death experiences from out-of-body experiences. The dying feel themselves lifted or propelled out of the body and begin their passage into death through a seemingly endless tunnel. Some people describe it as a tube, a shaft, a cylinder, or a funnel, all of which are circular or moving in a circular or spiral pattern. All attest that they proceed at a rapid speed, comparable to being in a jet plane or roller coaster. They may find themselves steeped in pitch-black darkness or nothingness within the tunnel, but some see a speck or beam of light way ahead.

Either before or following the propulsion, they are treated to a review of their life, generally from babyhood through present time. It is a visual presentation, shown in flashbacks, similar to the old TV program *This Is Your Life,* with Ralph Edwards. All events that have taken place, no matter how trivial, are recorded. They may appear in chronological order or simultaneously and are shown in black and white or "living" color. One man reported that the images appeared as continuous paintings all along the inside of the tunnel.

When the dying person reaches the end of the tunnel, a variety of experiences may occur. Nearly everyone claims to see lights of a brilliance not found on Earth; they can be white or gold or silver. Some refer to the light as a being of incredible warmth and compassion. Also seen are landscapes of compelling beauty, brilliantly clear in color yet unearthly in their intensity. Some give descriptions of magnificent gardens or meadows with the most exquisite flowers and shrubbery. Some see extraordinary sunsets or rainbows of unusual colors and some see castles in the clouds, bathed in bright lights and of astonishing beauty. Others may hear enchanting music—tunes unlike anything they have heard on Earth—of such beauty and harmony that it surpasses every other sound. Some hear bells ringing or tinkling or the sound of organs, trumpets, or harps.

Shortly after, they notice figures coming toward them. They may recognize departed loved ones—family and friends who, though in spirit form, look the same as they did on Earth. Sometimes they meet strangers who identify themselves as their guides or assistants. Those who were deeply religious on Earth may encounter images of saints and other holy ones. Almost everyone is overcome by intense surges of love and peace and longs to rush forward to be embraced. But they are urged not to come nearer. "You cannot stay—not now," they are informed gently but firmly. "You need to return to Earth to finish what you set out to accomplish" or "There are those on Earth who still need you. You must go back to help them until they are ready to find their own way." Most people say they were dismayed that they had to return and wanted nothing more than to remain in the afterlife forever. They were reluctant to again take up their pain-ridden existence, but they had no choice.

Near-death events are not experienced in the same sequence by everyone, and some recall only fragments of what took place. Not everyone who is pronounced dead, resuscitated, and brought back to life remembers what occurred. Some feel it was a dream or a hallucination. Many have not the slightest recollection of anything happening before coming back into their body. It is possible that those who do not remember choose to forget for reasons of their own.

We seem to hear mostly about pleasant and illuminating near-death experiences, but not all of them are. I, for one, can attest to it. Mine happened during one of the many times in my life when I felt I had reached rock bottom. I was only twenty-four years old but my future looked dim and grim. It was 1948 and my husband was in Israel (then Palestine), helping to fight the Arab invasion. I had not heard from him in three weeks and presumed he was dead. I was living in New York with my mother and was eight months pregnant. I was suffering from an infected wisdom tooth and my dentist was afraid to pull it out in the conventional way. He referred me to a New York clinic that specialized in extraction using nitrous oxide—also known as laughing gas! They apparently gave me one whiff too many—because I died!

It may have lasted no more than a minute, but I knew for sure that I was dead. I saw my whole life flashing by as though a tape was being fast-forwarded—every moment, detail, and event was recorded from my birth to the moment I lost consciousness. It went by at lightning speed, but it was very clear to me. I saw nothing in my entire life that had been joyous. When the tape ended I felt myself pulled or sucked into a spiral that was rotating at an unearthly velocity and had no bottom. I was certain that I was to remain in this eddy for eternity and I asked, "Why?"

The answer was, "Because!"

I remember coming back, screaming at the top of my lungs, and found the entire staff crowded around me, watching in horror. They must have been aware that someone had goofed, because they began to hug and solace me and supply me with milk and cookies. They even took me home in a cab. After that I dreaded the thought of anesthesia or other unconsciousness-producing methods. I stopped being afraid of death only when I got in touch with my spirit guides, who assured me that no one gets stuck in the tunnel—every one of us arrives to see the light.

I have also looked death straight in the eye while I was conscious, and I want to share with you that it was not all that scary. It happened when I was trapped in a burning building and the only escape was a window that had always been stuck. I was awakened one winter night shortly before six a.m. by shouts of "Fire!" I smelled the smoke and saw flames peeping through the door sill. I'd gone to sleep very late, so I seriously considered going back to sleep in my nice, warm bed. I rationalized that dying in my sleep was preferable to jumping from the top floor into the icy winter air, given the probability that I would be smashed to pieces.

"We all have to die sooner or later," I told myself. "It might as well be now." I was unafraid. It was only when a picture of my family flashed before my eyes that I felt obliged to try to survive. "I can't do it to them, " I decided as I jumped out of bed and smashed the window with my fist.

* * *

Life and death are not opposites, and birth and death are really one and the same. You could reverse things and say that death is the entrance rather than the exit; this concept would help you to face the transition as painlessly as possible. Both the dying and the survivors can become aware that death—like birth—can be considered the beginning of the eternal cycle of existence.

I wish that someone (preferably a person with clout and distinction and many impressive professional degrees) would institute classes for the terminally ill and their caretakers similar to Lamaze classes for mothers and their helpers. The person facing death could be instructed in breathing techniques and other tranquillity-promoting exercises, and those who care for them would learn how to ease their path to the spirit world. Training could be provided for medical personnel, family and friends to help the dying be physically comfortable, emotionally secure, and spiritually supported through their transition. Everyone concerned could be taught to discuss all aspects of the impending death. Some private practitioners are beginning to do this sort of work, but as far as I know it is not yet being conducted on a large scale or in public institutions.

It would also be great if thanatology could be initiated as a course in public schools. It would undoubtedly enable young people to proceed through life without fearing death and help them value their life more highly. The subject of death seems frightening only because we don't understand it. We don't need to dwell on it, but we should be able to discuss it openly and intelligently and become aware that the fear of dying is mainly the fear of letting go of what we consider to be reality.

I am not assuming that everyone is afraid to die, even if they don't have a metaphysical understanding of the nature of death, and relate to it purely on a rational level. But for all those who feel queasy even thinking about death, I suggest that you may wish to practice letting go of thought. You actually experience a kind of death each night when you go to sleep; *there is little difference between death and the dream state*. Some religious sects and primitive tribes believe that we die each night. When they awaken in the morning they are so happy to be alive that they sing and dance or give praises to their God or gods.

No one can guarantee that we will wake up in the morning. Anything can happen during the night—a building can collapse on us during an earthquake, a fire can consume us, we can be struck by lightning, be murdered, or have a heart attack. It may be improbable, but it is far from impossible.

We can release the fear of death through meditation, which helps us to learn to surrender to the unknown while we are still in the body. We can experience the same sensations we have when dying in the letting go that occurs during deep meditation. In this state you are able to sense being in suspension, devoid of conscious thought or other mind activity. You can train yourself to separate from mind, body, emotions, and surroundings by using all your tools—mantra repetition, deep-breathing methods, watching the breath, imagery techniques, or prayer recitations at a steady rhythm. Required are patience, persistence, and some uninterrupted time in which to enter a truly deep state of meditation. Once you enter that state of pure nothingness that is devoid of fear and leads to unexpected heights of existence, you will understand that there is no reason to be afraid of death.

You can also prepare yourself mentally and emotionally here on Earth so your transition into the afterlife can occur smoothly and peacefully, without confusion. The way to go about this is to wipe the slate clean, put your house in order, and tie up loose ends. Making sure your insurance premiums are paid up, your will is completed, or your burial plot is reserved can be helpful, but it's not the whole picture.

It is essential to forgive with all your heart each person on Earth, whether they are family, friends, or strangers. You need to particularly forgive those you deem undeserving and unforgivable—the murderer, the child molester, the warmonger, the tyrant—every criminal you consider evil and monstrous. Stop being influenced by those who condemn them—society, the media, religious or political leaders—regardless of how qualified you think they are to judge. Recognize that nobody can truly judge another and it is not your place to do so.

Not only that, righteous or justified anger or thoughts of revenge and bitterness stand in the way of your own progress. Let go of all grudges, especially prolonged ones: they poison your system and stunt your spiritual growth.

Don't worry or speculate about the offenders; they will have to account for themselves sooner or later.

Of utmost importance is to forgive *yourself* for every action, thought, or deed that you are ashamed of, regret, feel guilty about, or have tried to forget about. It is excruciating to leave this life with regret for not making amends for damaging thoughts and actions. I urge you to make a list of every misdeed you can think of and have accused yourself of. Write down everything you remember, no matter how trivial. Then correct what is still correctable, and forgive yourself for what is beyond repair. You don't need to don sackcloth and ashes or perform complicated rituals of penitence. A sincere apology coupled with a clear awareness of why you acted in ways that caused pain to others or yourself will help release each incident. Afterward, erase the list, tear it up, or burn it, and celebrate this new freedom from your past by loving and hugging yourself and those around you.

You don't have to wait until you are dying to do this. Begin now. You may have to repeat the process before you leave Earth, but it will become easier each time and the list will shrink. Doing this while you still have the chance will give you the freedom to face death unencumbered.

I hope that you are convinced that the dead do not die—they just go on—and life continues as a never-ending soap opera! The scenery will change and the action will vary, but the basic themes weave through all the performances on a myriad of stages. Other cast members may be let go and replaced, but be assured that you will remain in your role as leading character. Without you there would be no play.

CHAPTER NINE

KARMA AND REINCARNATION: YES, VIRGINIA, YOU *DO* CHOOSE YOUR PARENTS

Even though you may have firmly made up your mind that life is senseless, that death is the ultimate destruction, and that the riddle of existence cannot be solved, I beg you to reconsider. Let me assure you once more that I was the original disbeliever, even when I first became involved with Yoga.

The concepts of karma and reincarnation are synonymous with Hinduism, and therefore Yoga; I thought they were interesting, but quaint, and not at all relevant to a Western mind. The incarnations of Vishnu, Shiva, Rama, and Krishna seemed to be nothing but whimsical folklore depicted in bizarre art forms throughout India. I maintained that the idea of reincarnation provided an excuse for the Indian masses to cop-out in this lifetime, convinced that they would do better next time around.

I also felt that the belief in karmic retribution perpetuates the caste system with its degradation of the Untouchables. Although the Indian government has passed laws granting this group an equal place in society, in actual practice the ancient restrictions still prevail.

The *Bhagavad Gita* states that release from karma lies in impersonal detachment from action. Orthodox Hindus who take this idea literally can display indifference and callousness toward those who suffer. They take it for granted that all unfortunates suffer as an atonement for their misdeeds and should therefore be despised and left to their misery.

Hinduism also forbids the slaughtering of cows, and even rats are protected. These creatures, even if they are starving and diseased, are left to roam the cities and countryside, where they eat crops, spread pestilence, and are a general nuisance. Killing them is karmically taboo; doing so means risking reincarnation in animal form.

I used to reason that the recall of past-life experience could be explained by genetic memory, dreams, or subconscious childhood impressions. I was fond of pointing out that, without eyewitness accounts, there is no scientific evidence of reincarnation. Besides, I never found references to this phenomenon in Western culture: Even if I had confronted a karmic experience, I would have ignored it, due to my lack of awareness and my disbelief. Like most of my generation, I knew only what I had been programmed to know by society, and my Judaic upbringing negated most emphatically the concept of reincarnation. I had reasonable counterarguments from my Yoga colleagues who believed in karma and reincarnation, but I clung to my rational thought—until I received a rude awakening through Doris Collins.

I came to accept that, while *karma is* a Sanskrit word and is linked to Hinduism and Buddhism, it is also the cosmic principle of universal law. It implies total responsibility for one's actions. It is the explanation and justification for good and bad fortune during one's lifetime. It can be interpreted as *action and reaction*, cause and effect, the boomerang or echo principle—what you throw into the wind comes back to you.

In the Bible, karma is reflected in the adage: "As ye sow, so shall ye reap." Karma is a system of higher education whereby you choose a set of circumstances in which to learn your lessons. It is the sum of all your thoughts, words, and deeds in this and previous lifetimes. It is a force generated by consciousness that conditions this and future lives.

Once I did see the light, the idea of rebirth of one's soul into a new body made total sense to me. It provided me with a logical explanation for the phenomena surrounding death and the unequal opportunities present for the living. For the first time I was able to view my life in its proper perspective. I discovered that the tragedies I had to endure were not just part of an unfair deal, but merely a series of logical events. I learned that great thinkers such as Plato, Socrates, Voltaire, Schopenhauer, Emerson, and Thoreau all believed in reincarnation, as did practical men like Benjamin Franklin, Mark Twain, Arthur Conan Doyle, Henry Ford, and Edgar Mitchell.

As I started to become accustomed to this new framework, I met more and more people who shared my beliefs. I also came to realize that *my parents, husband, children, relatives, friends, acquaintances, and lovers all came into my life for a reason.* I knew for certain that whatever happened to me or anyone else in this life is not a matter of chance, coincidence, or predisposition—and there are no accidents! Good or bad luck or fate doesn't just happen—they are self-destined.

An intellectual giant like Einstein, or an artistic genius like Da Vinci is not just born that way—their talents are developed over a series of lifetimes. We know that Mozart composed symphonies at age seven. To accomplish this, he had to know orchestral composition, chord structure, transposition, and counterpoint. We are incredulous and can offer no logical explanation, so we call him unique, incredibly talented—a *wunderkind*—rather than admit to the possibility of previous lives.

I doubt that there is anyone, no matter how skeptical they are about reincarnation, who does not have personal evidence of a former lifetime. We all have experienced déjà-vu: *seeing faces, places, events, and objects we are certain we have seen before.* All logical explanations fall by the wayside and "coincidence" does not suffice. How often do you meet someone for the first time and immediately know that he or she is not a stranger! Both of you may wrack your brain to determine where you have met before, but you cannot find the answer. You may not ever meet again, or you become better acquainted and discover how much you have in common.

It can also work the other way. You could encounter a person who you dislike instantly, who may arouse in you animosity and aversion seemingly beyond your control. They may have done nothing to slight or hurt you, but you always feel uncomfortable in their presence and do your best to avoid them.

These meetings can occur in your childhood or in later years, and can result in lasting friendships or prolonged relationships of hatred. They don't happen by accident. These people, and virtually everyone of importance who comes into your life, is an associate from a former lifetime. It is usually those who annoy and upset you and who you detest the most with whom you have unfinished business to work out. The ones you run away from are the ones you need to cultivate, to go out of your way to become close to and help them to find their path. They offer your most important lessons.

If you come across someone to whom you are immediately drawn and recognize you have been closely connected in previous lives, that person can be considered a soulmate. A soulmate may be in your life already as your father, mother, sibling, or other relative. You will be immensely compatible, share many of the same feelings, likes and dislikes, and be happy in each other's company. You function on the same vibrational level, and the two of you are part of each other's destiny. You can have one or more soulmates in your life, and they could be of the same or opposite sex. Even if you don't remain together physically, you will harmonize in mind and heart for the rest of your life, and probably for lives to come.

Aren't there cities, countries, or certain areas that seem to be so familiar that you are certain you've been there before? You may attribute the sensation to dream images, fantasies, photos or postcards you have seen, or descriptions you might have heard. You are unable, however, to shake the feeling that you have come home. Sometimes you may experience an unexplained longing for a country you have never been to, and feel yourself drawn to its language, people, artistic and cultural expressions, and customs. At times you recognize public buildings or dwellings and landscapes in actual or picture form as sites that you seem to recall from your past. As with people, you may not always be comfortable with what you meet.

I have traveled extensively throughout Latin America and rarely was it by my choice. I never felt at ease with the natives, or their culture and customs, and made no effort to learn to speak Spanish. I disliked their food and late-dining habits and usually suffered some kind of intestinal upset while there. At one time I found myself on a tour to the Yucatan in Mexico, where we visited the ancient city of Chichen Itza. Walking among the ruins, I experienced an uncontrollable sensation of horror, with chills running down my spine. I felt myself choking and becoming dizzy and almost fell to the ground. I begged one of the tour guides to lead me out of the compound. Being familiar with Mayan history, I knew for sure that I had been one of the virgins who had been slain as a sacrifice to the gods.

One of the most forceful arguments against the possibility of previous existences is that no one remembers their past lives in the present one. But most people don't remember the events of their babyhood either. You would also draw a blank if you were questioned what you did on August 7, five years ago, unless a significant event such as a birth, death, accident, or marriage occurred.

However, it has been scientifically established that early-childhood events can be recalled through hypnosis. Evidence for this can be traced back to Mesmer in the eighteenth century, and was underscored and strengthened by Freud in the twentieth. A number of psychotherapists and nonmedically-trained hypnotists have achieved amazing results in restoring mental balance using hypnosis. Today, unerring proof exists that hypnosis, properly applied, can transcend time and take people back to lives they have lived aeons ago. Attested and authenticated documentation can be found in many libraries.

Many people are probably most familiar with *The Search for Bridey Murphy,* published in 1956. Morey Bernstein, a businessman, practiced hypnosis as a hobby and experimented on Virginia Tighe, a young woman from Colorado. In the presence of witnesses, Bernstein put Tighe into a deep hypnotic trance and regressed her in time. He recorded her accounts of a previous life from childhood until death. She was able to recall her existence in Ireland in the nineteenth century as a lass named Bridey Murphy, and remembered in detail the events of her life. It seems that records were later discovered in Belfast that proved that indeed such a person had lived there at that time.

Many other popular books on the subject of reincarnation have since appeared in print. Widely read is *Many Lives, Many Masters,* published in 1986, written by Brian L. Weiss, M.D., a traditional therapist who was ignorant of and uninterested in parapsychology. He was distrustful of anything that could not be proven by bona fide scientific methods.

One of his patients, who he calls Catherine, consulted him on a regular basis for eighteen months but was unable to respond to conventional treatment. Her symptoms of anxiety, unexplainable fear, panic, pain, and phobia became worse instead of better, and she could hardly function in everyday life.

In desperation, Dr. Weiss resorted to hypnosis and effected a breakthrough that exceeded his wildest expectations. To his amazement, he was able to regress Catherine to earliest childhood and eventually to a variety of lives she had lived before. While in a deep trance, she spoke of a series of lifetimes that extended back to antiquity. She claimed to have lived eighty-six times, both as male and female, in great wealth or abject poverty, in ignorance or highly cultural surroundings. She spent an ancient lifetime as an embalmer in Egypt, and recalled being a prostitute in Spain, a housewife in Britain, and a cavalryman in Russia. She had also been a Japanese scholar and a Gaelic shepherd.

Catherine often recaptured the way she had died—at a young or old age, violently or peacefully. She was also able to get in touch with enlightened entities, her guides or masters, who interpreted the relevance of her previous relationships to her present life and explained the principles of reincarnation. With the help of her doctor, she learned to unearth the reasons for her present mental illness and how her troubles were related to past-life experiences. She recovered completely and became happy and fulfilled.

Dr. Weiss also changed profoundly. While being regressed, Catherine managed to discover the root of some of *his* problems and helped him to face and solve them. He traded his skepticism for a spiritual awakening, and his life and career took on a new meaning.

In the New Age of the seventies and eighties, past-life therapy became a popular method of therapeutic healing. Experts on the subject flocked to the scene and many who had practiced or studied hypnotism hung out their shingles with a new addition: "Regression." The curious knocked down their doors and entertained each other with past-life experiences. Those who were not sincerely dedicated to the technique as a therapeutic modality enjoyed the more frivolous aspect of past lives: Many were told of, and boasted of, having been a famous historical figure—Alexander the Great, Cleopatra, Socrates, Napoleon, members of a royal family, often Jesus or Mary Magdalene.

Yes, you guessed it, I was right in there, lying on a couch or the floor, being hypnotized, taken back in time, shelling out shekels for services. It was relatively easy for me to go deep down under, and I remembered quite a few of my past incarnations.

I still see myself as a Moroccan warrior on horseback. I was young, tall, and handsome, with a full black beard, as I rode out through the archway of the town, swinging my sword. I wore a jaunty red cap with a tassel, a red uniform embroidered with gold braid, and high black boots. Women looked at me adoringly and called to me, and I pretended not to notice them as I galloped into battle—where I got myself killed.

I vividly recall being an eighteenth century abbess in Austria. I was dressed and veiled from head to toe in black, in scratchy material of many layers. It was summertime, and I was itchy and hot, but I was trained to suppress my physical discomfort and present a dignified image. I was fifty years old, and I had entered the convent at age sixteen because I was forced into it by my mother. She was convinced I was too ugly to find myself a husband. I was miserable but kept it to myself. Instead I willed myself to be obedient and disciplined, and I worked myself up to my superior position. I was in charge of the novices, and terrorized them all. Prayer, meditation, and rituals had no effect on my personality. I never experienced love and dwelt on resentment and hate. I died at age sixty of a gallbladder attack.

Like Catherine, in Brian Weiss' book, I, too, was a female embalmer in ancient Egypt. The picture came through extremely clear, in technicolor. I was a physician, which most likely was required of an embalmer of that period. I was thirty-five years old and not married, although I was quite attractive. I was rather dark skinned, with jet-black straight hair cut in bangs and falling to my shoulders. I wore a white knee-length tunic belted with a cord, and sandals laced up to my calves. I could see myself standing in the shade of a pyramid, removing intestines from the body of a high-born person, drying and carefully wrapping them in some of kind of leaves. The sky was brilliant blue without a cloud and the sun was brutally hot. I was resigned to my life and dedicated to my profession. I have no recollection of how I died.

While I thought these and other past lives experiences were interesting and informative, they provided no insight or understanding into the dilemmas I had to cope with in my present existence. I felt there was really no sense in knowing who you used to be just to make idle conversation. But, with the help of Doris Collins, I was able to remember other lives and their pertinence to some of my predicaments in this one.

I learned, for instance, that in the seventeenth century I was a ballet dancer in France. I was obsessed with my art and myself and cherished and catered to my body to the extent that I had neither time nor interest for anyone else. This may have been the reason I felt the need to smash up my body in this incarnation.

I also saw myself as a red-faced, big Englishwoman of wealth and title, riding a horse and cracking a whip. I was in total control of an enormous estate, which I ruled with an iron hand. I was so demanding and cruel that everyone—my husband, children, and servants—went out of their way not to anger me. I especially terrified my small daughter. She had a speech defect I couldn't tolerate, and I kept her in isolation and treated her like an outcast. Doris suggested one reason she returned to this life as my youngest daughter was to get even with me.

I found it difficult to comprehend that despite the fact that Doris, acting as a medium, discovered other people's past lives in her readings, the everyday Doris, at the time I met her, did not believe in reincarnation. It wasn't until 1982, when she and her husband Philip visited Israel, that she changed her mind. She had read about Masada, the amazing fortress in the Judean desert. It was the scene of a mass suicide by Jewish zealots to avoid capture by the Romans two thousand years ago, and she was eager to visit the site.

It was an arduous climb for her (today they have elevators), because she was troubled with hip problems at the time, but she felt it had been worth the effort. As she looked over the wall of the fortress, she saw what looked like an ancient encampment for a battle. Roman soldiers were everywhere and advancing up the steep mountain. She clearly heard the tumult and battle cries. She saw herself as an old woman with a scarf wrapped around her head, lifting up an enormous stone and hurling it over the wall. She was among other women who took turns throwing boulders and rocks at the Roman soldiers. She knew for certain then that she had been a Jewess in one of her previous existences, which possibly explained her close relationships with so many Jewish people in her present one.

I believe that regressions are of value only if relevant to present-life issues. They don't have to relate to calamities or earth-shaking matters, but knowing about past lives can often help you better understand yourself and the people you love. Everyone has behavior patterns and quirks that cannot be accounted for by something happening in this lifetime, and you don't always need to consult a licensed psychotherapist for interpretations and answers. It is not that difficult to enter into an altered state of consciousness, and a reputable hypnotist, psychologist, medium, or psychic specializing in past-life therapy can assist you. You can also train yourself to recall segments of your past while in meditation.

This is an example of how a regression can favorably influence and change your everyday life. It happened to friends of mine who were kind enough to share their experiences. Joan used to be driven crazy by Hal's habit of amassing food and other provisions. He would be frantic unless the refrigerator and pantry were crammed to overflow. Whenever they needed to travel to visit friends or family, or simply went for an afternoon drive in the country, he would pack their station wagon to the brim with food and drinks, blankets, first-aid kit, and other paraphernalia. They usually showed up late for their appointments.

She insisted that he see a therapist to possibly uncover something from his childhood that accounted for this mania. No, his parents had provided plentifully for the children and he had always had enough money throughout his life to take care of his needs.

Upon the advice of a friend, they went to see a past-life counselor. Hal went along willingly because by this time he realized that his obsession was abnormal. They discovered that he had been a prospector in the wild country of Nevada around 1850—and not a very successful one. One day he heard about a possible gold strike that could make him very rich if he got there ahead of anyone else. Within ten days of walking, he ran low on supplies. On the twelfth day he lost his footing and fell down a mountainside and apparently broke his leg. He desperately hoped that someone would find him, but no one came. When he ran out of food and water he died of thirst and in great pain.

What Hal encountered during that session was the voice of greed dominating the voice of reasonable caution, and he was able to see how this was a theme in his current life as well. He realized he would ignore warning signals of danger and avoid discomfort by overcompensating with such behavior as stuffing the refrigerator and the car. The logic of his conscious mind was that if he had sufficient provisions with him at all times, he would be safe. Unaware of the root of the behavior, he had repeated it for years. Hal now realized that he had to address this basic issue and see that when he wanted something badly enough he could silence the inner voice that wanted to protect him.

For some people, making the connection between a current behavior and a past-life incident can be so powerful that the problem disappears immediately. The very acknowledgment of the pattern unlocks its hold, and it no longer needs to be played out. For others, seeing the past-life incident is the first signal that it's time to take an in-depth look at how the habit can now be released. In either case, once a lesson is learned, we set ourselves free of patterns that are painful and unnecessary. After integrating what he had discovered in the session, Hal felt comfortable at home and at ease traveling with a normal amount of provisions.

But the other benefit of past-life work is even more profound. In fact, I would say the most important advantage of past-life work is its ability to generate understanding, compassion, and forgiveness. It is not too extreme to say it could be a major key to healing the divisiveness that has set people against each other down the centuries and torn this planet apart. The reason is simple, and reflected in the words of one of the great teachers and masters, Jesus: "And why beholdest thou the mote that is in thy brother's eye, but considerest not the beam that is in thine own eye? Or how wilt thou say to thy brother, 'Let me pull the mote out of thine eye'; and, behold, a beam is in thine own eye."

Simply put, when you have extensive knowledge of your past lives, you discover that just about anything that anyone has ever done throughout history, you have also done during one life or another. It can be said that those who call for revenge or harshly judge others are ignorant of the fact that they themselves probably have performed similar actions in another lifetime. When you live in the awareness that every one of us has been both perpetrator and victim, it is difficult to condemn other people.

As long as people on Earth are not conscious enough to act responsibly, a legal system will be needed to assess people's behavior and treat them accordingly. But clear vision and discrimination are not the same as judgment. Judgment includes the elements of self-righteousness and condemnation, and neither the perpetrators of a wrongdoing nor the victims who suffer by their deeds gain anything through it.

Unfortunately, those who consider themselves victims often believe that their pain can be salved by having the offender punished or even executed. This only karmically links those involved more tightly. Understanding and eventually forgiveness will need to occur so that both souls can continue their journey without the need to hurt each other anymore. In addition, when the issue is truly healed through forgiveness, a similar incident will not have to recur in this lifetime or later in the next.

When we leave each incarnation, the soul must review all karmic ties or misdeeds that have been ignored on Earth. Nothing compares to the torment and pain that may be experienced when a past life is reviewed in the spirit world and all wrongdoing is brought to the surface and seen in its proper light. Hell can symbolically be likened to the self-evaluation that souls who have been destructive must undergo when they enter the other dimension. This examination can cause the soul to be overwhelmed with guilt, remorse, anguish, emotional turmoil, and self-loathing, as well as frustration that it is too late to amend the past.

While we are in bodily form, we lack the insight to evaluate the extent of harm and injury we have caused others. When on Earth, we cannot truly identify with another person's psyche and emotions. There are exceptions, however: some lay people *do* have the ability to tune in to others. It is also possible, through psychotherapeutic training, to identify with another person's thought system and personality. But the average Earthling can relate only to his or her own thoughts and feelings and develops a well-defended excuse system for all his actions and behaviors.

Nobody believes himself to be bad, evil, mean, cruel, selfish, abusive, or destructive; each person carries his own justification in his mind. Liars, cheats, thieves, murderers, child molesters, warmongers, or tyrants—all those who commit a felony, atrocity, or transgression—do not necessarily grasp the extent of their violation. While they may repent their crime, especially when caught and convicted, they manage to justify their actions to appease their own conscience. Juvenile delinquents or drug addicts can blame their parents, environment, and social standards for their transgressions; murderers may plead temporary insanity or hold the influence of liquor or drugs responsible for their acts, and rapists may justify their behavior by claiming they have uncontrollable raging hormones. A dictator is always convinced that it is the evil of others that motivates him to attack or destroy.

Other examples may be judged not as harshly by society, but can nevertheless cause lasting harm to the victims. This may be a male who impregnates a female and refuses to be responsible, a fiancé who doesn't show up for the wedding, someone who cheats on a husband or wife, or even those who stand up their date. These men may feel like macho jocks, the women like liberated females, and none of them consider that their shoddy behavior can lead to emotional devastation for the betrayed.

But once one is in spirit form, all excuses and justifications fall to the wayside, as the soul realizes the extent of pain and sorrow he or she may have inflicted on others. It may not necessarily be a heinous crime for which one needs to repent; recognition of carelessness, negligence, neglect, or disregard may engender the same feelings. One may also realize that it was wrong to have ignored or been indifferent to another's plight and misery. Souls can also become aware of having been cruel to animals and destructive of nature, perhaps not deliberately but nevertheless unfeelingly.

When a soul experiences being overwhelmed with remorse for past misdeeds and desperately wishes to set things right—the path is open! Each soul gets its chance for penitence—to return to Earth or another planet to amend its transgressions and absolve itself of all self-accusation. Karma is not doled out; it is self-induced. It is never punished or forced upon you, but it is the way for you to settle the score.

It is, however, of value only when the odds are favorable and the time is conducive for your return to Earth. You also need to gain a certain awareness and understanding and make proper preparation for your return to bodily form. Unfortunately, not everyone listens to the inner voice or the advice of wise counsel, but instead rushes right back into action. Those who have been impatient and impetuous on Earth will most likely be quick to reincarnate and make the same mistakes all over again.

The ones who have made the effort to adjust to the spirit world and are willing to abide by its order—the majority of newly arrived souls—realize there is no urgency to reincarnate because there are no time limits and existence is eternal. While they are made to understand that they are free to return at will and most are eager to do so, they agree to bow to a higher knowledge and wisdom. However, it is sometimes advisable for souls to reincarnate immediately; I have been told about a soul that was aborted and needed to return to the same mother.

A hundred or even a thousand years can elapse between incarnations before conditions are conducive, and most souls are prepared to wait it out. They will spend their time prudently by availing themselves of all the methods of learning, progress, and advancement that are offered to bring them closer to their goal of enlightenment.

It seems quite possible that the spirit world is equipped with a giant computerized system or an automatic processor that contains all statistical data pertaining to everyone and everything in existence. In metaphysical lingo, the categorized information about each human on Earth and other planets is referred to as the Akashic Records. These would be celestial files in which every characteristic, thought, and action of each person in the material world is available for psychic observation. Many think that a panel reviews the information of those who wish to reincarnate. It is up to the individual soul to make the decision, but the experts, assisted by an advisory board, will most likely start you on your way.

An abundance of helpers are available in the spirit world: a wealth of teachers, loving companions, and impartial consultants to guide you. It may be a long time, possibly aeons, before the right environment is located in which you can carry out your intentions, but *you will be assisted in assembling the necessary ingredients and the proper setting for your rebirth.* They will help you choose the time, geographical and cultural milieu, as well as the race, sex, social position, physical and mental traits, parental lineage, and heritage that are to your best advantage. Each detail will be matched and assessed. Your life on Earth (or another planet) is carefully planned and follows a precise outline.

It is unlikely that such a complex system was set up by one God, but rather by a contingent of wise, learned entities who collaborated and combined their talents throughout the ages. I personally consider it logical to assume that our advanced technology of computer science and industry was handed down to us by higher forces; I also think that the astonishing expertise of a wizard like Bill Gates was not inborn but predeveloped.

In the scenario presented in the film *Defending Your Life,* you appear before a court with a prosecutor and a lawyer to defend you. You are judged and accordingly advanced or demoted in relation to how much courage you displayed on Earth. *Courage means not being afraid to take chances* and overstep unreasonable, confining societal boundaries that we tend to observe while in the body. When we limit ourselves by being careful and safe throughout our life, we stifle our growth and progress. Of course it is, after all, only a movie. No judge or jury exists on the other side to condemn or exonerate you for your mistakes on earth. You are the only one who can assess yourself—evaluate your past life and express how you wish to proceed in the next incarnation. The possibilities are endless, and you have all the assistance you need to advise you on how to best fulfill your purpose.

I can also picture the heavenly advisory board as a giant theatrical company or motion picture production similar to a Cecil B. DeMille spectacle, with a producer, director, technicians, and cast of thousands. But it is you who choose your role and it is you who decide who will play your parents. To explain why, as children, we may not always feel close to our parents, and why they in turn may be disappointed with us, let me quote the words of Kahlil Gibran, from *The Prophet:*

> Your children are not your children. They are the sons and daughters of life's longing for itself. They come through you but not from you, and though they are with you yet, they belong not to you. You may give them your love but not your thoughts, for they may have their own thoughts. You may house their bodies but not their souls, for their souls dwell in the house of tomorrow, which you cannot visit, not even in your dreams.

You don't always assume the role of the repenter and you sometimes return to Earth as the one who was abused to teach the offender a lesson. Often you feel impelled to go back for the sole purpose of helping someone else fulfill *their* karmic destiny. I can also believe that a casting problem could arise and that sometimes souls are urgently needed to take the part of the villain. Is it possible that someone was chosen to or volunteered to play Hitler?

Karma can also be overcome by whole groups or tribes who choose to reincarnate together to amend a despicable action of the past. A prominent ultra-Orthodox rabbi in Jerusalem has recently incited a wave of furor and indignation among world Jewry. He publicly asserted that the Jews who perished in the Nazi holocaust needed to atone for the atrocities that they had committed in another lifetime.

You don't necessarily need to suffer when you return to Earth; you could choose to go back for a triviality or for the sole purpose of having a good time. We all come across someone among the living whom we regard as lucky or blessed. Only good things happen to these people. Their life flows smoothly; they are always happy and cheerful, and enjoy themselves immensely.

Not everyone is eager to reincarnate. Some souls, either voluntarily or upon the advice of counselors, decide to wait for loved ones on Earth who will need help to ease their transition when they arrive in the spirit world. It may interfere with their own progress, but they are glad they can be of service. They may also choose to stay to welcome the new arrivals just to show them a familiar, friendly face. (I am positive that my mother will still be there to greet and hug me.)

Some have already determined on Earth that they no longer wish to return, and are waiting to progress to higher planes. Others may decide on arrival in the spirit world, or as they become accustomed to the spirit world, that any of their remaining karma can be dispensed with in the here-and-now. While this is possible, it is an arduous process. Most souls are discouraged from this undertaking and advised to go back once more.

There are those among my acquaintance who feel they have achieved what they set out to do and are well advanced on their spiritual path while on Earth. They have made up their minds that all their karmic debts are paid up, and that they no longer need to return to the world of chaos. However, when they reach the spirit world they may find that they incorrectly assessed their progress and do need to go back. (At this time of my life, I am inclined to think that I myself may have to come back again. I could, however, still change my mind.)

Each return trip to the world of illusion is a progression; you never go backward, even if it seems to be so. While we may appear to have regressed to lower levels of consciousness, the opposite is true. Material or social circumstances do not count. You may have been a nabob in a past life and are now a pauper; once brilliant and educated and now ignorant and illiterate. Your physique was at one time healthy and strong and in this lifetime you are sickly and deformed. It is not the picture you present but the lessons you have to learn and the obstacles you must overcome, that will diminish your karmic obligations. *We deliberately choose the circumstances that will best serve us to advance spiritually and bring us closer to our goal of supreme fulfillment.* Karma is the opportunity for growth and development and it is often the severity of the lessons that furthers and speeds up our progress.

There are no mistakes in the reincarnation scheme; this can be most difficult to comprehend while you are in the illusion. "Why is this person beautiful, rich, and successful and why am I such a poor slob experiencing nothing but misery?" you may ask. Why do some people have everything and others nothing at all? Why do people exist in war-torn countries, why are children starving in parts of the world, why are human beings exposed to ugliness, violence, and disaster? These are universal questions.

Is everything in the world unjust and unfair, and are we just helpless bystanders? It's not that way at all! You can look for someone to blame for your own adversities, *but you are totally responsible for your beauty or ugliness, your failure or success, and the whole course of your life.* We do not need to feel responsible for others' pain unless we have caused it or contributed to it in some way. But we can do what feels right to us to ameliorate the suffering of others. "All ye can overcome," says the Lord in the Bible, and no truer words have ever been recorded.

To proceed in the right direction, first accept that which you may think of as a cliché: Outside appearances and circumstances can never compensate for inner peace and happiness. You cannot deny that the most gorgeous, talented, and popular girl of eighteen could be on the brink of suicide and that an aged, blind, or crippled person can feel secure and peaceful within. The latest, most expensive automobile might be envied by others but may bring no joy to the owner, whereas a homeless person pushing a shopping cart through the city streets may take great pride in his or her possessions. A child raised in poverty can happily play with pebbles, twigs, and sticks, and another, surrounded by expensive toys, could be whiny and miserable. *It is the way we feel about ourselves that breaks the pattern of false societal conditioning and starts the ball rolling in the right direction.* The only reason we are on Earth is to change our way of thinking, and this is the place where we have the free will to reshape our destiny.

Whatever part in your play or movie you took on to act out your *karma,* you can trade it in once it has served its purpose. It might have been a heavy one—a suffering, laboring, grieving, emotionally shattering role, but you have the option to end it at will while still on Earth. You can choose to rise above your karmic circumstances and your handicaps whenever you wish to do so. There are people born in slums, growing up without proper care and nourishment, illiterate and with all odds against them, who made their way from rags to riches. Some who are blind, without voice, or without hearing have achieved vocational success, and there are those born without hands who have learned to write and paint with their toes.

While you may not reach perfection in your physical state, you can come as close to it as you desire. We cannot achieve the impossible—we cannot see if our eyes are irrevocably damaged, hear if the eardrums are destroyed, or grow limbs that are missing. We do not, however, have to accept traits in ourselves that do not please us. For example, we don't need to state, "I am stubborn because I am a Taurus" or "I am an Aries; that is why I am so impatient and bossy." Instead, as an indication of your spiritual growth, you might say, "I used to be a Gemini, two people, always divided. But I have now unified myself." We can change everything about ourselves that does not please us and we can accept and live with what is not changeable.

Karmically speaking, no one takes on more than can be handled in one lifetime. Those who seem to be the victims of all the miseries in the world often have the ability to endure them. I have been told during a spiritual reading that I took on more than I could chew in my present incarnation, that I was warned about this by my advisors but that I paid no heed. My stubborn desire to get everything over with in one fell swoop has undoubtedly caused me much pain. Yet, somehow I managed to get through the extremely difficult times.

You are here on Earth to improve your attitudes, realize true values, and better understand yourself, but you can also choose to accept and cherish yourself as you are. *You need first and foremost to be happy and at peace with yourself and then go on to lead your fellows onto the path.* We all need to help each other, because interdependence brings us closer to our spiritual goal. It is the law of the Universe. We don't always accomplish what we hoped to resolve in a given lifetime, but there is always another chance. If we make a mistake, we are allowed to come back to correct it.

You signed a contract before you were born agreeing that you would follow the rules and regulations and do your best. You also engaged in a contract when you went to school: promised to listen to the teacher, study earnestly, and obey. But your mind was not always on the subject and you probably got distracted by the other kids. The purpose of the journey on Earth is to become a bit wiser each time and ultimately to discover the truth of existence. You don't need to consciously know your mission on Earth, but if you offer kindness, honesty, compassion, and help to everyone you meet, you are definitely on the way to earning your brownie points. We need to free ourselves of envy, resentment, and malice toward human beings, in action and in thought, and realize that karmically sound emotions are forms of love.

Not all messengers from the spirit world agree with each other about the various aspects of karma and reincarnation we on Earth are curious about. It is likely they each offer their own interpretations about certain subjects. A question of interest to many is, if time on Earth is only linear, is there a sequence to reincarnation? While it is generally accepted that time is indeed an illusion, and that past, present, and future exist in three-dimensional reality only, opinions differ. Some believe that each lifetime follows the next in sequential order until the path leads us back to the Source.

Others maintain that life and death are in constant rotation, occurring in a circular motion without a beginning or an end: Even if the ultimate is reached, one begins the cycle of spiritual evolution over and over again. Another opinion is that all time exists simultaneously, so all events in the Universe happen concurrently—just as dreams tumble upon each other. In this way of thinking, souls experience all incarnations at the same time.

An intriguing question is, if we can choose our time of birth, can we also choose when to die? Again, the answers vary. Some insist that all details about present-life existence are predetermined in the spirit world.

But others among the wise disagree. They are convinced that, as we have the power and jurisdiction to end our karma on Earth, we can end our life as well (I am not referring here to suicide). They insist that those who have fulfilled their karmic objectives and are eager to return to the spirit world don't need to stick around.

They are also certain that the ones who are still needed on Earth are able to prolong their life at will. I, too, am inclined to think that way, though I don't think this holds true for everyone. Some die before they think they will, and others live longer than they intended. But it is undeniable that there are many who defy all the odds against them. They live through the fiercest battle in war, or remain unharmed in a plane crash and unscarred in other disasters. Millions perished in concentration camps, but others prevailed through the horrors. Many who survived perilous situations in ways that are seemingly unexplainable attest that they were either unafraid or else made a conscious decision to remain alive. A friend of mine, together with her mother, spent two years in concentration camps where everyone around them died and there was no hope of rescue. She was only eleven, but she decided that she and her mother would survive.

I personally believe that we can forestall death if we have set an important goal to fulfill or if someone else desperately depends on us. While we cannot prevent death, we can nevertheless postpone it.

I am sure pet lovers want to know: Do animals reincarnate as well? Again, opinions differ. Some believe the original soul progressed from mineral to plant to animal life and then into human form, so that all of us, at one time, were part of the animal kingdom. Some who have been regressed report recalling life in animal form, and others who feel particularly connected to their pets are positive about a past-life as an animal.

I would estimate the majority of the enlightened deny the theory that humans and animals are karmically related. They feel it is karmically taboo to maliciously harm or kill an animal, or any other living thing, but emphasize that these creatures are a less developed species than ours. Some say that animals have no soul, others insist they have. As far as I can determine, animals do incarnate, but on their own level. While they lack a human form of intelligence and reasoning and act purely by instinct, they most likely do have a soul. Western thought does not accept the Hindu idea of transmigration, which includes the concept of rebirth into an animal body under certain conditions. Most teachers say that we never backslide but go up and up eternally.

There are, however, two queries about reincarnation whose answers are unanimously agreed upon by all consultants from the spirit world. The first is, "When do we no longer need to return to Earth?" The answer is, "Your karmic structure is completely dissolved when you decide to finish it once and for all—that is, when you have finally fully experienced and accepted your own perfection and divinity."

And the second, "What can we do to speed up the process?" The reply is: "*Learn to live in the now.* Love your life and yourself in it. Don't look for sadness, and if you're not happy, do something about it! Forget about the past and don't worry about the future—enjoy each moment! You cannot change a single event or thought from the past—it is finished, dead. The future is fiction, projection, expectation. Don't waste a moment of your precious time on Earth on idle speculation—and *live and cherish each day as if it were your last.*"

About the Author

I am a survivor of Nazi terrorism, as well as a devastating accident which fractured my body and psyche. And I have overcome numerous other tragedies which occurred during my lifetime.

I was very fortunate to discover yoga and, through its practice, achieve wholeness, success and lasting peace of mind. I became a teacher and owned and directed Yoga For Long Island, the largest school of its kind in the country. It was an extremely successful institute, especially through the seventies and eighties when yoga was at the height of its popularity. I hosted my own radio program, appeared as a guest on various radio and TV talk shows, and was acclaimed as *the* expert on Yoga.

I wrote *Yoga and Common Sense* in 1970, published by Bobbs-Merrill. It went into three printings and was translated into several languages. It was acquired by Lancer books and appeared in a soft-cover edition, and was later revised and re-published by Bobbs-Merrill in 1977. In 1991 Carol Publishing Group (Citadel Press) published *Fitness For the Unfit*.

I returned to New York from the San Francisco area where I was engaged in giving lectures and seminars on the subjects of holistic living and Eastern philosophy. While in California, I made radio and TV appearances and was featured in numerous newspapers and magazines throughout the country. At present I teach yoga classes at senior centers in Manhattan and at the New York Lighthouse and am still actively involved in the New York Yoga scene. Last year, I presented my own Yoga program on public television and plan to resume it in the near future.